Banking in China

Palgrave Macmillan Studies in Banking and Financial Institutions

Series Editor: Professor Philip Molyneux

The Palgrave Macmillan Studies in Banking and Financial Institutions is international in orientation and includes studies of banking within particular countries or regions, and studies of particular themes such as Corporate Banking, Risk Management, Mergers and Acquisitions, etc. The books will be focused upon research and practice, and include up-to-date and innovative studies on contemporary topics in banking that will have global impact and influence.

Titles include:

Yener Altunbus, Blaise Gadanez and Alper Kara
SYNDICATED LOANS
A Hybrid of Relationship Lending and Publicly Traded Debt

Santiago Carbó, Edward P. M. Gardener and Phillip Molyneux
FINANCIAL EXCLUSION

Franco Fiordelisi and Philip Molyneux
THIRTY YEARS OF ISLAMIC BANKING
History, Performance and Prospects

Philip Molyneux and Munwar Iqbal
BANKING AND FINANCIAL SYSTEMS IN THE ARAB WORLD

Alfred Slager
THE INTERNATIONALIZATION OF BANKS
Patterns, Strategies and Performance

Mario La Torre and Gianfranco A. Vento
MICROFINANCE

Franco Fiordelisi and Philip Molyneux
SHAREHOLDER VALUE IN BANKING

Banking in China

Violaine Cousin

palgrave
macmillan

First published 2007 by
PALGRAVE MACMILLAN
Houndmills, Basingstoke, Hampshire RG21 6XS and
175 Fifth Avenue, New York, N.Y. 10010
Companies and representatives throughout the world

PALGRAVE MACMILLAN is the global academic imprint of the Palgrave Macmillan division of St. Martin's Press, LLC and of Palgrave Macmillan Ltd. Macmillan® is a registered trademark in the United States, United Kingdom and other countries. Palgrave is a registered trademark in the European Union and other countries.

ISBN-13: 978–0–230–00695–9 hardback
ISBN-10: 0–230–00695–7 hardback

This book is printed on paper suitable for recycling and made from fully managed and sustained forest sources.

A catalogue record for this book is available from the British Library.

A catalog record for this book is available from the Library of Congress.

10 9 8 7 6 5 4 3 2 1
16 15 14 13 12 11 10 09 08 07

Printed and bound in Great Britain by
Antony Rowe Ltd, Chippenham and Eastbourne

To Ewald,
For all his patience and love.

Contents

List of Tables

List of Figures

List of Abbreviations

A-IRB	Advanced Internal ratings-based (approach)
ABC	Agricultural Bank of China
AMC	Asset Management Company
Art.	Article
Basel I	Basel Capital accord of 1988
Basel II	New Basel Capital Accord (2004)
BCBS	Basel Committee on Banking Supervision
BCG	Boston Consulting Group
BCP	Basel Core Principles
BIS	Bank for International Settlements
bln	billion (defined as 1,000 million)
bp	basis point(s)
BoC	Bank of China
BoD	Board of Directors
CAR	Capital adequacy ratio
CBRC	China Banking Regulatory Commission
CCB	China Construction Bank
CCBs	City commercial banks (preceded by a place name, it is written in the singular and refers to the city commercial bank in that locality)
CEQ	China Economic Quarterly
C/I ratio	Cost income ratio
CIRC	China Insurance Regulatory Commission
CNY	Chinese Yuan; also Renminbi (RMB)
CSRC	China Securities Regulatory Commission
E&Y	Ernst & Young
EAD	Exposure at default
EU	European Union
EUR	Euro
EVA	Economic value added ®
FDIC	Federal Deposit Insurance Corporation
FC	Finance company
FI	Financial institution
F-IRB	Foundation Internal ratings-based (approach)
GARP	Global Association of Risk Professionals
HK	Hong Kong

HKD	Hong Kong Dollar
ICBC	Industrial and Commercial Bank of China
IIF	International Institute of Finance
IMF	International Monetary Fund
IRB	Internal ratings-based (approach)
JSCB	Joint-stock commercial bank
LGD	Loss given default
LLP	Loan loss provisions
M	Maturity
MIS	Management information system
mln	million
NBFI	Non-bank financial institution
NDRC	National Development and Reform Commission
NPA	Non-performing assets
NPC	National People's Congress
NPL	Non-performing loan
p.a.	per annum
PBOC	People's Bank of China
PD	Probability of default
PRC	People's Republic of China
PwC	PricewaterhouseCoopers
QFII	Qualified Foreign Institutional Investor
OECD	Organisation for Economic Co-operation and Development
RAROC	Risk-adjusted return on capital
RBC	Risk-based capital
RCC	Rural credit cooperative
RCU	Rural credit union
ROA	Return on assets
ROE	Return on equity
RWA	Risk-weighted assets
QIS	Quantitative impact studies
S&P	Standard and Poor's
SA	Standardised approach
SAFE	State Administration of Foreign Exchange
SASAC	State-owned Assets Supervision and Administration Commission
SB	Supervisory Board
SME	Small and medium enterprises
SOE	State-owned enterprises
SOCB	State-owned commercial bank

TIC	Trust and investment corporation
TVE	Township and village enterprise
UCCs	Urban credit cooperatives
WTO	World Trade Organisation

Introduction

As many articles and books on China point out in their introductory sentences, China has witnessed stellar economic growth since the early 1980s. GDP growth was high, around 7–10% in each year during that period. However, looking at the banking system in China gives quickly the impression that China is more *un géant aux pieds d'argile*: a gigantic economy and impressive economic prowess supported by a frail banking system. "Technically insolvent, riddled with corruption and bear[ing] the imprint of socialist economic planning" (Kynge, 2002), to name just a few of the reasons why it is so frail. Or should we compare it, as Boston Consulting Group (BCG) (2005) did, to a casino, because it is so vast, complex, highly liquid, fraught with risks and with many participants placing their bets?

Chinese banks have managed in recent years to shed some of their fragility. Banking reforms gathered pace as the state-owned banks were incorporated and listed on stock exchanges, as the disposal of non-performing loans (NPLs) entered a new stage by developing new methods such as securitisations, and as other commercial banks found new ways to raise fresh capital. Not only have Chinese banks become more market-oriented and market-driven, their environment has also changed with them. Now Chinese banks can rely on more adequate regulations, as supervision has matured and the focus turned towards risk management and internal controls. Banks also found they have more leeway in determining their business scope and interest rates. Even the credit cooperative sector has experienced major advances with the deepening of the structural reforms.

China's banking system has a central role to play in the development of the country. Jing Xuecheng wrote in 2005:

> First, finance is the motor of modern economic activities and the lifeblood of the economic cycle. [...] Second, finance has a core function in the distribution of market resources. [...] Third, finance is a powerful lever in the macroeconomic regulation of the national economy. [...] Fourth, the reform of the financial structure is the precondition to the deep-seated adjustment of China's economic structure. [...] Fifth, the opening of the financial services sector is the point of support for when the national economy faces the

> challenges of the WTO entry. [...] Sixth, the financial security is the key to one country's economic security. (pp. 30–33)

Further, Xiao Zhuoji (2006: 46) adds, "The overall weight and the structural changes of the financial markets have a decisive influence upon the ability to change and the main indicators of a country's financial condition." China's banking system is of crucial importance, but not only to China anymore.

Because of its recently won importance in the world economy, China's banking system is also important internationally. If Chinese banks fail, what would this mean for the Chinese economy and its enterprises, what would it mean for other parts of the world? While a full failure is unlikely, it is still necessary to look at the small print, at the details of the banking system fabric to understand where its challenges lie and where solutions might be found. Could the Chinese banks emerge from their technical insolvency to become banks well recognised on the world stage? Just as China is emerging economically and politically, could its banks follow a similar path in the years ahead? How much has the banking system changed over the last few years? Did the reforms work well, do they work in depth? Or should we expect more financial scandals in the future?

The aim of this book is to offer an in-depth analysis of the Chinese banking sector, of its challenges and the reasons for its present form as well as the implications for reform. Over the next chapters, this book will answer all the crucial questions raised above.

After a brief introduction on the size and main indicators of the Chinese banking system, the analysis will move on to the financial infrastructure in which Chinese banks operate. The financial infrastructure is understood as a broad arrangement of external factors, such as the legal and regulatory environment, which includes not only the regulators' role and their work as well as bankruptcy and deposit insurance regulations, but also the changing functions of the central and local authorities as well as the more recent role played by foreign investors. Indeed banks are influenced in their behaviour not only by bankruptcy regulations and legal mechanisms but also by their ultimate shareholders.

The third chapter will discuss the most important issues Chinese banks face. These are specific to banks in China and include a problematic financial intermediation capacity, poor asset quality and deficiencies in corporate governance. Chinese banks are, for now, faced mostly with credit and operational risks. As will become clear in reading this chapter, the banks have not yet mastered these fully.

Part 4 will concentrate on the diverse types of banks existing in China. Every bank is different, but still banks can be grouped into five different types to simplify the analysis. These groups of banks show not only commonalities but also stark differences in their business approach as well as in their specific operating environments. The main types analysed here include state-owned commercial banks (SOCBs), joint-stock commercial banks (JSCBs), city commercial banks (CCBs), rural credit cooperatives (RCCs) as well as foreign banks.

Because Chinese banks have not yet had time (and in some cases the chance) to readily master the management of credit and operational risks, it is important to analyse further the upcoming challenges to the Chinese banking sector as well as possible responses or new developments. The main challenges come from three areas: developing retail banking at the product or customer level, dealing with Basel II for risk management issues, and the threats and opportunities posed by World Trade Organisation (WTO) membership. Each of these developments is expected to have a major influence on Chinese bank strategy and performance in the future.

Note: The present book reflects the events and knowledge of the author up to June 2006. Send any questions, queries, suggestions and feedback you may have to cousinviolaine@yahoo.com.

Part I
Setting the Stage

1
Structure of the Banking System

For those acquainted with the Chinese banking industry, it is becoming easier to find positive and forward-looking words to describe developments in the industry. More and more reforms have been introduced and this is at a growing pace; however, Chinese banks still face a number of challenges, such as insufficient capital, government interference, poor risk management practices and large chunks of NPLs.

This chapter will set the stage by discussing the broad features of the Chinese banking system and the different institutions that operate in the system.

For reference, Table 1.1 presents a range of economic and financial indicators for China.

Table 1.1 Macro-economic indicators for China (2004)

Real GDP (bin CNY)	12,471
Real GDP % change	9.5
Goods exports: volume % change	23.8
Goods imports: volume % change	22.9
Trade Balance (mln USD)	58,982.3
Total External Debt (mln USD)	233,187.8
External debt as % GDP	13.7
Reserves excluding gold (mln USD)	614,474
Equity market capitalisation (bln USD)	447.7
Gross domestic investment % of GDP)	45.2
Gross domestic saving (% of GDP)	48.1
Population (mln)	1,300.0
Per capita GDP (USD)	1,308.3

Source: IIF, 2005.

The Chinese banking system has been transformed from a mono-banking system (a single bank) into a multitude of banking institutions managing CNY 37 trillion in banking assets (by the end of 2005). As many other things in China, the banks are huge, as are the problems they carry with them.

1.1 Historical developments

To understand the evolution of the banking system, it is necessary to have an insight into the historic legacies of the Chinese banking system. Deng Xiaoping is often quoted in this context as having said that "banks should be changed into real banks", because in the past "our banks were money printing enterprises, cash vaults, but not real banks" (Jing X., 2005).

The Chinese banking system was long organised around the People's Bank of China (PBOC), which was established in 1948 and assumed for some 30 years the functions of commercial bank, supervisor and government treasury. Starting from 1979, with the opening and reform policy introduced by Deng Xiaoping, the PBOC was given the function of a supervisory body and of a central bank, while commercial activities and treasury functions were transferred to other newly (re-)established entities. This process was finalised with the establishment of the PBOC as a central bank and of the Industrial and Commercial Bank of China (ICBC) as an independent entity in 1984.

Reform efforts can be subdivided into three phases.

In the first reform wave spanning between 1978 and 1993, the banking system moved from a mono-bank system, with the PBOC at its core, to a two-tier system when the four state-owned commercial banks (SOCBs) were formerly established as independent entities (still under the trust of the Ministry of Finance and the State Council[1]). This phase prepared the environment setting for future reforms.

A second series of reforms from 1994 to 2000 entailed a progressive move towards less administrative and more independent banking operations. The banking system thus reflected lesser budgetary constraints. In 1995, the *Commercial Banking Law* and the *Law of the People's Bank of China* (References for laws 1 and 3[2]) were issued to establish the legal underpinning for banking in China. Policy banks were established to take over the policy lending practices of SOCBs, and asset management companies (AMCs) were further established to orchestrate the transfer of NPLs of the SOCBs.

The 21st century saw the beginning of a new phase in banking sector reforms with the progressive move towards the WTO agreement on which most of the motivation for reform is based (Griffiths, 2005). In this last phase only, observers are able to distinguish reform efforts that run deeper into the banking system and even at times in banking practices. Evidence of this can be found, for example, in newly promulgated laws and regulations, in the introduction of foreign entities as new stakeholders and in the management of banks. Reforms, however, never went as far as to close down a large bank or as to open fully the banking market.

1.2 Organisation and structure of the banking landscape

Financial institutions

As of October 2005, the Chinese banking system was made up of some 35,000 financial institutions (CBRC, 2006a). The main institutions in terms of size and weight in the banking system are as follows:

- the 4 state-owned commercial banks (SOCBs)
- the 3 policy banks
- the 13 joint-stock commercial banks (JSCBs)
- the 115 city commercial banks (CCBs)
- the 30,438 rural credit cooperatives (RCCs).

No less important are the 3 state-owned policy banks, the recently established 57 rural commercial or cooperative banks, and finally the remaining 709 urban credit cooperatives (UCCs) (Figure 1.1).

The SOCBs, JSCBs and CCBs accounted for 73.4% of all banking assets at the end of 2005 (their respective market shares are 52%, 16% and 5%) (Table 1.2).

The SOCBs hold a majority share of the banking assets; however, this strong position is weakened by the lack of sufficient capital, high NPLs levels and the banks are characterised by an important involvement of the state (with all the positive and negative implications of government ownership).

The JSCBs were established between 1987 and the mid-1990s. They are thus mostly free of policy lending and credits to large opaque state-owned enterprises (SOEs). Consequently their loan portfolios are healthier. However, their networks are not as extensive and their weight in terms of market share is not as strong. In the last 9 years, only one fully new bank,[3] Bohai Bank, was granted a new banking licence (opened in early 2006).

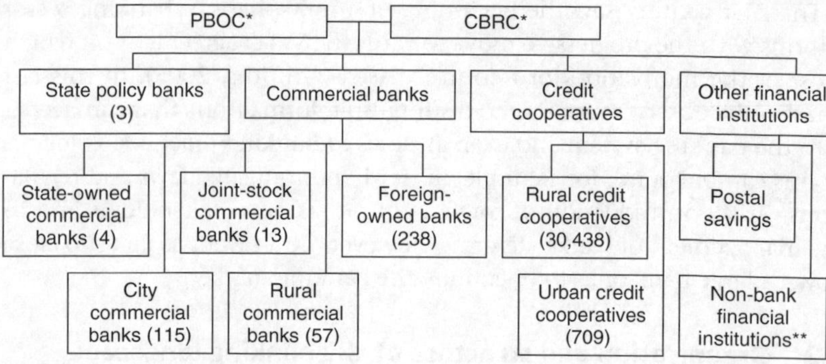

Figure 1.1 The structure of the Chinese banking system.
* PBOC – People's Bank of China; CBRC – China Banking Regulatory Commission. Both regulatory agencies are described in detail below.
** To these can be counted the 59 Trust and Investment Companies (TICs) (see below), 74 finance companies, 12 financial leasing companies and 5 automobile financing companies.
Source: based on CBRC, 2006a.

The CCBs were established in the late 1990s in urban areas following the merger of most UCCs. The formerly 3000 plus UCCs were merged into some 112 CCBs. Because of their often close links with local and provincial governments and their related enterprises, the banks' loan portfolios are often loaded with NPLs. Together with rural institutions, these serve mainly local enterprises, while SOEs and large corporates turn to larger banking institutions for their financing needs.

The RCCs are financial institutions set up in rural areas for collecting the rural population's savings and lend mainly to agriculture projects and township and village enterprises (TVEs). The lending decisions in these institutions are highly influenced by local governments and the quality of their loan portfolios is low.

Finally, *foreign institutions* are mostly branches of large foreign banking corporations and a few small joint-venture banks.[4] These were set up after the reform of the banking system was initiated. For a long time these faced various degrees of restrictions. Thus most are located in wealthier provinces and their scope remains small.

State-owned policy banks include the Agriculture Development Bank, the Export–Import Bank of China and China Development Bank and are in charge of specialised lending on behalf of the central government and do not have profit-making as their goal. They were established in 1994 and took over policy lending functions from the SOCBs. Their funding comes from the issue of bonds. These policy banks lack adequate capital funding and a strong branch network to reach out to their target groups.

Table 1.2 Banking industry in China

Year	2005				2004			
Bank type	**Total assets (CNY bln)**	**Number of institutions****	**Market share (%)**	**Average assets by institution (CNY bln)**	**Total assets (CNY bln)**	**Number of institutions****	**Market share (%)**	**Average assets by institution (CNY bln)**
SOCBs	19,658	4	52.46	4,914.49	16,932	4	53.58	4,233.00
JSCBs	5,813	13	15.51	447.12	4,697	11	14.86	427.00
CCBs	2,037	115	5.44	17.71	1,706	112	5.40	15.23
Others*	9,963	31,445	26.59	0.32	8,264	34,506	26.15	0.24
Total	**37,470**	**31,577**	**100**	**1.19**	**31,599**	**34,633**	**100**	**0.91**

* Others include state-owned policy banks, rural commercial banks, rural cooperative banks, urban credit cooperatives, rural credit cooperatives, foreign banks, postal savings as well as non-bank financial institutions (for the last two types, these are included except in the number of institutions).
**Number of institutions as of October 2005 and August 2004.
Source: Based on figures from www.cbrc.org.cn.

Although not within the scope of this book, *non-bank financial institutions* (NBFIs) should be noted. The most important ones are trust companies and credit guarantee companies. The regional Trust and Investment Corporations (TICs) were established at the beginning of the reform era in 1986 to finance local long-term projects and provide short-term corporate loans. The funding came from institutional liabilities and deposits (but no private deposits) as well as bond issuances. These rapidly became the target of influence of local and regional authorities, because the funds could be directed at projects and enterprises that were not within the scope of the official state credit plan (Grimm, 2005). However, these lost their importance with the collapse in 1998 of Guangdong International TIC to which many foreign institutions had provided credit lines. The credit guarantee industry developed from the necessity to support the development of small and medium enterprises (SMEs). Most of the multitude (around 5000) of these credit guarantee companies are owned by their local governments. Their function was, until the cap on interest rates was removed, to offer financial support to enterprises which were deemed too risky by mainstream banks. They now stand at crossroads and it can be expected that the industry will shrink in the next years as it re-focuses its strategy.

1.3 Key indicators of the Chinese banking system

China is one of the largest countries in the world and its banking sector reflects the country's geographic size. Banking assets made up 240% of GDP at the end of 2005, and at the same time loans outstanding made up 125% of GDP (Table 1.3). These percentages are some of the highest

Table 1.3 Relation between GDP, M2 and banking assets in China

in CNY bln, %	**2003**	**2004**	**2005***
Real GDP	12,895	14,197	15,603
M2	22,172	25,411	29,876
Total assets	27,640	31,599	37,470
Total loans	15,900	17,736	19,469
Assets as % of GDP	214.34	222.57	240.14
Loans as % of GDP	123.30	124.93	124.78
M2 as % of GDP	171.94	178.98	191.47

* 2005 figure for GDP is an estimate.
Source: Based on data from www.cbrc.org.cn, www.pbc.org.cn and IIF, 2005.

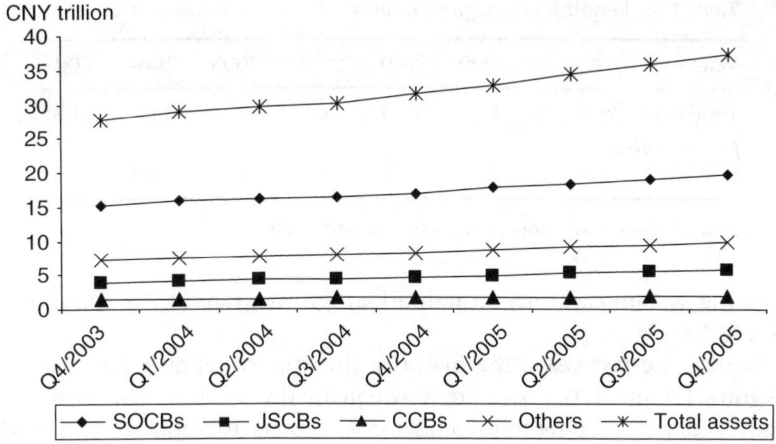

Figure 1.2 Banking asset growth in China.
Source: Based on data from www.pbc.org.cn.

in the world. These features highlight the importance of banks for the country.

The Chinese banking system has witnessed a 19% growth between 2004 and 2005, not an unusual growth. During the period 1997–2002, assets grew on average by 14% yearly (Figure 1.2) (BCG, 2002).

Growth in the Chinese banking industry is not evenly spread (Table 1.4). Most new loans in 2004 came from SOCBs (46%) and from JSCBs (21%). The stronger relative growth was seen at JSCBs which hold 17% of all loans in China, while state-owned banks hold 82% of all loans.

McKinsey estimates that bank lending needs to grow by 15% a year to ensure a 7–8% GDP annual growth as targeted by the central government (Bekier *et al.*, 2005). However, the analysts suggest that the

Table 1.4 Banking asset growth in China (half-yearly growth rates)

	Jan.–Jun. 2004	Jul.–Dec. 2004	Jan.–Jun. 2005	Jul.–Dec. 2005
	(%)	(%)	(%)	(%)
SOCBs	5.95	5.18	8.38	7.12
JSCBs	13.49	8.43	11.66	10.83
CCBs	4.50	11.65	5.40	13.26
Others	8.66	6.13	10.87	8.73
Total assets	7.62	6.23	9.36	8.43

Source: Based on PBOC and CBRC data.

Table 1.5 Lending yearly growth rates

Year	2000	2001	2002	2003	2004	2005
Total loans (%)	6.0	13.0	16.9	21.1	11.6	9.8
for comparison						
Real GDP % growth	8.4	8.3	9.1	10.0	10.1	9.9

Source: Based on data from IIF 2005 and from www.pbc.org.cn.

banking system can only sustain a loan growth rate of 7–8% annually (Table 1.5).

Within the last years, the maturity structure of lending has changed (Figures 1.3 and 1.4). Loans are now equally divided between short-term and medium- to long-term ones (45%). Loans to industry and trade account for 27.2 and 21.5% of all loans respectively (Euromonitor, 2004).

The growth rates for short-term loans are much lower than for longer-term loans.

The stronger growth for long-term loans can be explained (Liu L., 2004), despite the higher risks and the lower actual returns achieved on these, by the strong correlation between the loan growth and the growth of infrastructure projects, by the strong bias towards larger enterprises which are still felt to be safer borrowers than smaller ones (their borrowing requirements are likelier to entail larger longer-term loans),

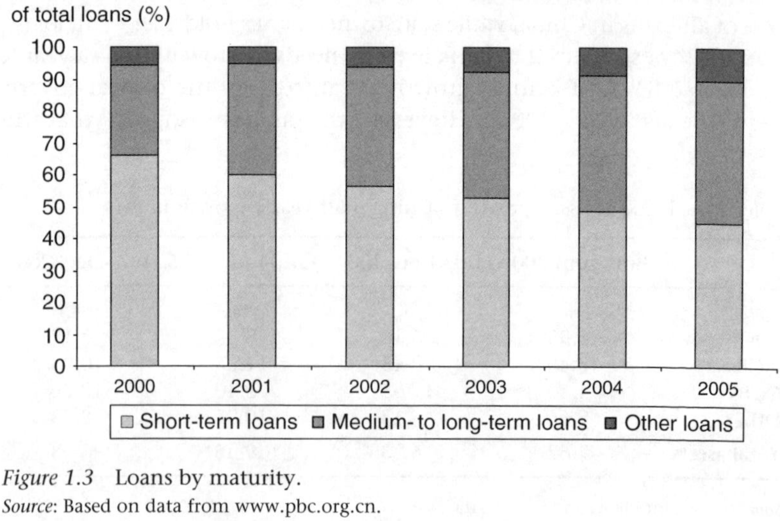

Figure 1.3 Loans by maturity.
Source: Based on data from www.pbc.org.cn.

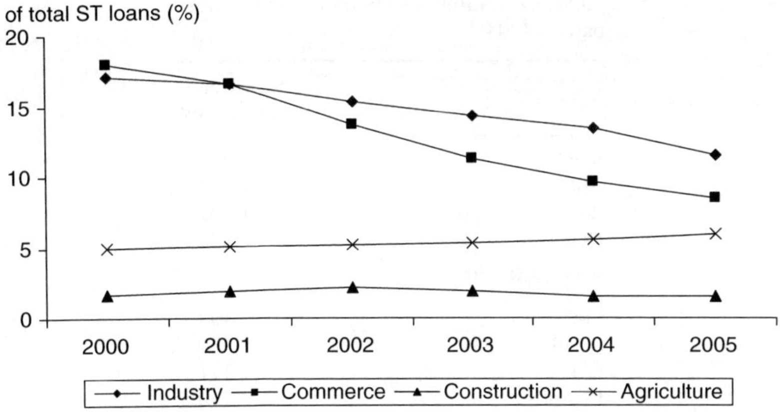

Figure 1.4 Short-term loans by sector.
Source: Based on data from www.pbc.org.cn.

Table 1.6 Growth rates based on loan maturities (year on year growth)

	2001	2002	2003	2004	2005
Total loans (%)	13.03	16.90	21.10	11.55	9.77
Short-term loans (%)	2.40	10.28	12.68	3.80	0.71
Medium- to long-term loans (%)	40.48	23.97	30.34	17.81	17.09
Other loans (%)	1.01	46.17	42.00	32.67	24.94

Source: Based on data from www.pbc.gov.cn.

and finally by the strong growth in consumer mortgage loan growth (Table 1.6) (75% of consumer loans, with maturities ranging from 10 to 30 years).

Geographic scope

The SOCBs have the most extensive branch networks and are present throughout China, although recently they have reduced the number of branches (especially in rural areas) to make their networks more efficient.

The JSCBs are active in large commercial urban centres, while CCBs are limited by law to conduct banking business in their local area (these geographic constraints have been eased since December 2005 for healthier banks) (Table 1.7).

Table 1.7 Number of branches in Chinese banks (2004)

	Number of branches
ICBC	21,223
ABC	31,004
BoC	11,307
CCB	14,585
Average SOCBs	*19,530*
BoComm	2,403
SPDB	329
CITIC	391
Everbright	410
Minsheng	219
Huaxia	243
Merchants	411
GDB	487
Industrial	294
SDB	255
Average JSCBs	*544*
Average	**10,037**

A list of acronyms for the banks' names can be found in the annex.
Source: Based on data from www.stats.gov.cn.

Rural banking institutions are, as their name suggest, located in smaller cities and villages in rural areas, but also around larger urban centres. They are limited to their local area for business.

Foreign banks have less restrictions on where they can operate since the entry of WTO. Progressively all of China has been opened to foreign-invested banks. However, foreign banks typically are located in large economic centres in coastal areas such as Shanghai, Beijing and Shenzhen. Some only have representative offices with no branches.

Banking performance rankings

Various studies (Zheng Y., 2005; *The Banker* [Chinese], 2006) have recently published rankings of Chinese banks. When it comes to market influence, international market competitiveness, technological competitiveness, the SOCBs do better than JSCBs. The latter's strengths lie overall in capital adequacy (BoC and CCB improved significantly their capital adequacy but only recently), asset quality, profitability, liquidity management, human resources strengths, financial innovation, service quality, corporate governance and the strength of internal controls. In all these areas the rankings give the first four to five places to JSCBs. These results are consistent over time as shown by earlier rankings. Overall the competitiveness listing ranks three JSCBs as the most competitive banks in China.

A separate ranking for CCBs shows that the most competitive ones are located in Shanghai, Tianjin, Hangzhou, Beijing and Nanjing. The ones based in large economic centres or in provincial capitals have the strongest market presence. They are also more likely to show better capital adequacy and lower NPL ratios. The best CCBs show results comparable to those of the healthier JSCBs.

1.4 Reform of the Chinese banking sector

The aim of the financial sector reforms is to increase the efficiency of the financial system while preserving the financial and economic stability and improving the development of the economy (Jing X., 2005).

> The fragile banking system is the long-term secret worry of the already tattered Chinese economy and poses the largest potential threat to the Chinese macroeconomy, the financial stability and the long-term economic growth. (Hu Z., 2005)

For many observers, China's economic reforms have been remarkable by any standards. However, reforms have not been equally deep and broad in all sectors of the economy. This has resulted in China's financial sector lagging behind other economic sectors. One reason behind this late start may be found in the centrality of banking to the Chinese economy, meaning that the Chinese leadership did not dare introduce major banking sector reforms as they wished to preserve the status quo. Another reason for the slow rate of reform of the banking industry compared to other sectors was that the state did not wish to lose control over financial flows and resource allocation (for both central and local authorities). A third reason for the slow pace of reform relates to the challenge posed by the large unprofitable SOEs, which are also seen as of paramount importance to the state. Reform of the banking system could not go ahead without a concurrent reform of SOEs. Finally, as in many cases where reforms are required, there was a reluctance by politicians to recognise that reform was necessary and a general reluctance to abandon established practices.

Systemic risk

The banking system is the source of financing for enterprises but as well the source of systemic risk to the economy as a whole (Longueville and Ngo, 2004). The central role played by the banking sector but at the same time its poor incentives to introduce sound banking practices highlight the vulnerability of the country to banking crises. Not only is the banking system central to China's economic development, but also it is concentrated on a few poorly managed banks. Each of the larger banks weights heavily on the banking system and also on the consideration of authorities for systemic risk (i.e. ensuring financial stability and avoiding bank runs or bankruptcies).

Table 1.8 Herfindahl index for the Chinese banking industry (2004)

2003	0.3419
2004	0.3805
2005	0.3730

Source: Based on PBOC and CBRC data.

Systemic risks are also influenced by the fact that regulatory capacity and enforcement of regulations (due to implementation and interpretation discrepancies) are still weak.

Allocation of resources and banking sector reform

As mentioned above, the choice of reform of the banking system is clearly linked to the reform of the whole economy. Some legal and economic experts discussed the current allocation of resources in China (*Caijing Magazine*, 2005b). For them, before the reforms started, the government was the creator of wealth and investment, there was no differentiation among legal, economic and administrative activities. All were integrated into one entity. As such it made no difference if loans were repaid, because they represented only a money transfer from one state pocket to another. Now, however, the question of resources allocation (land, labour and capital) has become crucial. The government still has the final say in many issues relevant to the allocation of resources despite the need for it to move towards a service function, rather than a control function. The market has not yet had the chance to allocate resources efficiently.

This also applies to the banking sector. Allocation of important resources is still not separated from state affairs: loans are directed at infrastructure investments or some 50% of loan portfolios are geared towards state enterprises; important positions in banks are filled with government officials and so on. Private or foreign shareholders and depositors are left with little choice and say in governing financial institutions.

Impetus for banking sector reform

In an interview (Ling H., 2005a), Zhou Xiaochuan, PBOC's governor, underlined the importance of internal and external (from the point of view of the banks) factors which made reforms possible and which heightened the pace of reforms. After the Asian crisis, Chinese banks (mainly the state-owned ones) faced a strong decline in asset quality on their portfolios and became increasingly aware of the necessity and urgency to take steps to improve internal controls. Zhou Xiaochuan identifies three further factors: the introduction of much more efficient accounting standards, the introduction of the internationally prevalent loan classification standards (details are given in Chapter 7) and finally the setting of clear reform goals for SOCBs at the central level.

In order to make the reforms work at all levels and in all places, the central government and the regulators put pressure on local governments to push through reforms and make the banking system leaner. Just as other large SOEs, banks suffered from similar ills (such as government interference, weak management incentives, poor corporate governance, etc.) which made the reforms of the banking system a corollary to reforms in SOEs. Other factors that have helped start the reform process include such factors as exchanges with foreign experts, the better education that new leaders have enjoyed and so on.

Current reform focus

Liu Mingkang, Chairman of the banking regulator, outlined the way ahead for SOCBs: increase market value, put the customer at the centre, cooperate with strategic investors, improve the fruits of cooperation and introduce higher technology standards. For rural financial institutions and postal savings reforms, the focus of China Banking Regulatory Commission (CBRC) will first lie in the reduction of NPLs, the diversification of risks and avoidance of further industry concentrations, the reduction of corruption cases and finally the reduction of the riskiness of poorly managed institutions (CBRC, 2006a,b).

In an interview in February 2006 (Ye W. and Hu J., 2006), Wu Xiaoling, Vice-governor of the PBOC, briefly outlined the steps ahead for reforming the financial sector in China. For banks, she underlined the importance of increasing competition as well as the need to introduce market discipline in banks.

Currently, the basic methods for reforming the state-owned commercial banking system are as follows (Hu Z., 2005 as well as Zhang J. *et al.*, 2006):

- financial restructuring (财务重组) to resolve as soon as possible the historical burdens through recapitalisation and stripping of bad loans (with the help of central authorities);
- fundamental reform of the traditional bank ownership structure (银行结构重组) and operational mechanisms to achieve a sound corporate governance through the transformation of the capital into shareholding capital (including the introduction of international strategic investors, introduction of Central Huijin (see Part IV for details) as representing the Chinese state, etc.); and
- strengthening market controls for banks, ensuring that banks are committed to continued reforms, strengthen and consolidate the reforms' latest results, through the public offering of shares (上市冲刺, while this is not an aim in itself).

The last 10 years have showed that superficial and cosmetic changes such as financial restructuring alone cannot guarantee improvements in state-owned entities. Two bailouts at the SOCBs did not decrease the number of scandals and thus reforms must run much deeper within the system. And this is not a question of whether sufficient money is available to support such expensive actions (as funds are available for now). Rather it points at the long-term pointlessness and inefficiency of short-term superficial actions on a stand-alone basis. Short-term bailouts are needed, to give banks the chance to have a fresh start and to get the authorities to take responsibility for years of policy lending. What would be, however, more important is to ensure that a precondition for a bailout is the implementation of high governance and risk management standards, of less government interference and so on.

One response to this is the introduction of foreign shareholders. With their help, capital can be further replenished, and they will also make international initial public offerings (IPOs) more attractive. In addition, foreign investors will bring forth advanced management experience (for credit decision-making, risk management, internal controls, financial products, IT, etc.) and in general will act as a catalyst for reform (Hu Z., 2005).

Many reforms were more cosmetic in nature, scratching the surface, with transfers of funds from one entity to another. These demonstrations of goodwill did not, however, induce the expected results. A sound banking system can only establish itself on sound governance and management practices. This is something that the Chinese leadership seems to have come to realise in the past years.

Reforms took a long time to take off. Vested interests and lack of understanding of the need for reform and the direction to be taken, all these factors surely impeded the start off of banking market reforms. While reforms are being recognised as inevitable for the banking system in China, a lot remains to be done as will be showed in the following chapters.

As Hu Shuli (2006), managing editor of *Caijing Magazine*, wrote after the Bank of China IPO: "In terms of the reform of the Chinese banking system, wasted resources are huge, history is long, inter-relations are great and indeed it is a 'fight to win or die', there is no room left for failure." She further wrote that while financial restructuring exercises at the banks involved large sums, the restructuring of internal mechanisms is inevitable.

Part II

Financial Infrastructure

The second part of this text presents the financial infrastructure surrounding Chinese banks. Their environment is not solely determined by the current legal and regulatory framework. It is also largely influenced by other factors, such as the interest rate setting environment, exit mechanisms and role of important shareholders in banks, in particular the Chinese state and foreign owners.

2
Legal and Regulatory Environment

The legal and regulatory environment plays an important role and influences the daily work as well as the work culture in which Chinese banks evolve. This chapter will first describe the regulatory authorities and their work up to now. It will then turn to their supervisory instruments: mainly banking regulations and the interest rate setting environment.

2.1 Regulatory authorities

The financial sector is regulated by one bank (the central bank or PBOC) and three commissions (regulatory commissions for banking, securities and insurance), 一行三会. The banking sector is mainly under the supervision of the PBOC and the CBRC.

In the past 3 years, Chinese regulatory authorities have showed that they are progressively moving towards supervision based on legal and market principles, away from administrative controls, that targets the reduction of the overall riskiness of the financial system (Xiao Z., 2005).

People's Bank of China

The PBOC was established in December 1948. For a long time it served three main functions: commercial bank, government treasury and supervisor of the financial system. Gradually the introduction of reforms has reduced its roles to that of a central bank.

The PBOC is an administration with ministerial rank working under the leadership of the State Council. This means that the final decision and approval power lies with the State Council, rather than with the central bank itself. PBOC reports to the State Council to get its approval on all important issues, for example setting interest rates, money supply targets and exchange rates. PBOC's capital is held by the Chinese state. Its governors are nominated, appointed and removed by the Premier and approved by China's legislative body, the NPC.

PBOC is responsible for formulating and implementing monetary policy and its goal is to ensure the stability of the financial system. It has some major functions: issuing local currency, administering its circulation, implementing monetary policy through administrative and market-driven mechanisms (reserve requirements, interest rate setting, etc.), managing China's foreign exchanges and gold reserves, and regulating the inter-bank market (the Chinese inter-bank market is underdeveloped and can therefore only serve the short-term finance requirements of banks).

Since the establishment of a specialised regulator for banks (see p. 23), PBOC does not interfere in the daily supervision of financial institutions. However, it often discusses general issues, such as the strategic direction of reforms and their goals, and retains the role of lender of last resort (Xiao Z., 2005). Because it has the responsibility for the stability of the financial system, it also needs to evaluate the riskiness of the financial system to prevent and solve financial crises (Xiao Z., 2005; PBOC, 2005d). Its responsibilities are closely linked to managing systemic risks inherent to the system.

Instruments used by PBOC have evolved but it still uses a mix of administrative and market-driven instruments for policy purposes. Market-driven instruments and mechanisms used to influence financial flows came in the mid-1980s. A first step was made with the introduction of minimum deposits and reserves requirements as well as discounting activities. These mechanisms became necessary with the end of the Credit Plan (see Annex) and increased opening and diversification of the banking sector.

The PBOC has a number of instruments through which it can intervene in financial markets:

- interest rates (until recently also through interest rates controls), and window guidance (a softer and less frequently used version of the Credit Plan)
- minimum reserve requirements
- rediscounting
- central bank re-lending[1] and
- open market interventions.

The last three instruments have been used more often in recent times (Wei W., 2005). Administrative measures are used whenever required to support SOEs' reforms, to support the state sector in general or to direct funds to specific economic sectors or regions.

Concrete examples show that the dividing line between market-oriented and administrative instruments is not clearly drawn: PBOC increased its required deposit rate for commercial banks from 7 to 7.5% to stem the strong loan volume growth in 2004 and increased the lending rate by 27 basis points (bp) at the end of April 2006. Administrative controls were introduced as well to reduce lending in overheated sectors such as real estate and construction.[2] Finally the impact of market instruments is reduced by the fact that the Chinese economy still depends to a large extent upon administrative steering.

China Banking Regulatory Commission

To increase the independence of the central bank and the efficiency of the regulatory function, the central government established in March 2003 the CBRC. The CBRC is the supervisor of financial institutions,[3] under the leadership of the State Council.

Its goals are stated in the *Law on Banking Supervision and Administration* (References for laws 2[4]) and these include making sure financial institutions keep to the law, ensuring the stability of their operations and the trust of the public in such institutions. Furthermore the Law aims to ensure fair competition among institutions and raise their competitiveness (Art. 3). CBRC's responsibilities include the defining of relevant rules and regulations for supervising financial institutions in China, licensing financial institutions,[5] conducting off-site and on-site supervision of all financial institutions, approving the adequacy and qualifications of senior management in these institutions, and making proposals for resolving banking crises or high risk situations in the banking system. Overall, CBRC remains focused on shortening the existing gap between Chinese and international banking practices. This involves resolving issues related to NPLs, capital adequacy, corporate governance and, in general, effective financial intermediation. Liberalising and opening gradually the banking system is seen as an effective way of enhancing its capacity.

To establish a differentiated and more focused supervision (分类监管), CBRC is divided into four operational departments (as opposed to research and administrative departments): the first one supervises SOCBs, the second JSCBs and city commercial banks, the third credit cooperatives, and the newly established fourth (April 2006) the policy banks and the postal savings.

The creation of a specialised regulatory agency for financial institutions in China is thought to have had a positive impact on the reforms of the Chinese banking system (Shih, 2005). It has reduced conflicts of interests and increased the focus on asset quality.

The CBRC's establishment reduced internal conflicts of interests that existed when PBOC was the central bank and the industry regulator at the same time. The establishment of CBRC as an entity independent of the PBOC ensured that it is more credible when calling for reform (Shih, 2005), because it has no mandate to save failed institutions (unlike PBOC), and it does not have shareholding interests in the institutions (such as PBOC, which has such interests through the Central Huijin Investment Co., a wholly state-owned investment vehicle, see Part IV).

With its independence, the improvement of bank asset quality has been promoted more strongly and is independent from monetary policy (Shih, 2005). The reduced NPL levels hint at success (although the reliability of official NPL data is open to question). CBRC has also been given some power and responsibilities to increase its force de frappe, for example by approving the appointment of bank directors.

However, two outstanding issues have yet to be resolved. The first one is the fight against corruption. This area is the responsibility of the Audit Office of the People's Republic of China (PRC) as well as of the central authorities' own watchdog, the Central Disciplinary and Inspection Committee (Shih, 2005). The definition of responsibilities has yet to be drawn clearly. The second issue is that CBRC still lacks the human and financial resources[6] as well as sufficient knowledge and experience in bank supervision to fully enforce the new regulations, especially those concerning risk management. While new regulations give the CBRC the power and means to enforce new standards and to introduce new practices in Chinese banks, the real power gained by CBRC will depend on how its professionalism is perceived by the market.

Regulatory instruments

In February 2004, CBRC published its rating system for assessing commercial banks (excluding the SOCBs, References for laws 29). It is similar to the CAMELS system (Table 2.1) employed in other developed countries (*The Asian Banker*, 2004b). Scores are attributed depending on quantitative and qualitative assessment of the banks' capital adequacy, asset quality, liquidity management, profitability, market risk, and

Table 2.1 Bank assessment system CAMELS

Weights	Capital adequacy situation 20% Asset safety situation 20% Management situation 25% Earnings situation 20% Liquidity 15% (Sensitivity to market risks assessment not yet included because not deemed a major issue for the moment)		
Overall and single factor assessment	Level 1 Level 2 Level 3 Level 4 Level 5	over 85 75–85 60–75 50–60 below 50	Excellent Good Special Mention Substandard Bad
Period of the assessment	One year		
Disclosure	Assessment results will be announced to related sectors		

Source: References for laws 29.

overall management. Each area has a weighting ranging from 15 to 25% (Marshall *et al.*, 2004a).

From 2007 onwards, this new CAMELS system will be supported by a set of newly published risk-based supervisory indicators (Table 2.2) that will apply to all Chinese commercial banks (References for laws 5).

Table 2.2 Risk supervision in banks

Risk aspects	**Measurement/Definition**
Risk level 风险水平	Liquidity (ratio, gap), credit (asset quality, client exposure), market (forex, interest rate sensitivity) and operational risk indicators (loss rate)
Risk migration 风险迁徙	Measured through the migration rate of loans between performing and non-performing grades as well as among each categories of the loan classification
Risk prevention/offsetting 风险抵补	Measured by the ability of the bank to make profits to cover losses (C/I Ratio, ROE, ROA, CAR and LLP)

Source: References for laws 5.

Regulators' independence

To ensure institutional, personal and functional independence of supervisors, regulatory authorities should be free from influence of local authorities and other government departments. The independence of the regulatory authorities largely depends upon their role and position as well as scope for action.

The de iure independence which is written down in the relevant regulations and laws (References for laws 2, Art. 5) does not guarantee a de facto independence. While the promulgation of the *Law of the People's Bank of China* and the *Law on Banking Supervision and Administration* has enhanced the regulators' scope for action, both remain under the influence of the State Council. These regulations have not regulated conclusively the status of either PBOC or CBRC. Parts of these laws do point to some degree of independence, while other parts refer to the strong position of the State Council or other ministerial agencies and their instructions. For some important decisions, regulators are required to get the approval of the State Council first.

Both regulators, PBOC and CBRC, are established under the State Council and are subordinate to it. Committees in both PBOC and CBRC also are mostly staffed with personnel from the Communist Party chosen by the State Council. Furthermore, the capital of the PBOC is fully in the hands of the state, under the State Council. The regulations do not give any details of the duration of a chairman's or governor's term; the person can be removed or transferred whenever deemed necessary. Through the committee for monetary issues, the National People's Congress also gets an opportunity to oversee the work of the PBOC (Grimm, 2005; Wei W., 2005).

Political influence is also eased by the fact that the organisational structure of the PBOC runs almost in parallel with that of other administrations (although now regional offices do not report anymore to provincial governments). Theoretically any type of political influence at local level is forbidden. However, while local authorities rewarded PBOC branches with special treatment for their employees and facilitated their work, they require in exchange support for large financing projects (Grimm, 2005, gives some examples of local political influences). No study has yet been undertaken to analyse the influence of local governments on the activities of CBRC; however, such influences can reasonably be assumed.

As a result from the strong influence exerted by the State Council, PBOC and CBRC cannot be made fully accountable for their policies and actions. Their subordination to the State Council reduces the degree of achievable functional, institutional, personal and financial independence. Local authorities also influence the regulatory authorities where and when deemed necessary.

Other regulatory agencies

Apart from being under the regulatory authority of the PBOC and the CBRC, banks are, depending on the scope of their funding, also regulated by the China Securities Regulatory Commission (CSRC), which is in charge of regulating the securities markets.

Furthermore, they may also fall under the regulations of the State Administration of Foreign Exchange (SAFE), which manages currency reserves and the exchange rate (under the PBOC umbrella). Other departments or ministries also influence the banks' operating environments: the Ministry of Finance is responsible, among others, for promulgating accounting and tax rules and the National Development and Reform Commission (NDRC) is responsible for enterprises finance issues.

Various commentators, such as Xiao Z. (2006), note the lack of established communication and coordination among the different regulators and authorities. This often leads to contradictory situations and adds workload for the regulated entities, which often have to report the same or similar information to a number of different agencies. The differentiated supervision increases focus and specialisation but at the same time acts in some cases as a barrier to development and innovation.

2.2 Important commercial banking laws and regulations

Overall, China is progressively moving away from decree-based towards rules-based regulation. In their daily work, PBOC and CBRC issue administrative rules that should help implement and regulate the laws issued at a higher level. The most important laws and regulations of the PRC include the *Law of the People's Bank of China*, the *Commercial Banking Law* and the *Law on Banking Supervision and Administration*. These all aim to improve the level of banking sector supervision.

The *Law of the People's Bank of China* (References for laws 3) regulates the status of the PBOC as well as the sharing of responsibilities with CBRC. PBOC is responsible for realising the goal of currency stability, but this is more than often pushed in the background for the sake of economic growth (influence can be taken directly by the State Council to which it directly reports). The law also details the instruments PBOC can use to take up its responsibilities. PBOC shall not give any guarantees to outside entities and should not lend funds to other entities other than banks. When suspecting problems in one bank which might endanger the financial stability, PBOC can inspect the bank, with the authorisation of the State Council (Art. 34). PBOC shares with other central banks of the world common functions as a banks' bank.

The *Commercial Banking Law* (References for laws 1) provides details of the requirements for operations of commercial banks and includes general provisions for depositors' protection, licensing, prudential supervision and so on (Table 2.3). The law gives commercial banks the needed operational independence and protects them from any outside interference. The law stipulates that banks have to bear the risks they incur and notes that they should make independent lending decisions based on the borrower's creditworthiness.

Table 2.3 Summary of capital requirements for commercial banks licences

Institution type	**Min. registered capital**	**Min. operating capital for branches***
JSCBs	CNY 1 bln	CNY 100 mln
CCBs	CNY 100 mln	
UCCs	CNY 50 mln	
RCCs	CNY 1 mln	CNY 0.3 mln
RCCs unions	CNY 1 mln	
Combination of RCCs and unions	CNY 10 mln**	CNY 1 mln**
Rural credit unions	CNY 5 mln	
Rural cooperative banks	CNY 20 mln	CNY 1 mln (outlet: CNY 0.5 mln)
Rural commercial banks	CNY 50 mln	
Cooperative FI's savings branch	–	none
Foreign invested bank	CNY 300 mln	CNY 100 mln***
Sino-foreign bank	CNY 300 mln	CNY 100 mln***
Foreign finance company	CNY 200 mln	
Sino-foreign finance company	CNY 200 mln	
Foreign banks' branches	CNY 100 mln	

* Making up no more than 60% of the HQ's capital.
** May be adjusted by CBRC but cannot be less than half that amount. SOCBs branches require the same operational capital than for JSCBs. Further capital for new business lines or expansion of business lines is not required.
*** Further outlets in one city where a branch is already established can be opened with an operating capital of CNY 10 mln.
Source: References for laws 14.

Commercial banks are defined as receiving deposits and lending to the public, and providing settlement services as well as other financial services (Art. 2 and 3). Banks are required to analyse their borrowers before extending loans (Art. 6). Requirements for establishing a commercial bank include having a professional senior management team, as well as having adequate registered capital, shareholders and a complete organisation. Changes in name, business scope, important shareholders, capital and so on have to be approved by CBRC. As Art. 34 states, "A commercial bank shall conduct its loan business in accordance with the need for the development of the national economy and social progress and under the guidance of the state industrial policy" – it therefore, however, remains unclear how free a bank can operate. The situation of SOCBs is clearer: "A commercial bank owned solely by the state should provide loans for special projects approved by the State Council. Losses resulting from such loans shall be compensated with appropriate measures taken by the State Council" (Art. 41).

Commercial banks cannot engage in trust, insurance and securities businesses. They cannot invest in real estate other than for their own business needs, nor invest in other entities such as other banks or real sector enterprises. For trust companies, securities firms, commercial banking stays well off-limits. Services are cross-sold through strategic partnerships. At the beginning of 2006, regulations permitting the establishment of financial holdings (to consolidate a wide range of financial services) had not yet been finalised. Dissolution of commercial banks requires the approval of PBOC.

The *Law of Banking Supervision and Administration* (References for laws 2) is important because it clarifies the legislation for banks, defines the role and position of supervisors, outlines the responsibilities of regulators, defines regulatory measures and instruments and finally supports international cooperation (Liu X. and Liu S., 2004).

The *Law of Banking Supervision and Administration* introduces the CBRC as the new supervisory authority for financial institutions incorporated in the PRC under the leadership of the State Council. CBRC is assigned the responsibility for monitoring banking risks, protecting the interests of all stakeholders (and especially those of shareholders) and maintaining the security of the banking system. Article 3 promotes this idea: "objectives of banking regulation and supervision are to promote the safety and soundness of the banking industry and maintain public confidence in the banking industry".

To supervise banks and fulfil its responsibilities, CBRC can promulgate rules and regulations (Table 2.4), authorise or not the operations of institutions, and review the institutions and their managers through on-site and off-site examinations (Art. 16–23). As sanctions, CBRC can suspend activities or managers, restrict business scope and powers or withdraw licences. In the case of a financial institution threatening the social order, or violating laws, CBRC can also order its closure. Banks in

Table 2.4 Main regulations concerning banking business in China

Time of issue	Subject of rules/regulations
2001	Loan categories classification
May 2002	Information disclosure rules
June 2003	Pricing of financial services
September 2003	Management of Rural Commercial Banks, Rural Cooperative Banks and RCCs' legal entities
October 2003	Lending limits and authorities for group exposures
December 2003	Law of the People's Bank of China (first promulgated 1995) Law of banking supervision and administration Foreign shareholdings Commercial Banking Law (revision from 1995)
February 2004	Capital adequacy Camels system for JSCBs
March 2004	NPLs and write offs Corporate governance at CCB and BoC
April 2004	Related parties and insider transactions
June 2004	Subordinated debt issuance
July 2004	Due diligence in lending business
August 2004	Auto loans (also November and October 2003)
September 2004	Real estate loans risk management Supervision of foreign invested banks
January 2005	Market risks management in commercial banks Assessment of internal controls in commercial banks
March 2005	Derivatives products transactions Operational risk management
July 2005	Small loans
September 2005	Board of directors at JSCBs
November 2005	Asset securitisation
January 2006	Licensing rules Indicators for risk-based supervision

Some of the most important of the above-listed regulations are analysed in the following chapters, where relevant.
Source: www.cbrc.org.cn, www.pbc.org.cn.

difficulties or in a credit crisis can be taken over by CBRC, under the State Council, or can be restructured (Art. 38).

The *Law of banking supervision and administration* as well as other recent new regulations (such as the one concerning capital adequacy) marks a fundamental departure from previous regulations and supervisory approaches. They take different approaches by introducing explicit wording, and not just general principles. Such laws also pave the way for more independence of the regulatory authorities.

Prudential indicators

Prudential indicators were published in 1995 by PBOC and in early 2006 by CBRC (Table 2.5). Until just recently, prudential indicators were not really enforced. Only the re-publication of prudential rules by the newly established CBRC has improved prospects for thorough enforcement.

Table 2.5 Prudential indicators for banks

Capital adequacy ratio	>8% (core capital >4%)
Loans to deposit ratio	<75%
Loans over a year to deposits over a year	<120%
Current assets/current liabilities	>25%
PBOC reserves and cash held/deposits	>5–7%
Single client exposure	<10% of bank capital
Single group exposure	<15% of bank capital
Ten largest clients exposures	<50% of bank capital
Inter-bank loans/inter-bank deposits	<8%
Shareholder loan	<100% of paid-in capital
NPL ratio	<5%
NPA ratio	<4%
Core liabilities to total liabilities	>60%
Percentage of liquidity maturing in 90 days to liquidity gap for 90 days	>10% (on- and off-balance sheet)
Aggregated forex exposure	<20% of bank capital
Operational costs and depreciation	<45% of operational income
Return on average assets after tax	>0.6%
Return on average equity after tax	>11%
For loans and assets the loss provisions	>100% of the required provisions
Credit exposure to one related party/group	<10%/15% of the bank's net worth
Credit exposure to all related parties	<50% of the bank's net worth

Source: References for laws 5 and 17.

2.3 Lending and deposit rates

The PBOC has four types of interest rates instruments at its disposal for policy purposes (*China Securities News*, 2006):

1. the on-lending interest rate, which it uses when lending to selected financial institutions;
2. the rediscounting interest rate, which is used to rediscount financial institutions' bills;
3. the deposit reserve interest rate (the deposit reserve ratio was 7.5%. For those institutions with a capital adequacy ratio (CAR) lower than 8%, the ratio is 50 bp higher. A lower rate of 6% is applied to credit cooperatives), which is the remuneration of the reserve requirements with the central bank; and finally
4. the interest rate for deposits above those of the reserve requirements.

In April 2006, the respective interest rates were 3.33, 3.24, 1.89 and 0.99%. The base lending rate was 5.85% and the base deposit rate was 2.25%.

The basis rates of the PBOC also can influence banks' behaviour. Banks lack the right incentives to lend more of their deposits to enterprises. Since deposit rates at the central bank are as high as 1.89% and those in the exchange markets are between 2.2 and 2.3% (while bank accounts deposit rates are a mere 0.72%), banks sometimes prefer to earn their interest income in markets safer than lending (Liu L., 2004).

Until 2004, to ensure an inexpensive financial support to enterprises and to retain some power over terms and uses of loans (Girardin, 1997), PBOC authorised only a small band within which interest rates could move compared to the base rate. Furthermore as fees can only be charged within the narrow scope defined by PBOC (banks only started in May 2006 to charge ATM fees, for example), lending pricing did not take into account creditworthiness and the scope for competition was reduced.

Until the early 1990s, the interest rates on loans to SOEs were extremely favourable as rates for working capital loans to non-state enterprises were typically 20% higher (Huang *et al.*, 2005). The ceiling on interest rates further discriminated against lending to SMEs and non-state enterprises (Lu S. F. and Yao Y., 2003). The ceiling meant that the artificially lower rate could not compensate banks for taking higher risks when lending to SMEs.

Since 29 October 2004, commercial banks in urban areas have been free to set interest rates.[7] However, a ruling by the Chinese Supreme

Court a few years ago has set the definition of a usury rate as being equivalent to four times the base rate set by PBOC (Jiang X. and Ding C., 2004).

In September 2005, PBOC reported that the average fixed and floating loan rates (one year, local currency) were 6.17 and 5.87% respectively, that is respectively only 1.11 and 1.05 times the benchmark rate (PBOC, 2005b). The same report shows that around 22% of banks have on average set their loan rates lower than the benchmark, while 25% have chosen to set loan rates at the benchmark. At most, 28% have made a 30% upward adjustment. The remaining has set higher rates on average.

Furthermore, a few months earlier, the PBOC allowed banks for the first time to choose together with their clients the repayment frequency, the frequency for resetting floating interest rates and for choosing between fixed and floating rates for identical financial products.

Lending interest rates at banks have changed only a little since the removal of the ceiling. Overall banks still lack the tools to price their loans according to the risks incurred, therefore the effect of the interest

Table 2.6 Interest income weight at selected Chinese banks

Bank name	Interest income weight (%)	Year
ICBC	95.66	2005
BoC	85.32	2005
CCB	90.97	2005
ABC	96.37	2004
Minsheng	95.43	2005
Merchants	88.75	2005
SPDB	83.23	2005
Huaxia	99.00	2005
Industrial	96.27	2005
SDB	89.59	2005
CITIC	72.42	2005
BoComm	90.00	2005
12 CCBs	96.66	2004

Definition: Interest income weight = net interest income/(net interest, financial, provision and other income).
Twelve CCBs include those in Beijing, Shanghai, Chongqing, Xi'an, Dongguan, Dalian, Hangzhou, Nanjing, Ningbo, Shenzhen, Tianjin and Wuxi. All of them are located in large urban centres which are also relatively wealthy and most are located in coastal areas.
Source: Own calculations based on data from banks' annual reports.

rate liberalisation has not yet been felt. Market mechanisms are being introduced, but have not yet taken root.

2.4 Credit registries

The PBOC has established in 1997 a centralised database for bank loans.[8] By the end of 2002, the system covered most of China (with 334 cities) for corporate bank loans. The system does not cover inter-company trade transactions or loans to individuals. As of March 2004, the system covered 4.27 mln borrowers and transactions amounting to CNY 13,700 bln. In 2002, for example, the system was checked 4 mln times and the monthly average number of checks is 0.3 mln.

The database includes information on the borrower (name, address, loan registration number, industry, some general financial data and pending law disputes), on the loan (amount, currency, status of repayment based on the five loans classification, maturity) and on the collateral provided (guarantor details, mortgages, amount valued). Normally the potential borrower presents its loan registration card (provided by PBOC) to the potential lending bank (almost all commercial banks are participating), which then will check online the records of the borrower. When granting a loan, the bank submits the necessary information about the transaction and the borrower to the PBOC.

Credit registries for consumer loans or individual loans were established in a rudimentary form in Shanghai (there the first steps were made in 2000) and Beijing. PBOC has established a nationwide credit registry, called the *State Credit Bureau*, for all loans to natural persons (supported by a foreign credit bureau). At the beginning the system included seven cities (in Beijing, Chongqing, Shenzhen, Xi'an, Nanning, Huzhou and Mianyang) and all commercial banks with a branch there (i.e. some 15 SOCBs and JSCBs and 8 CCBs).

The system was fully operational in January 2006 and already could boast data on 340 mln individuals and credit records for 35 mln private borrowers as well as including some CNY 2200 bln in consumer loans (i.e. 97.5% of all consumer lending).[9] Daily inquiry requests are around 110,000 (Marshall *et al.*, 2006). As a result of the establishment of this database, the costs to banks for loan decision-making are expected to fall by 80%.

The information includes general information on borrowers (name, address, work unit, identity number), loan information (lending bank, amount, maturity, loan type, repayment method and records) and credit card information (issuing bank, limit amount, repayment records).

At a later stage it could also include records on payment of bills (telephone, electricity, etc.). It could also include a scoring system for borrowers. Apart from this new system, a large number (about 200) of small credit investigations companies have been established over the past years in China. However, the largest credit investigation company has operating revenue of only CNY 20 mln.

In March 2006, PBOC announced that the enterprise database and the consumer registry will be merged into one comprehensive system starting from mid-2006 (*SinoCast China Business Daily News*, 2006).

The main challenges in setting up these institutional arrangements are the data security and information disclosure issues[10] as well as the combining of registries data with rating or scoring data. Yu Yan (2003) argues that the paucity of information provided for each borrower and the diversity in terms of quality of the submitted data reduce the influence of the system on risk management and on reducing bad repayment practices.

2.5 Credit rating industry in China

Central to the measurement and management of credit risk is the role played by external credit rating agencies. The first step to establishing a credit rating industry was made in 1987 with the issuance of regulations on corporate bonds (corporate bonds outstanding accounted for only 1% of GDP in 2004). However, the industry took until the early 2000s to really take shape (Chen and Everling, 2002) and still does not have a dedicated regulator (rating agencies are under PBOC, as well as two other government agencies, see Zhao Y. and Fu T., 2006).

Credit rating agencies in China rate long- and short-term corporate bonds, their issuers, loan certificates[11] as well as financial institutions and enterprises. There are numerous domestic credit rating agencies in China,[12] established by local authorities, universities or research institutes (Table 2.7). Most are small and lack professional experience. Many have only a regional or industrial focus and have not established any name in the market to speak of. The Chinese credit rating industry is a highly fragmented market and lacks coverage (Zhao Z., 2003).

Apart from lacking recognition, trustworthiness and visibility (Jing X., 2005), these agencies also suffer from the lack of interest of Chinese investors in ratings (most agencies have few subscribers) as well as the reluctance from Chinese enterprises to publish internal information. The rated universe in 2003 was estimated by Wu Jian (2005) at 6.5% of the banks' borrowers, compared with 43 and 44% in the USA and

Table 2.7 Six largest domestic credit rating agencies and their business scope

Name	Start time	Main shareholders/Capital	Branches and staff	Business scope/focus
China Chengxin Securities Rating Co. Ltd.	August 1999	Cinda AMC, Shanghai Securities Co. Ltd. Shanghai Chengxin Investment Co. Ltd. China Jiade International Auction Co., Orient AMC. Fitch Ratings has withdrawn from this investment and was replaced by Moody's for 49%.	21 branches, 40 professionals	Bonds, loan certificates, investment funds, structured finance, investment and corporate banks, credit information service. 25% market share for corporate bonds, 75% market share for bonds issuance.
Dagong Global Credit Rating Co. Ltd.	March 1994	Beijing Xing Hong Liang Investment Mgmt Consultants, and Beijing Da Gong Xin Yuan Credit Rating Consultant. Strategic partnership with Moody's (never really used). Capitalisation CNY 31 mln.	12 branches, 5 senior officers, 120 staff, CNY 31 mln of issues rated	Mainly consulting to setup internal rating systems. Bonds and securities, investment funds, corporate banks, preferred shares, rating for industrial and commercial companies, credibility assessment for introducing foreign capital, feasibility studies, asset valuations.
Shanghai Far East Credit Rating Co. Ltd.	March 1988 in Shanghai	Since Feb. 2002 strategic alliance with Xinhua Financial Network (owns 40%). Capitalisation CNY 15 mln.	7 branches, 60 staff, 196 issuer ratings (most unsolicited), rated 16 corporate and convertible bond issues	Listed companies, loan certificates ratings in Shanghai, corporate bonds, investment and corporate banks, credit information service, SME ratings, lending portfolios ratings, unsolicited ratings.

China Lianhe Credit Rating Co. Ltd.	1997 in Beijing	Registered capital CNY 30 mln.	26 branches, 205 staff, 30 credit analysts, up to now 24 ratings for bonds issued and 27 ratings for transferable securities	Market leader in ratings for corporate bonds, rating of corporates and financial institutions, also active in building credit registries, credit ratings and credit research, 50% market share in 2004 for corporate bond issues, 33% in 2004 for transferable corporate shares.
Golden Credit Rating International Inc.	2001 in Beijing	n.a.	11 expert staff	Several types of ratings and consumer credit data services as well as corporate ratings and FIs ratings.
Great Wall Credit Rating Co. Ltd.	1992	China International Project Consulting Co., Central Securities Registration Settlement Co, Beijing Securities Co. Ltd. and Beijing Foreign Commerce Service Centre. Partly supported by PBOC.	10 branches, 35 specialised or expert staff	Chinese banks, project finance rating, corporate ratings, securities and bonds ratings, change ownership evaluation.

Source: Based on Chen and Everling (2002), Wassmuth (2004) and Hong W. (2004) as well as own research.

Europe respectively. Most domestic rating agencies have not yet found the right balance between objective rating and sales leads (Lee, 2006).

Apart from the domestic agencies, some international credit rating agencies are represented in China: Standards and Poor's, Moody's and Fitch Ratings. Of the potential 8 mln corporates that could be rated, only less than 100 have an external credit rating from an international credit rating agency (Baglole, 2004). Due to the lack of transparency and openness of Chinese issuers, the rating process is rendered difficult and even impossible (Baglole, 2004). Credit rating agencies tend to focus on larger and better-managed enterprises, where depth of disclosure is higher (According to verbal regulators' guidance, inter-bank bonds cannot be rated by international agencies, see Lee, 2006). In order to protect their reputation, agencies are moving prudently in the Chinese market by declining work where information is insufficient. Moody's has entered in April 2006 a partnership with China Chengxin Securities Rating Co. Ltd.

In the short and medium term it is highly unlikely that a significant number of enterprises, especially smaller ones, will get an external rating. Thus the rating universe cannot be expected to grow substantially.

3
Exit Mechanisms in Banking

As mentioned by Wu Xiaoling in an interview (Ye W. and Hu J., 2006), the banking industry in China needs a functioning and efficient exit mechanism: "In a market economy, only if there is a pressure to exit a market, there is a good incentive for operations; [the pressure] improves the healthiness of operations of financial institutions, optimizes the allocation of financial resources, and protects the system from financial instability."

Exit mechanisms for banks are part of the legal infrastructure and come mainly in two forms: through bankruptcy proceedings and through deposit insurance. By way of these, the state does not need to interfere directly in banking sector exits, and leaves the operations to independent institutions such as the courts and deposit insurance funds.

3.1 Deposit insurance

In 1993, the State Council outlined its intentions to build a deposit insurance scheme in order to preserve the financial stability of the system in times of crises. In 1997, a working group was established with the aim of reviewing the possibility of establishing such a scheme. After the large increases in non-performing assets (NPA) following the Asian crisis, the state stepped in to support bankrupt entities.

Preliminary conditions and regulations that deal with the guarantee of bank deposits have been promulgated. CBRC, CSRC, PBOC and the Ministry of Finance jointly issued in November 2004 an *Guidelines on acquisition of individual claims and clients' securities transactions settlement funds* (References for laws 20). It aims to protect the interests of small depositors and investors, the stability and continuous operations of securities markets, the stability of society, to raise the risk awareness and the market discipline and decrease moral hazard. The *Guidelines* stipulate that full compensation would be required for commercial banks' and RCCs' deposits and related interest. Deposits eligible are those of individuals (including also trust transactions and securities). For all deposits before the 30th of September 2004, the deposits and securities transactions of customers amounting to less than CNY 100,000 are fully covered by the insurance scheme. Above that amount, 90% will be repaid. The responsibility is now not the sole responsibility of local governments, but with both central and local government who share costs (for securities and savings deposits the central government carries the costs, for all other deposit types the costs are covered 10% by the local government and 90% by central authorities). However, there are no provisions for deposits after that date (30 September 2004) and 90% is a large portion (Ye W. and Hu J., 2006). It is therefore important that a deposit insurance scheme is established and that banks get special attention in the upcoming revised bankruptcy law.

The idea of a deposit insurance scheme resurfaced in 2004 and is being currently discussed in the press: a scheme is said to be awaiting the highest approval (Chen Y., 2004). A compulsory system is envisaged, which would be similar to that of the USA. It is expected that different premium rates will apply, depending on the bank's CAR (Yue G., 2005). The fund to be created would be under the State Council.

Experts have warned that such a scheme offers a market exit mechanism but also increases the risk of moral hazard and of using people's money to save bankrupt banks (Wang C., 2005 and *The Economist* 2006b: the scope of the deposit insurance scheme will probably determine the amount by which moral hazard will be influenced). In establishing such a scheme the authorities will first need to clarify its funding mechanism (probably with a mix of banks' and government's contributions) and the scope of participation. In addition, the relation between the deposit insurer and the state-owned banks would need to be clarified (as they both would have similar owners, OECD, 2005). Various commentators suggest that the new scheme should have independence from authorities (Deloitte & Touche, 2004).

A deposit insurance scheme could remove the competitive advantage of SOCBs: SOCBs' deposits enjoy the implicit guarantee of the state, something that is not available to other commercial banks (even if state support would be likely).

3.2 Bankruptcy

Bankruptcy is a double issue for banks, in terms of the impact of the failure of enterprises as well as banking institutions themselves. As illustrated in the *Doing Business Report 2005* of the World Bank (WB, 2005), it takes 25 procedures and 241 days in China (compared with 62 procedures and 30 days in OECD countries) to enforce a commercial contract and the average cost amounts to 25.5% of the debt to be enforced. Bankruptcy proceeds take in China on average 2.4 years to complete and cost 22% of the value of the underlying assets (compared with 1.5 years and a cost of 7.4% in OECD countries). The recovery rates achieved by investors are around 31.5% (compared to 73.8% in OECD countries).

Bankruptcy of enterprises

The current *Bankruptcy Law* (also see Annex) has a number of constraints from the point of view of creditors: registration of collateral, seniority ranking and the protection of creditors, the likelihood for realising collateral, and the enforcement of courts' rulings.

Currently, there is no way in China to centrally register collateral. Normally banks can only register collateral locally and at different administrative units for different types of collateral. Such lengthy processes make it more cumbersome to take collateral.

In the current bankruptcy proceedings of enterprises, seniority is determined politically (Art. 156): first come salaries and social security payments, then the claims of the state for tax payments (followed by any other state claims). This endangers the protection of creditors' rights and has been discussed in many essays (WB, 2000; Wormuth, 2004), but no concrete steps have been taken to reform current legislation and it does not appear that changes can be expected in the near future. Treatment of creditors also varies according to location. Bankruptcy proceedings are more an "administrative process" rather than a way of protecting creditors' rights (WB, 2000).

The third constraint stems from the outlook for recovery which further waters down creditors' expectations. It is largely unlikely for financial institutions to recover their claims and thus the incentive for starting bankruptcy proceedings is low.[1] For real estate, because it represents only land use rights (limited to 50 or 70 years depending on the use of the property) and not land ownership, bankruptcy proceedings can mean that local authorities seize without any compensation the user's rights and sell them again.

A final problem is that even once the details of the proceedings have been settled and that creditors can be assured of their repayment, enforcement remains problematic and in many cases no repayment takes place.

When banks act as creditors, they are increasingly becoming "passive creditors" (Goodhart and Zeng, 2005) and prefer not to push for bankruptcy, which is a lengthy and expensive process. Much less resource-consuming is to continue to provide lines of credit to the said enterprise in the hope that one day the outcome of a restructuring (that is likely to be the preferred option by the authorities, especially when the enterprises is large enough or of relative importance to the locality) will enable the borrower to repay. In many cases, this does not even appear to influence asset quality (nor, until recently, managers' bonuses) (WB, 2000).

Proceedings for banks

Bankruptcy proceedings are not only important when banks act as creditors, but also when they are the debtors. Two sets of regulations are important for banks: the *Bankruptcy Law*, although it does not specifically deal with the bankruptcy of banks and the *Rule on Dissolution of Banks* (References for laws 31). However, these regulations are not frequently used for banks. More often the authorities use an administrative decree rather than legal means to resolve problems faced by individual banks, in complete disregard of economic and market principles. The reason for preferring such methods is the stated goal of social stability.

Often in the past, sound financial institutions were ordered by regulators to merge or take over failed banks in their area (Table 3.1). This was the case in 1997 when Hainan Development Bank was asked to take over UCCs which had suffered a run, or in Chengdu where Chengdu City Commercial Bank was asked to take over the failed Huitong Urban Credit Cooperative in 2000 after a liquidity crisis. In the first case, Hainan Development Bank was driven into bankruptcy by the take over and was finally closed down in 1998 (Zhao S., 2004). It was the first official closure, but not a true bankruptcy. Chengdu City Commercial Bank is still digesting the failed Huitong cooperative and is still feeling the negative impact on its business and its future development.

By way of removal, dissolution, closure or bankruptcy, between 1997 and 2001, the central bank has dealt with 427 smaller financial institutions which were conducting illegal or irregular operations or which were unable to repay their debts. It also closed some 28,588 informal rural (rotating) funds or credit associations. In 2001, through name

Table 3.1 Selected rescue activities of bad banks in recent years in China

Bank name	**Year**	**Rescue method**
Qingzhen Hongfeng RCC	1996	Payment crisis. Merged to Guiyang CCB in 1999
Haikou UCCs (33)	1997	Closed. Takeover by Hainan Development Bank
Hainan Development Bank	1998	Closed. Relending by PBOC of CNY 4 bln
Zhengzhou Rural Cooperative Bank	1998	Run in 1998. Fully taken over by PBOC in 1999
Various FIs in Enping City	1998	CCB branch removed, ABC branch cleaned, 20 UCCs closed. Total loss to PBOC CNY 6.8 bln
Guangxi Beihai City Cooperative	1998	12 closed, 2 had their licences withdrawn
Hunan Changge UCC	1998	Operating without licence, closed down
Guangzhou Shantou Commercial Bank	1999	Payment difficulties. Restructuring
China Investment Bank	1999	Bought by China Everbright Bank (CEB). Provisions at CEB increased by CNY 7.3 bln and bank is still struggling
Huitong UCC	1999	Payment difficulties. Merged into Chengdu CCB

The list does not include rescue activities for securities firms, insurance companies, trust and investment companies.
Source: Based on information from Zhang. H. and Cheng. M. (2003), as well as author's own research.

changes, forced mergers, acquisitions, and restructurings, it disposed of 766 UCCs. In 1998, it closed down a further 239 TICs (Yu N., 2005d). Only Guangdong ITIC[2] was allowed to go bankrupt in the past (it did not hold any public deposits).

In China, as in many other emerging or developing countries, larger financial institutions facing financial difficulties are rescued and supported by the state. Adherence to the "Too big to be allowed to fail doctrine", however, creates moral hazard problems and reduces incentives for introducing best practices in banking. Thus recently, Chinese regulators have made calls for increasing market discipline and reducing the likelihood of administrative state bailouts.

In a speech in December 2005, the Chinese regulators somewhat changed their stance towards failed smaller banks. They warned those high-risk banks[3] that they may be closed altogether (CBRC, 2005a). In these cases, the resolution will involve the repayment of debts (according to the percentage of debts to assets) to natural persons by local authorities (using central government special loans as well as using re-discounting by the central bank). The closures may, however, also include the mergers or restructuring or rescuing in some form or another for some of the UCCs.

In 2005, Tang Shuangning, CBRC's vice-chairman in charge of CCBs supervision, clearly outlined measures to support the worst performing CCBs[4] (Liu Y., 2006): "Seek support, Add strength, Grasp the focal point and Reduce risks (求支持、加力度、抓重点、解风险)." "Seek support" means looking for the support of local authorities. "Add strength" means increasing NPLs disposal and the reduction of other inherited risks. "Grasp the focal point" means focusing attention on the reduction of high risks. "Reduce risks" is self-explanatory. Closure is only the last option when nothing else has worked and all other ideas and measures have been exhausted.

For the upcoming bankruptcy law (see Annex), Chinese banking regulators are working with those drafting the law to integrate a special article concerning banks, and creditor rights should receive better protection. Finally, Chinese regulators are also working on creating a nationwide collateral registry, although the timing is unknown.

Issues and constraints in current bankruptcy proceedings

The administratively run bankruptcy proceedings for banks and for enterprises discourage sound banking practices. First, these impact negatively on the incentives for banks to learn and to avoid bankruptcy. Second, the costs of bankruptcy proceedings for enterprises are often higher than those of keeping credit lines open.

Ba Shusong and Chen Hualiang (2005) discuss the impact of rescuing bad banks on the reputation of the authorities. If strong authorities are seen as saving bad banks from bankruptcy, then other banks will have less incentive to learn from experience and markets will become less efficient. As a consequence, the default probability of banks increases. A small change in the authorities' behaviour can have a large impact on their reputation. A loss in reputation is linked to higher costs for the authorities and to higher wealth losses to society (the resulting moral hazard is a cost of saving the bad banks). This creates an accelerating vicious circle. This issue has been recognised by a number of high-level financial regulators, but concrete action has not been yet taken (Ba S. and Chen H., 2005).

It is also questionable if functioning bankruptcy proceedings for banks would represent a sanctioning mechanism for the largest of them. Chen X. (2005) has illustrated that a state-owned bank would in a case of failure represent such loss to the state, that that state will ensure that the bank is kept afloat. Thus even threats by the authorities to close a large bank are often not credible.

Despite a few improvements that have taken place in the financial infrastructure of the Chinese banking system, banks still have too few incentives to introduce best practice. While rules and regulations have become more detailed and target risk management practices and enhance prudential benchmarks, serious moral hazard problems still remain in the system. Unless appropriate market-based bankruptcy proceedings and deposit insurance systems are established, these serious moral hazard problems are unlikely to be reduced.

4
Role of the State

The state[1] has a very influential position and permeates all of the Chinese banking industry. The state is shareholder, lender of last resort and also influences strategic, operational and managerial decisions throughout the banking system.

The state is a major player and owner not only in the banking industry. This assertion is also true for the whole financial system. The Chinese state also has a dominant position in stock markets[2] where it is the indirect and direct owner of most shares listed (81%). Further to these, it is also dominant in regulation and supervision of all entities active in the financial system due to the reduced independence of regulators. The state's influence permeates the whole financial system.

4.1 Financial influence

Apart from the four SOCBs (where it had as of May 2005 82% of SOCBs' capital; Chu *et al.*, 2006b), the three policy banks are also under direct government ownership (under the State Council, China's highest political body, or the especially established Central Huijin Investment Co., which is itself also under the State Council). The state also holds banking assets indirectly through local governments and SOEs as is the case in most JSCBs and CCBs. The Chinese state holds between 95 and 99% of all banking assets (Bekier *et al.*, 2005 and OECD, 2005). The only bank whose capital is in majority privately held is China Minsheng Banking Corp.

Apart from having a controlling equity stake in the banking sector, the Chinese state has also provided generous financial support to financial institutions. In 1998, the state issued fresh capital amounting to CNY 270 bln to the four SOCBs. In 1999, it issued CNY 1.4 trillion in securities to support the transfer of NPLs from the big four SOCBs to their respective newly established four AMCs. In 2004 and 2005, it spent a total of USD 60 bln in foreign reserves to recapitalise the Bank of China (BoC), China Construction Bank (CCB) and ICBC. Furthermore it also spent CNY 168 bln to support the reform of RCCs (Yu N., 2005d). Overall, up to 2006, the state has spent around CNY 2.3 trillion to support the banking system (i.e. some 21% of China's real GDP in 2003).

Researchers at Deloitte & Touche (2004) have estimated that the Chinese authorities will need some USD 662mln to further reform different parts of the Chinese banking system: USD 56 mln will be required to bring corporate governance and human resources systems up to international best practices, while the development and establishment of management information systems (MIS) will require USD 246 mln and that of risk management systems USD 360 mln. Two thirds of that sum would be earmarked for SOCBs.

None of the Chinese commercial banks has its liabilities guaranteed by the state. However, the state has a long history of financial support, thus the state acts as an implicit guarantor. By law, neither central nor local authorities can provide guarantees for bank loans. However, this is practised in a number of financing arrangements (through related firms) to support local economic development (Guo Q. *et al.*, 2006b as well as Sun M., 2006). These guarantees can be used to pressure borrowers into repaying debts but have no legal value. Recently the central authorities have required local governments to stop such practices and reiterated their stance by declaring that guarantees issued after the 26th of January 2006 were void.

While central and local governments may be seen as "saviours" in terms of financial support to the system, they can also be viewed as "wrongdoers" in terms of interference, destroying incentives to introduce best practice and establishing an environment where moral hazard predominates.

4.2 Influence on decision-making

Before the start of the reforms in 1978, the banking system was just one of many parts of a huge state administration. Financial flows were organised around the planning exercises for the whole economy and flows were directed to specific industries and regions based on political decisions. Since then, the authorities have remained influential in the decision-making process of banks, especially larger ones. While the credit plan system (see Annex) has been removed, practices remain, especially for large government projects and SOEs (in disregard of creditworthiness and repayment ability and willingness). This is not only the case with central authorities, but also with local ones.

The Chinese state has business interests. As illustrated by Shih (2004), the Chinese authorities can obtain private gains and advancement through bank loans. He showed that more loans (+4.4%) were likely to flow to a specific province when that province was headed by a party official with ties to the central leadership. Another way of increasing the flow of loans is to generate more revenues for the central government (Shih, 2004). For many local governments a tight grip on bank's lending decisions can help develop the local economy by securing financing for infrastructure projects and real estate development (Table 4.1) (local governments have a monopoly on land, and thus on land prices and land transfers; *The Economist*, 2006h).

In some cases, the state appeared to use bank lending to compensate for lower levels of government-spending and government-financed projects. Thus local authorities needed to take more influence on the lending decision and process, to politicise lending (Heilmann, 2005). At the same time this weakens the power and pressure that regulators can put on local financial institutions. While corporate governance mechanisms have limited the influence channels of party and local governments, these have not been removed completely (Heilmann, 2005). This creates conflicts between managers and shareholders when having different interests and loyalties.

The Chinese state also has personnel interests in the banks. For state-owned banks, as the majority or sole shareholder, the authorities have the right to choose senior managers. For example, all senior managers and board members of the four SOCBs are appointed by the State Council. This is in line with the government's policy of choosing senior managers and board members reflecting political credentials rather than business acumen.[3] The authorities also have the power to remove or transfer the managers as they see fit, in *all* banks in China: some 80%

Table 4.1 Lending yearly growth rates

Year	**2000**	**2001**	**2002**	**2003**	**2004**	**2005**
Total loans (%)	6.0	13.0	16.9	21.1	11.6	9.8
for comparison						
Real GDP % growth	8.4	8.3	9.1	10.0	10.1	9.9

Source: Based on data from IIF 2005 and from www.pbc.org.cn.

of CEOs and 56% of senior executives in SOEs are appointed by the party (Pei M., 2006b). Under such conditions, managers are given the incentive to reach a higher position in their (political) career rather than profit maximisation (Goodhart and Zeng, 2005). The high level of decentralised management in Chinese banks makes it even easier for these authorities to intervene efficiently at branch level. Since 1993, the influence of local authorities over the choice of bank managers has been forbidden, but unofficially influence channels remain lively (Grimm, 2005).

Finally, the influence of the Communist Party should not be underestimated. Formally, it operates at local level through "financial services offices" which are set up to provide administrative services to financial institutions (such as encouraging their establishment in certain geographic areas). Its work in local level financial supervision can be influential (Heilmann, 2005) and is often orchestrated through local governments' finance bureaux and diverse work commissions. In financial institutions, party committees do influence the appointment and removal of senior bank managers and branch directors in local banks by proposing managers and reviewing preliminary applications[4] (which are then submitted to CBRC for final approval). Party committees can also influence strategic lending decisions if necessary. This involvement undermines the establishment of corporate governance structures.

A good example of the authorities' influence on the banks' internal management and decision-making process can be illustrated by the latest loan growth in the banking sector (Guo Q. *et al.*, 2006a). The increase of 6% in the first quarter of 2006 was mainly led by fixed investments growth, reflecting efforts of local governments to secure loans for their local investment projects.[5] These investment projects are called "打捆贷款" "bundle loans" and amounted to some CNY 1 trillion for the first 4 months of 2006 (typically these loans have 10-year maturities; Sun M., 2006). This increases the banks' exposure to local authorities (the loans are often collateralised with land based on the assumption that prices will continue to rise) as well as to certain industries (such as infrastructure and energy).

The lending activities of China Development Bank, a wholly state-owned policy bank, provide another example (Zhang Y., 2006). In a number of cases it has taken indirect stakes in CCBs (such as Deyang, Changchun and Chongqing) to help in the restructuring efforts. Normally funding is channelled through a local investment or AMC and is agreed upon in cooperation with the local authorities (which often also guarantee repayment and offer land collateral for loans).

The loans are also tied to conditions, and progress on the restructuring of the bank has to be shown. While such examples may increase the opportunities for restructuring CCBs, it does not resolve the fundamental question of the state's interference and does not build up strong mechanisms for appropriate banking reform.

The influence of the authorities is in some cases welcomed by the banks themselves (Luo J., 2002a). Banks have a number of reasons for supporting state involvement as this can help with restructuring efforts and the local authorities as shareholders put little pressure on managers to address NPL problems. Since local authorities' ownership rights are not explicitly defined (most local banks were only recently incorporated and before that they were part of local governments' budgets), these still have strong administrative power in decision-making but put less stringent disclosure and governance requirements on the banks. Finally, banks require local government participation to resolve NPL issues that they have helped create (Luo J., 2002b).

4.3 The role of the regulators

Banking regulators have a difficult position: they are part of the state apparatus and are under its leadership, at the same time, they should be in a position to oversee banks independently to create a real sanctioning mechanism. There are a number of issues that pose a threat to this.

The first issue are the different incentives of the state compared to regulators. This is especially true for local governments and also for central authorities and the Communist Party. In fact many SOEs will face a more difficult environment in terms of credit lines and financing if banks are required to reform their risk management standards. To protect them from these challenges, local governments could intervene in their favour at banks in their area. Influence is prohibited under the banking law; however, the reality is different.[6]

Furthermore the commitment of the Chinese authorities to reform the banking system can be questioned in view of the priority given to social stability. This is especially true when it comes to SOCBs where the state has a stronger influence and this also explains the difference in regulating SOCBs and JSCBs. The central government is expected to step in, should the need arise, in order to preserve social stability.

Another challenge that Chinese regulators face is the usual use of administrative controls rather than market-oriented instruments. Administrative controls are, for example, still widespread to curb lending in bullish times. The newly issued regulations take a different approach by moving towards a more qualitative supervision, and remove the dependence on and the leeway of local authorities. It remains to be seen how much power local authorities will be prepared to yield.

The current situation in the Chinese banking system has created a number of perverse incentives. First, higher risks can be incurred. Because the state has also been supportive in the cases of smaller financial institutions running into difficulties, all banks show a higher readiness to incur higher risks. Second, banks have incentives to publish low and decreasing NPL ratios (to reduce the level of regulatory scrutiny as well as to increase the reputation of the bank with the authorities and depositors).

4.4 Rationale behind the influence of the state

A number of experts think that if China is not to repeat the mistakes of the past and to ensure a sound banking system, it would be best if the state withdrew from the banking sector – progressively handing over its role and shareholdings to private investors, which would bring the right incentive mechanisms into the system (Yang D., 2004).

During the NPC sessions in March 2006, the Chinese leaders took the opportunity to reiterate both the need for reform in Chinese banks and the need to retain controlling ownership in the four state-owned banks (*Xinhua's China Economic Information Service*, 2006; *AFX Asia*, 2006a). Wen Jiabao was quoted to have added, "First, we will firmly press ahead with the shareholding reform of state-owned commercial banks, [...]. While keeping a controlling share in the state's hands, we will work to improve the banks' ownership structure."

The Chinese banking sector is of crucial importance to the financing of enterprises and thus economic development and growth. It appears that the state would be more than willing to rescue large institutions to guarantee social stability. In view of these considerations, the Chinese authorities are unlikely to relinquish their grip on decisions and capital in banks, especially the larger ones. Such channels enable them to ensure that their interests are still taken into account.

Furthermore, the Chinese authorities have had, up to now at least, the administrative and financial means to support their influential position. The state has been able to maintain its dominant position by building barriers to entry and competition in banking and through its involvement at all levels of bank hierarchies (and in all kinds of decisions) (Boyreau-Debray and Wei, 2005). Another factor that has helped it maintain such a strong position is linked to its financial resources. With the huge reserves (USD 875 bln in May 2006) and other resources generated by economic growth, China has been able to support its controlling position financially as well.[7]

Thus for the time being, the Chinese authorities have pushed through reforms with little interest in reducing state ownership (only minority stakes have been sold) and interference. Some timid steps have targeted the efficiency of state ownership and interference, for example by centralising the supervisory and appointment functions at the central government level (Fang X., 2005). However, the authorities at the local level have not yet relinquished their substantial influence (Heilmann, 2005).

Reforms in the Chinese banking system are unlikely to be deeply rooted until the authorities choose full privatisation. As Steinfeld wrote (2005: 51), "unless the government fundamentally relinquishes control over financial flows and allows marketisation to proceed, capital will continue to be allocated in an extremely inefficient manner". But the centrality of the banks to Chinese economic development makes it impossible for the Chinese state to withdraw from its overreaching support commitment. This further reduces the incentives of banks to follow better banking practices. Even a stock market listing and a partial privatisation cannot remove the distortion of incentives for SOCBs (market domination, for example, remains).

5
Foreign Banks in China

5.1 Historical developments and rationale behind entry

Since 1991, when the Asian Development Bank acquired a stake in Xiamen International Bank, foreign banks have started buying stakes in the capital of Chinese banks. Most of the deals have taken place in 2004 and 2005, after CBRC raised the ceiling on individual stakes to 20% and overall on foreign stakes to 25% in the capital of any type of Chinese bank (including RCCs) in December 2003.[1] Further to this, in January 2006, CBRC announced that foreign investors can invest in "up-to-now off-limits" A-shares.[2] Overall, individual foreign institutions' stakes range between 2 and 20%. As of May 2006, foreign investors had taken equity stakes in 25 Chinese banks (approved) and their equity participations amounted to some USD 20 bln.

The intentions of foreign investors differ depending on the type of investors (international banks, specialised financial institutions and even government backed entities): some may be more interested in developing a sound bank in the long term, while others are more interested in a short-term return on their investment. Their intentions result not only in different stakes and control levels (Yu N., 2005b), but also in targeting different institutions (investors in the SOCBs are mostly new to Chinese banking and are not direct competitors of the banks, *The Economist*, 2005b). The interests of foreign investors are to increase the scope of their business, to deepen their entry into Chinese markets, to prepare for a further increase of the stake whenever the ceiling is removed or relaxed, to form strategic partnerships and to exchange information and customers in order to profit from China's economic growth (He L. and Fan X., 2004). In the area of business cooperation, foreign entrants are currently interested (in this order of priority) in the credit card business, mortgage lending and related securitisations, private banking, insurance products and finally fund management.

Overall Liu Lei *et al.* (2005) find that foreign ownership's impact will ensure less government interference and a more stable financial system. The Finance Minister, Jin Renqing, said in May 2005: "China has foreign currency reserves of USD 700 bln. So it does not need the USD 1–2 bln investment in Bank of Communications from HSBC. What we need is the management and technology, because the authorities do not want to have to recapitalise this bank every other year" (Huan G., 2005).

The interest in Chinese banks (including SOCBs, JSCBs, and CCBs, but even RCCs) is the result of the relaxing of foreign ownership rules in banking assets, the increased importance of capital adequacy, the support of regulatory authorities for such deals and the overall interest in Chinese banking as a future growth market. For Chinese banks the interests are fourfold: first foreign ownership provides new financing (diversifying funding sources, increasing capital adequacy to support growth), second it can enhance corporate governance structures (including risk management and performance incentives systems), thirdly it enables the transfer and introduction of new technology and products (drawing on expertise and state-of-the-art management systems), and finally the foreign brand name can also be attractive in terms of obtaining customers and increasing international funding opportunities. Another factor could also be the increased expected business independence for the investee banks in relation to the local and central authorities (He L. and Fan X., 2004).

In terms of the prices paid by foreigners for Chinese bank acquisitions, the new entrants require discounts to account for the costs associated with NPLs, expensive social security systems, labour policies, weak management systems and various tax issues. However, the share prices of Chinese banks can also attract premiums – mainly related to the large deposit bases and future prospects of the investee bank (Liu L. *et al.*, 2005). Foreign investors (obviously) take a detailed view of corporate governance and business development issues in the context of the acquisition (Table 5.1).

However, not all commentators see foreign entry in a positive light (Yu F., 2005). Some believes that the prices paid were too low and foreigners stand to gain substantially with relatively low costs.

Table 5.1 Foreign shareholdings in Chinese banks (up to May 2006)

Target bank	**Time**	**Investor**	**Percentage stake**	**Nominal amount**	**Approval stage, possible stake increase**
Shanghai Country Commercial Bank	Feb. 2006	ANZ	Around 20%		Not yet approved
Ningbo Commercial Bank	Jan.–Jun. 2006	Overseas Chinese Banking Corp. (OCBC, Singapore)	12.2%	CNY 570 mln	Approved, increase possible in principle
Hangzhou Cooperative Bank	Early 2006	Rabobank and IFC	Together 24.9%	CNY 125 mln	Formerly Hangzhou Rural Credit Cooperative Union
Liaoning Rural Credit Cooperative Union	Dec. 2005	Rabobank (NL)			To be acquired in 2006
Tianjin Rural Cooperative Bank	Dec. 2005	Rabobank and IFC			To be approved
Tianjin CCB	Dec. 2005	ANZ	19.9%	USD 120 mln	Approved
Guangdong Development Bank	Nov. 2005–Aug. 2006	(1) Citigroup, (2) ABN Amro or (3) Société Générale	Not approved		Up to 85% (1) with Carlyle and China Life, (2) with Ping An Insurance, (3) with Baosteel and Sinopec
Nanjing CCB	Sept. 2005	BNP Paribas	19.2%	USD 87 mln	Buying up part of IFC's stake, remaining at 5%.
Shenzhen Development Bank	Sept. 2005	General Electric	7.3%	USD 100 mln	Confirmed
Bohai Bank	Sept. 2005	Standard Chartered	19.99%		Confirmed. Established in Jan. 2006.

Table 5.1 (Continued)

Target bank	Time	Investor	Percentage stake	Nominal amount	Approval stage, possible stake increase
Huaxia Bank	Sept. 2005	Deutsche Bank and Sal Oppenheimer	9.5%, 4.5%	USD 220 mln, USD 104 mln	Confirmed, possible increase by Deutsche Bank
Bank of China	Jul. 2005	UBS	2%	USD 500 mln	Confirmed
	Aug. 2005	RBS, Merrill Lynch, Li Ka-Shing Foundation	10%	USD 3.1 bln	Confirmed (RBS only 5.16% or USD 1.6 bln, no increase option)
		TemasekHoldings (SG)	5%	USD 2 bln	
		Asian Development Bank	3.9%	USD 75 mln	
ICBC	Jul. 2005	Goldman Sachs, Allianz and American Express	10% (7, 2.5, 0.5%)	USD 3.8 bln	Confirmed and approved. (USD 25.8, 10, 2 mln)
CCB	Jun. 2005	Bank of America	9.10%	USD 2.5 bln USD 500 mln	Until 2010 possible increase to 19.9%
	Jul. 2005	TemasekHoldings (SG)	5.10%	USD 1.4 bln	Confirmed
Nanchong CCB	Jul. 2005	German DEG and Sparkassen International Development Trust (SIDT)	10%, 3.3%	CNY 30 mln, CNY 10 mln	Possible increase DEG: Deutsche Investitions- und Entwicklungsgesellschaft mbH
Hangzhou CCB	21 Apr. 2005	Commonwealth Bank (AU)	19.9%	USD 78 mln	
Beijing Bank (former Beijing CCB)	Mar. 2005	ING	19.9%	USD 1.78 bln	
		IFC	5%	USD 447 mln	

Ji'nan CCB	Nov. 04	Commonwealth Bank (AU)	11%	USD 17 mln	Approved, until 2008 up to 20%
Xi'an CCB	27 Oct. 2004	IFC, ScotiaBank (Canada)	2.5%; 2.5%	USD 53.76 mln	Will increase to 24.9%
Shenzhen Development Bank	Jun. 2004	Newbridge Capital (US)	16.5%	USD 150 mln	Possible. (Share lower after GE entry)
China Minsheng	Oct. 2003	IFC	1.60%	CNY 348 mln	No
	24 Oct. 2004	TemasekHoldings (SG)	4.55%	USD 110 mln	
Bank of Communications	06 Aug. 2004	HSBC	19.90%	USD 1.75 bln	
Industrial Bank	29 Apr. 2004	Hang Seng Bank (HK)	15.98%	CNY 2.7 bln	With the exception of a stock market listing, foreign investors have the right to sustain their current percentage stake
		IFC	4%		
		GIC Special Investments (Singapore government)	5%		
Dalian CCB	2003	SHK Financial Group	10%	n.a.	
Shanghai Pudong Development Bank	30 Dec. 2002	CitiGroup	19.9%	CNY 600 mln	Initially 5%, increased in 2006 to 20%, in the future at most 24.9%
Shanghai Bank	22 Dec. 1999	IFC	5%	CNY 182 mln	No

Table 5.1 (Continued)

Target bank	**Time**	**Investor**	**Percentage stake**	**Nominal amount**	**Approval stage, possible stake increase**
	30 Apr. 2002	IFC, HSBC and Shanghai Commercial Bank (HK)	12%, 8%, 3%	CNY 916 mln	No
Nanjing CCB	End 2001	IFC	15%	CNY 182 mln	No
China Everbright Bank	Dec. 1996	Asian Development Bank	3.29%	USD 1.9 mln	No
Xiamen International Bank	1991	Asian Development Bank	10%	USD 10 mln	–
Total (25)	**1991–2006**		**2–20%**	**USD 20 bln**	

Habib Bank of Pakistan is said to be interested in acquiring a stake in Urumqi CCB (possibly for a 20% stake or USD 20 mln). American United Bank is also said to have made a proposition for Shaoxing County Rural Cooperative Bank. Minsheng Bank is also said to be in discussion with Carlyle Group, Kohlberg Kravis and Roberts and Blackstone Group. Ping'an Insurance is also said to be in the approval process for a stake (possibly 60%) in Shenzhen Commercial Bank (which is also in talks with ScotiaBank). Recently, CBRC mentioned that some ten more CCBs are in talks with foreign investors, such as Dalian, Chongqing, Changsha, Wuhan, Nanchang, Quanzhou and Shenyang (CBRC, 2006c).
The above table does not include the stakes taken by foreign and domestic investors through stock market listings.
Source: Based on own research.

5.2 Critics to the introduction of foreign shareholders

The increased influence of foreign institutions in the Chinese banking system has been a controversial issue and voices critical of such developments have grown stronger. For example, while the foreign ownership plan for the BoC has been approved (involving Royal Bank of Scotland (RBS) and TemasekHoldings), it showed clearly that Chinese directors voted against the deal, because they feared that the commitment of foreign shareholders was not sufficient to bring reforms and new technology into the bank. The discussion which broke out in October 2005 reflected the growing worries of Chinese leaders with regard to foreign ownership. When RBS withdrew from an initial commitment to buy 10% and finally took only 5% in the BoC, this further increased state concerns over the scale and depth of the acquisitions (Yu N. and Ling H., 2005).

This incident was also accompanied by a series of articles critical of foreign shareholders' entry into the Chinese banking system (Yuan J., 2005; Yu Y. and Luo D., 2005a,b). The criticism is directed at three issues: first, the usefulness of foreign investors, second the sacrifice of Chinese banks and finally the stability of the financial system.[3]

First, various commentators doubt that foreign strategic investors can be useful to Chinese banks (无效论). Yuan J. (2005) refers to three areas: bringing in management experience, improving corporate governance and changing the credit culture. These, Yuan argues, are absolutely foreign to Chinese thinking and methods, and thus not applicable. Furthermore he thinks that foreign investors' management experience has impacted Chinese managers only in a superficial manner. Finally, he argues that NPL and corporate governance issues can only be resolved once the operating environment improves – both socially and politically. Concluding he observes ("with great pain") that China is not able to reform the banking system by itself and needs the help of foreigners. Other authors (Yu Y. and Luo D., 2005a,b) also hope that Chinese banks could be owned by the Chinese state and the management privatised. Others think that these views fail to recognise the reality which Chinese banks face (Hu Z., 2005; Li L., 2005b; Shu M., 2005). First, foreign investors do provide a learning opportunity for all, but still Chinese managers need time to capitalise on this. Foreigners can help push the establishment of some new mechanisms. Change should be seen as a long-term process whose effects are going to be felt in a few years at the earliest. Foreign shareholders can show other stakeholders how to discipline and supervise banks.

The second argument is that banks are being sold cheaply to foreigners (贱卖论) The authors compare the pre-IPO prices with the post-IPO ones and see windfall gains in the hands of foreigners. This argument has been widely criticised in the Chinese press. Pricing, it was answered, should be the work of investors and markets. Pricing was fair and competitive, as Chinese banks have had time to talk to numerous and diverse investors. Huan (2005) believes that prices should be judged in the long term: foreign investors have a lock-up period and have for most a long-term orientation. Furthermore it fails to recognise that foreign shareholders have given reputational strength to the banks seeking an IPO. Finally, the better return in the short term that foreign strategic shareholders have achieved is also a reward for their greater commitment to reform (technical assistance, large risks with small stakes, etc.) the banks that have been part acquired.

The third argument is concerned with financial system stability (威胁金融安全论). The argument goes as far as to assert that China's sovereignty is endangered by the entrance of foreign shareholders. A persistent argument is that foreigners are using Chinese banks to develop their own products and ideas so as to eventually invade the domestic marketplace. Finally critics believe that foreigners will slowly take over Chinese resources and wealth and walk away with all the riches (Yu Y. and Luo D., 2005a). These views are groundless because of the small shareholdings foreigners are allowed to take in banks. Furthermore financial stability is more related to monetary policy and openness than equity stakes in banks. The more open, the less the system will be prone to financial crises. And up until now the fragility and destabilising influences on the Chinese banking system are more likely to result from domestic problems (such as government interference, policy lending and corruption) rather than external problems such as foreign bank shareholdings.

Ba Shusong (2006a) also thinks that the arguments relating to "the sale of Chinese jewels to foreigners" are unfounded. The greatest threat to the Chinese banking industry comes from the banks themselves. Because they carry substantial NPA, waste people's deposits and so on, they put the whole system at risk. The cost of not reforming would be much higher than that of taking up the reforms.

5.3 Foreign investors' environment

Foreign investors in China are now facing a more critical environment. In this context, CBRC's leaders gave five guiding principles for judging foreign investors:

1. they should not get controlling stakes in large banks;
2. negotiations should follow market principles;
3. foreign investors should bring in strong management experience and technical skills;
4. the investing institution should be a large financial institution; and
5. the adequacy of the foreign investor should be tested in a strict review.

Further to these principles, minimum standards have been announced: investments should be for more than 3 years and for more than 5% stakes, the investing institution should bring forward a director to sit on the board; the institution should not have more than two strategic investments in Chinese banks and the foreign investors should bring technical and network support (*People's Net – Jiangnan Times*, 2005; Yu F., 2005). According to new licensing rules published in early 2006, foreign investors in Chinese financial institutions should have a long-term orientation, have a large asset base (at least USD 10 bln for investing in a commercial bank, less for rural institutions), have a good international credit rating, have been profitable in the last two consecutive years, show sound internal controls and enjoy a favourable (economic and supervisory) environment at home (References for laws 19).

Capital and expertise is what foreign banks are expected to bring, but not control. Control will remain in the hands of the state, for smaller and larger banks. The state regularly reiterates its unwillingness to relinquish full control. Such assertions have been heard from central bankers, bank regulators and other high ranking government officials. Most of the foreign influence is likely to be felt in the area of corporate governance.

With such small participation in the banks' capital, can foreign investors really make a difference? As of now, it remains to be seen how much influence and difference foreign investors can make in Chinese banks. Introducing sound banking practices could be challenging when facing the strong influence of the authorities.

Will the entrance of foreign investors mark the beginning of their end in China, as happened in numerous cases in the real economy? While Ningbo Bird Company was at first only a manufacturer for Motorola, it rapidly turned into a strong competitor. This is not the only case. And in a closer case (both in time and in terms of industry) foreign banks were signing partnership to market their mutual funds through Chinese banks, because these possess strong networks that can help achieve critical mass. But now Chinese banks are being allowed to create and promote their own mutual funds, and are making full use of this opportunity. Thus they have done for mutual funds what Ningbo Bird did with mobile phones: learned from the foreigners, and learned it so well that they can do by themselves, without any foreign help (EIU, 2006a).

The introduction of foreign investors and the opening of the banking sector to competition will not change much the position of the Chinese state.[4] Pei Minxin (2006a) writes that "[p]artial reforms have thus created a hybrid, albeit state-centred, system that allows these elites to perpetuate its privileges". For him, even foreign entry into banks' equity is only a way for the state to strengthen itself. As two China observers mentioned, "China's communist cadres have discovered that equity capital, like state banks' loans in the old days of central planning, does not have to be repaid. And while investors' funds do come with some strings attached, including international-standard accounts and disclosure requirements, this is a small price to pay considering how little control the state has had to relinquish in the process" (Mitchell T. and Lau J., 2006).

Conclusion

While the management of banks and the regulatory environment are gradually changing and becoming more market-orientated many issues remain unresolved. De iure, banks are responsible for their risks, gains and losses. The credibility of authorities until now has been undermined by repeated capital injections and other types of financial support as well as indirect support and influence from the state.

To create real incentives for sound banking, the state should move towards fuller privatisation (reducing ownership to levels below 50%), allow for more competition (encouraging the entry of new institutions), improve alternative financing channels, for example, through the promotion of greater capital markets activity and the venture capital industry, and also seek to diversify capital investments opportunities.[5] In addition, banks and other financial institutions should be forced to carry at least a large amount of the costs resulting from bad management (Chen X., 2005). All these could lead to improved efficiency in the financial system.

The wrong incentives for banking may retard liberalisation. These may delay the introduction of new practices (such as assessing the creditworthiness of borrowers) and retard the closing of the gap between Chinese and international banking practices. As long as the state remains a large controlling shareholder, conflicts of interests and interference (even if forbidden in theory) are likely to prevail. These conflicts will reduce the level of competition in the banking sector and the soundness of banks (because they will have fewer incentives to embark upon reforms).

Finally, so far strong economic growth has allowed the Chinese authorities to use widely available public funds to support its financial system: it is easier to solve problems by spending public funds than to attack the root cause of such problems. However, the sustainability of this situation is questionable. Various authors (Chen X., 2005, Melka and Xu, 2004 and Fan G., 2004 among others) have noted that in the short-term, financial resources are sufficient to support such expenses, but the sustainability depends on future economic growth and shock absorption capability of the system.

Part III
Specific Issues

As we have seen in Part II, Chinese banks are under the tight control and influence of regulators and authorities, but, in some other aspects, still operate in an unprotected environment (e.g. the lack of protection of creditor rights, limited operational and managerial independence, and lack of managerial responsibility).

These features give rise to a number of issues that are not only specific to China, but also common to many emerging markets or transition economies. To compensate for the lack of protection (in certain areas) as well as limited operational independence, banks and other economic entities or participants have to revert to a number of informal mechanisms, such as relationships and networks. These facts and mechanisms come to light in issues that will be reviewed here: distorted formal financial intermediation, high levels of NPLs, small capital bases, corruption and a dysfunctional corporate governance structure.

6
Financial Intermediation

6.1 Definition and measurement

Financial intermediation refers to the activity of (mainly) banks by which they allocate the funds received (deposits) to productive activities and at the same time monitor the behaviour of the receivers of funds (loans). At the same time as the transfer of funds takes place, a transfer and allocation or re-pooling of risks occurs. For the economy to grow, it is important that the allocation of funds is efficient and that financial intermediation runs deep (Cull and Xu, 2000). Poor financial intermediation can be the result of information asymmetries, loans rationing, mispricing of transactions, poor monitoring of behaviour, and so on. All other things being equal, banks should be in a better position to allocate funds than bureaucrats because of their expertise in the analysis and management of risks.

Table 6.1 Loans and deposits in China

Year end in CNY billion	**2000**	**2001**	**2002**	**2003**	**2004**	**2005**
Total loans	9,937.11	11,231.47	13,129.39	15,899.62	17,736.35	19,469.04
Total deposits	12,380.44	14,361.72	17,091.74	20,805.56	24,052.51	28,716.95
Loan to deposit ratio (%)	80.26	78.20	76.82	76.42	73.74	67.80

Source: Based on data from www.pbc.gov.cn.

For successful and efficient financial intermediation, the administrative steering and control of financial flows must be reduced to a minimum or scrapped completely. Furthermore, a functioning resources allocation requires high levels of transparency and information disclosure so that all market participants can be informed in a timely and thorough manner (Grimm, 2005). This information disclosure acts as a market discipline if stakeholders have the means to impose some kind of sanctions for the transmission of bad or misleading information.

Resources should be allocated to productive uses and at the same time should match the maturities of deposits to that of loans. Often in China, short-term funds are lent out for long-term uses, because the banks lack the knowledge to correctly assess borrowing needs or because authorities have restricted banks to short-term lending (then short-term funds are simply rolled over).

Financial intermediation is not only a function undertaken by banks. Capital and money markets, as well as venture capital for example, can also allocate funds to productive uses. Financial intermediation can also take some informal traits when family, friends or other unregistered entities, for example, support an enterprise financially (either with debt or capital).

The depth of financial intermediation in a country is generally measured as the percentage of total loans compared to GDP. Higher GDP per capita and higher economic growth are both positively correlated with a deeper financial intermediation.

Table 6.2 Relation between GDP, M2 and banking assets in China

in CNY billion, %	**2003**	**2004**	**2005***
Real GDP	12,895	14,197	15,603
M2	22,172	25,411	29,876
Total assets	27,640	31,599	37,470
Total loans	15,900	17,736	19,469
Assets as % of GDP	214.34	222.57	240.14
Loans as % of GDP	123.30	124.93	124.78
M2 as % of GDP	171.94	178.98	191.47

* 2005 figure for GDP is an estimate.
Source: Based on data from www.cbrc.org.cn, www.pbc.org.cn and IIF, 2005.

These figures, however do not reflect the quality of the financial flows allocation. The figures may be overstated by large corporate deposits in banks made in exchange for loans (MGI, 2006).

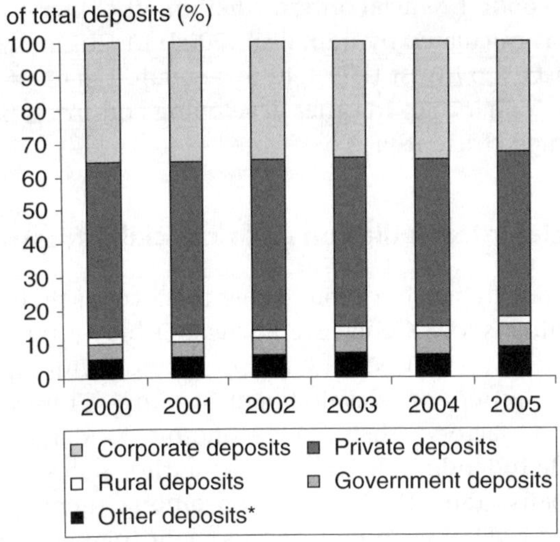

Figure 6.1 Deposits by origin.
* include trust deposits and other deposits.
Source: Based on data from www.pbc.gov.cn.

Since the available resources should be allocated to the most efficient and productive uses, the sector of the economy that is the most competitive and growing fastest should also receive a commensurate part of the funds in the financial system and the quality of the funds lent out should also be profitable (Figure 6.1).

Table 6.3 Enterprises by economic sector in China and their portfolio share (end-2004)

	Enterprises by economic sector (%)	Loan portfolio distribution	
		SOCBs average	JSCBs average
Manufacturing	20.1	22.29	30.50
Trade	17.6	9.97	12.07
Construction and real estate	4.4	11.37	14.80
Services	30.5	10.45	10.70
Public management and others	27.2	32.12	27.13
Total	99.8	86.2	95.20

Note: Services include health, research, education, IT, gastronomy and related services. Other sectors include mining, agriculture, power generation and transportation. The total excludes consumer lending. Figures in first column are based on number of entities.
Source: Based on data from www.stats.gov.cn.

Because of poor financial intermediation, the incremental capital output ratio as calculated by Ira Kalish (2006) in China is 4.4, meaning that China needs to invest USD 4.40 to generate USD 1 of growth. This is quite high, higher than in other developing countries, because funds are not allocated efficiently.

6.2 Financial intermediation and financial infrastructure

A number of researchers have found that the level of financial intermediation in China is low. Genevieve Boyreau-Debray (2003: 18) finds an "inverse relationship between the rate of financial intermediation and the level of economic development among Chinese provinces, suggesting that factors other than economic fundamentals play an important role in lending decisions". The author states that the health of Chinese banks (and the competition among them) goes hand in hand with the level of economic development (higher market concentration is positively related to lower growth). Finally, she finds that higher levels of interference from local governments, measured in terms of financial flows from the government to local banks, are likely to induce a lower level of economic growth. McKinsey analysts (Pitsilis *et al.*, 2004) observe that while private and collective enterprises generate around half of China's industrial output, they receive a mere 2% of the outstanding loan volume. After years of socialist state-led capital allocation, this points to a strong misallocation of resources.

On the other side of the financial intermediation spectrum, deposits are widely available (Figure 6.2). Banks are highly liquid and gathering deposits is an easy task: due to cultural factors (such as the preference for low risk investment products with stable, predictable and in some way guaranteed returns), the lack of social safety nets (for unemployment, illness, pension, accidents, etc.), the lack of alternative investment channels (lacklustre state of the stock markets, under-developed wealth management, highly volatile real estate markets, lack of corporate bond market, etc.), an implicit guarantee of SOCBs' deposits and large banking networks spanning the country. In addition, until recently fixed interest rates were standard (making shopping around for best rates a futile exercise) and Chinese have a high propensity to save (Chen X., 2005).

Scarcer deposits would oblige banks to make choices with regard to the most efficient allocation of these funds. Too much liquidity means that the banks can be relatively lax about fund allocation. If depositors

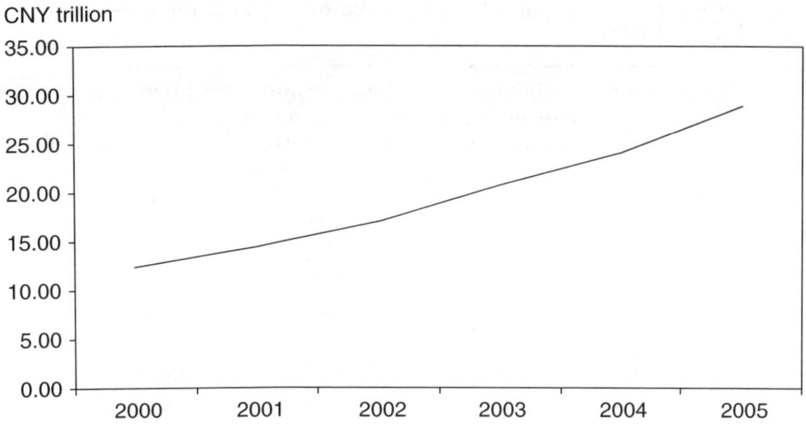

Figure 6.2 Total deposits.
Source: Based on data from www.pbc.gov.cn.

had more investment opportunities, this would provide a stronger control mechanism over intermediation.

Financial intermediation is biased against rural areas (Brandt *et al.*, 2005b). This is even true at rural financial institutions. The reason behind such discrimination is first that rural financial flows are static (each branch or cooperative has to rely heavily on its own deposits for lending) and second that interest rates are capped (remained in force in rural areas in 2004). This impedes the adequate remuneration of risk-taking activities and curbs lending.

When analysing financial flows within China, Boyreau-Debray and Wei (2005: 3) find that "the state-dominated financial system severely retards the efficient allocation of capital". They find that the numerous government interferences and the state-ownership of banks impair the efficient allocation of financial flows and resources. The importance of SOEs in one region also determines to a large extent the volume of financial flows (from government or banks).

Park and Sehrt (2001) also analyse whether the allocation of financial flows in China relies on policy motives. The tests they carried out show that policy lending is also strong in economically more developed areas and was stronger even after the formal end of the credit plan (and after the first bank bailout, see Lu *et al.*, 2005). They further find that in coastal provinces the rate of financial intermediation is actually negatively correlated to the rate of economic growth, thus suggesting that financial intermediation is not based on economic and financial

Table 6.4 Loan portfolio geographic distribution for selected banks (2005)

Bank name	**Beijing and surrounding provinces (%)**	**Shanghai and surrounding provinces (%)**	**Pearl Delta (%)**
BoC	14.98	33.45	20.67
CCB	13.71	62.98	16.64
ICBC	n.a.	n.a.	n.a.
ABC	n.a.	n.a.	n.a.
Average SOCBs	*14.35*	*48.21*	*18.66*
Minsheng	25.75	30.32	16.19
Merchants	0.55	84.37	18.02
SPDB	6.84	46.68	8.66
Huaxia	18.90	28.66	8.35
Industrial	9.68	43.58	15.90
SDB	3.85	76.46	23.19
CITIC*	17.57	31.69	13.56
BoComm	7.11	71.12	17.10
Average JSCBs	*10.38*	*54.45*	*15.34*
Average	**12.37**	**51.33**	**17.00**

Shanghai and Region includes Shanghai, Jiangsu and Zhejiang provinces.
* Figures for 2004. Figures for ICBC and ABC were never published.
Source: Own calculations based on data from banks' annual reports.

principles. Allocation of financial resources reflects SOEs' financing needs: large financial flows are directed towards SOEs in the reform process (Cull and Xu, 2000; Zhang L., 2005).

6.3 Enterprises financing

Chinese financial markets show some peculiar features: enterprises are served by a rather inefficient banking sector and cannot turn to debt or capital markets because of their limited capacity and development (Allen *et al.*, 2004). For many enterprises and individuals, self-reliance or support from other financing channels (e.g. inter-company lending, informal lending and authorities' support) have been the only means to participate and benefit from economic growth. Still the banking sector plays a central role and the economy grows at a high rate.

Table 6.5 Enterprises by ownership type in China (end-2004)

	As published in official statistics (%)	As represented in CCB's lending portfolio (%)
State-owned enterprises (SOEs)	17.7	50.61
Collective enterprises	29.9	2.67
Private enterprises	44.6	30.33
Foreign-funded enterprises	4.7	8.92
Other enterprises	3.1	7.47
	100.0	100.00

Calculations for the official statistics are weighted by the origin of capital. Breakdown for CCB's loan portfolio is given for reference only, and does not reflect the industry average.
Source: Based on data from www.stats.gov.cn and bank annual report.

The main borrowers of Chinese banks are SOEs, the private sector (mainly represented by smaller sized enterprises as well as collective enterprises) (Table 6.5) and private persons.

State-owned enterprises

The SOEs are often large enterprises with structures inherited from before the reform and opening policy. At the end of 2002, there were 159,000 SOEs in China (of which around half have reformed their shareholding structure) with assets of CNY 18 trillion, profits of CNY 379 bln (Green, 2004). After a policy of "grab the big fish and let go small fish" (抓大放小), most SOEs of lesser importance were privatised and reformed (Zhang L., 2005). The most important ones (172 companies with assets of CNY 9.2 trillion) are still in the hands of the state, managed through the State-owned Assets Supervision and Administration Commission (SASAC).[1]

The SOEs in 2003 generated only 17% of China's GDP (down from 80% in 1978, compared with half of the industrial output generated by private enterprises), but still employed 50% of the workforce and amounted to 57% of industry assets. Their performance is well below that of private enterprises in China: 3% return on assets (ROA) compared with 7% for private enterprises (Desvaux *et al.*, 2004).

SOEs, large and small, share a number of common challenges. They suffer from political interference (both at the local and national level), have unclear lines of control (often controlled and managed by one or more ministries or administrative units), have poor creditworthiness and repayment incentives (no hard budget constraint and cannot go bankrupt), are burdened with policy and social goals (generate employment opportunities locally and shoulder social and tax payments) and lack professional managers and functioning corporate governance structures. Thus the incentives to lead these enterprises in a commercial way are rather thin (Goodhart and Zeng, 2005) and the incentives for taking risks are high (expansion without a disciplining mechanism in the case of failure induces managers into taking upon riskier projects which may generate higher profits and at the same time raise their personal career prospects) (Chen X., 2005).

Last but not least, large enterprises such as state-owned ones are attracted to bank loans because they are relatively cheap (MGI, 2006) and less cumbersome compared to debt markets. Banks are the preferred partners for financing not only because of pricing, but also because of the historical relationship that bonds them, because of the similar administrative structures that still exist and the shared interests on both sides.

Such conditions naturally influence negatively their lenders, traditionally the SOCBs. While the riskiness of SOEs may be understood as low because of the high likelihood of being rescued, SOEs are partly responsible for the large volumes of NPLs in the SOCBs.[2] These SOEs are inefficient and draining available financial resources. On both sides, in the banks and in the SOEs, incentives for good management and professional work wear thin. The strong inter-dependence visible between SOEs and state-owned banks results in a strong correlation between reform of the banking system and reform of the SOEs. The SOEs remain, until their full restructuring into truly commercial entities, a major liability of the financial sector (and not an asset as would be the case with other corporate customers from the banks' point of view).

Private and collective enterprises

In June 2004, there were 3.3 mln registered private enterprises in China which employed 47.1 mln people. At the end of 2003, these had a production value of CNY 2008 bln. Most of them (56%) were located in developed eastern coastal provinces and were mainly engaged in manufacturing (38%), catering (24%) and social services (11%) (Miller, 2005). For example, SMEs in China accounted for more than 50% of GDP but received only 10% of all bank loans in 2004 (PBOC, 2004). Private enterprises are more efficient and more profitable: between 1998 and 2003 their ROA increased from 6.1 to 12.2% and their return on equity (ROE) improved from 3.8 to 12.2% (Dougherty and Herd, 2005).

Often, lending to private firms is seen as more risky because of their information opacity,[3] lack of collateral, lack of formal structures and good governance. Other factors also influence their access to loans: the operational and lending policies of banks (procedures do not differentiate among borrowers, industries, etc.), the incentive mechanisms for bank managers (often based on stable interest income generation and the avoidance of bad loans), the lack of widespread confidence in private enterprises, and the lack of a credit registry (Zhang X., 2004a).

Private and collective enterprises lack collateral which would be required to enhance their creditworthiness in the eyes of Chinese banks. Collateral is often required in the form of land[4] or buildings, the only type of collateral acceptable to many banks (Table 6.6) (OECD, 2005). Some banks in the coastal areas use other forms of collateral on a trial basis, such as inventory and movable assets. However, this cannot be expected to develop in the future, unless the necessary laws are implemented and enforced. With Chinese banks progressively relying more on cash flows for analysis and lending, the accessibility of credit

Table 6.6 Loan portfolios' collateralisation (2005)

Bank name	**Unsecured (%)**	**Guaranteed (%)**	**Other collateral (%)**
ICBC*	33.30	27.24	39.47
BoC	21.29	30.64	48.07
CCB	27.94	25.76	46.30
ABC*	n.a.	n.a.	n.a.
Average SOCBs	*24.62*	*28.20*	*47.19*
Minsheng	26.05	31.93	42.02
Merchants	27.77	38.06	34.16
SPDB	17.38	37.85	44.78
Huaxia	3.32	49.29	47.39
Industrial	18.12	38.15	44.78
SDB	14.66	32.80	52.54
CITIC*	26.24	37.97	35.79
BoComm*	22.01	42.52	35.47
Average JSCBs	*17.88*	*38.01*	*44.28*
Average	**21.25**	**33.11**	**45.73**

Other collateral includes all other forms of collateral, including pledges and real estate collateral. The figures include all forms of enterprises. Unsecured loans are often limited to SOEs.
* Figures are from 2004, thus it is not included in the average calculations.
Source: Own calculations based on data from banks' annual reports.

for enterprises other than SOEs should become easier and enable the further penetration of local banks (OECD, 2005).

All other things being equal, collective enterprises such as TVEs fair slightly better. TVEs belong to the population of the village or township in which they are established.[5] These represent a strong inflow of financial resources for townships and villages which saw their revenues decrease as a result of fiscal reforms. The TVEs generate profits that can be transferred to the township. The roughly 20 mln TVEs in China account for about 30% of the country's GDP (Dong and Featherstone, 2004).

The TVEs have a greater chance of getting a bank loan because of the protection from local authorities. Enterprises in rural areas have often relied in the past on their local governments to ensure sufficient funds. At the same time, these generated tax revenues and employment in their areas. However, they still suffer from the poor financial intermediation because most lending is directed towards urban areas. Banks implicitly analyse rural enterprises as being more risky and less worthy of loans. Apart from this bias, collateral also is an issue for TVEs. They also lack the ability to provide collateral and require stronger support and guarantees from local authorities (Kwong and Lee, 2005). The reform of banking practices is likely to encounter strong resistance in the short term in rural areas where TVEs' revenue and employment generation is necessary for rural development (Kwong and Lee, 2005).

Because of the wrong incentives both for banks and managers as well as the influence of politics and administration, lending is still geared towards large SOEs. Private enterprises and TVEs also need loans to grow but are unable to use formal decision-making channels to obtain a favourable decision in lending (lack of human and financial resources for loan bargaining). To ensure access to bank loans, private enterprises have to spend a large amount of their profits on diverse fees and entertainment[6] (respectively 68 and 15% of profits, Miller, 2005).

Importance of banks in financing enterprises

While Chinese enterprises heavily rely on internal finance or self-financing for their overall financing needs, bank finance accounts for a large part of external financing sources (Table 6.7). This can be explained by the under-developed debt and capital markets, capital account controls and the high level of liquidity in the banking system.

The financial intermediation function of Chinese banks is hampered by hidden information and hidden action (Longueville and Ngo, 2004).

Table 6.7 Sources of finance for Chinese and US enterprises

	Internal finance (%)	External finance (%)			
		Bank	Informal*	Supplier credit	Others**
China	70.07	10.17	5.93	2.41	8.67
US	52.88	21.47	2.94	6.62	16.09

* Informal lending is lending by money lenders or friends and family.
** These include equity, leasing, development bank financing.
Source: Based on Beck *et al.*, 2004.

Hidden information asymmetry results from the lack of tools available to the banks to control the veracity and completeness of the information submitted by potential borrowers. In fact, bank officers tend to build informal information networks to mitigate this risk, but their reliability is limited by the private interests of stakeholders in these networks (which may collude with those of bank officers). This issue is further worsened by the fact that loan officers lack skills and experience to recognise potentially bad borrowers. Other factors such as the lack of credit registries, inappropriate incentives on both sides and limited risk pricing mechanisms in banks also place a drag on the system.

The hidden action issue is also a strong challenge in China. Credit monitoring and controls are under-developed at best and loan officers rarely check the use of loan proceeds or the progress of an investment project. In fact they do not have any incentives to do so: there is no punishment for bad behaviour (such as loss of employment) and the bank will not be declared bankrupt when accumulating losses. Where bank managers are responsible for their unit's profitability, discrimination against SMEs is much less likely (Brandt and Li, 2003).

More stringent capital requirements have a potentially negative impact on the depth of financial intermediation: to comply with higher capital adequacy, one inexpensive way is to increase the portfolio of government bonds which carry a lower risk. It has been calculated that on average a deposit of CNY 100 is lent in the amount of CNY 50–60, compared with the CNY 70–90 international average (*SinoCast China Financial Watch*, 2006a).

6.4 Informal financial intermediation

China's rates of economic growth and the performance of its private enterprises are striking in view of its distorted financial intermediation.

One explanation is, apart from the reliance on internal funds generation (through profits), the strong informal lending sector.

Financial intermediation is developing in China on two tracks: one formal, dominated by the steering hand of the state; the other informal, dominated by networks and relationships among individuals, which has provided an alternative to the mainstream system. Both seem, however, to be necessary ingredients of China's economic success (Allen *et al.*, 2005).

Imperfect markets and weak institutions, such as in China, require entrepreneurs to establish informal networks (with friends, family, politicians, etc.) and institutions in order to fill the gap not yet closed by formal institutions and the rule of law, in order to achieve their economic goals and support their economic activities. Informal channels are a temporary, transitional but expensive and time-consuming instrument to compensate for the lack of formal functioning and efficient arrangements or contracts. The stage of development of an economy dictates the importance and scope of informality. While formal arrangements (such as the protection of property rights or of creditor rights) are substituted by informal ones in the short term, they are still a necessary requirement for long-term sustained economic development.

Informal lending has also developed because private funds have only few good investment opportunities: lending informally can bring as much as 20% p.a. compared to the 1–2% in a bank's savings account. For individuals it is also possible to participate in trust loans.[7]

Informal lending includes all financing and depositing activities that are not channelled through the intermediation of formal and regulated institutions.[8] Informal lending can take many forms: loan sharks, revolving savings associations,[9] pawn shops,[10] family and friends, other individuals (private, a firm's employees, bureaucrats, etc.) and other enterprises (including SOEs[11]) and so on (Tsai, 2001). Informal lending is especially lively in coastal areas and common in Guangdong and Wenzhou as well as in north-eastern provinces.

Informal lending started to grow strongly from 1997 onwards (Zhong W. *et al.*, 2004). Depending on the source, informal lending markets are estimated to amount to around CNY 950 bln to CNY 1 trillion, that is around 7% of GDP and 6% of all lending in China (OECD, 2005; Xu Y., 2006; Yao K., 2006). In rural areas it could account for as much as 70% of all lending (Yao K., 2006) and 60–70% of SME financing comes from informal lenders in underdeveloped areas, compared with 30% in other areas (OECD, 2005). Informal lending can account for as much as 45–65% of all financing for large SOEs but 90% for small enterprises

(Allen *et al.*, 2004, 2005). In some places it amounts to 44% of formal lending, but in especially lively places such as Wenzhou this percentage is closer to 80% (Niu M. *et al.*, 2004).

Informal credit markets showed interest rates 50–100% higher than the official rates (Lu S. F. and Yao Y., 2003): 15–24% p.a. depending on the area and the product (consumer purposes are generally cheaper than productive uses), but can also be as low as 5–10% (Bradsher, 2004; Niu M. *et al.*, 2004; Xu Y., 2006). Loan amounts can also vary widely: single loan amounts in Henan are at least CNY 4 mln (Guo L., 2005) while another survey found that enterprises draw on average CNY 10–30 mln (Niu M. *et al.*, 2004). The purposes of such finance are becoming more diversified: from the original consumer orientation (including education, housing, individual farming) and easing of short-term financial shortages (mainly for enterprises, both SMEs and TVEs) towards longer-termed productive operations (Niu M. *et al.*, 2004). There is no reliable data for delinquency rates in informal lending, but these are assumed by most researchers to be quite low.

Informal lending has some important virtues in the Chinese banking market. Informal finance relies solely on creditworthiness, is flexible and produces easily understandable information (no need to understand procedures, requirements, etc.). Furthermore, informal lending is efficient in allocating resources and funds and contributes strongly to local economic development (Guo L., 2005). Informal lending serves the financing requirements of all those excluded from the mainstream finance sector (such as individuals, small shops, SMEs, etc.). Informal lending also gives information on realistic lending interest rates. It can boost higher flexibility and faster response to firms' requirements (Guo L., 2005). Finally, it provides useful investment channels for idle funds and creates more impetus for reform in the formal lending system (Niu M. *et al.*, 2004).

But, informal lending also has some negative aspects. It adds pressure on sources of funding for formal banks, it represents foregone tax revenues for the authorities, interest rates can be usurious, it breaches with official development policies (runs contrary to any controls that governments tend to set upon financial flows), and finally limits the regulatory role of the authorities (Girardin, 1997).

Local governments have long tried to curb or to forbid informal lending (Tsai, 2001); however, they have recently changed their attitude to a more progressive one (Yu L., 2006) and have begun to informally monitor developments in informal lending (Balfour and Roberts, 2004). Having said that, attitudes still differ in regions and provinces and are also largely dictated by the liveliness of informal lending in that particular area and the attitude and support to private sector development of that particular local government (Tsai, 2001).

An efficient way to deal with the informal lending sector would be to increase the performance of mainstream banks, to increase their intermediation capacity, to improve the allocation of resources and capital, and to remove constraints on the country's financial infrastructure.

7
Non-performing Loans

A major and long-standing issue in the Chinese banking industry are its non-performing loans (NPLs). This problem is common to most banks, but is particularly acute in banks which are older and where state shares have more weight. The highest NPLs ratios are found in SOCBs, some CCBs and rural financial institutions (Table 7.1).

As for many banks their NPLs exceeded their equity in the past, the banks were technically insolvent and kept afloat only to avoid bank runs. Apart from weighing down a bank's profitability, high levels of NPLs also have the effect of reducing a bank's creditworthiness (which may lead to a rating downgrade or greater hurdles or costs in raising funds), increasing potential bank and system failure (through contagion) and negatively impacting economic reforms.

Table 7.1 NPLs holdings in China (end-2005)

	in CNY bln (%)		
Bank type	**NPL amount**	**NPL ratio**	**Share of NPLs**
SOCBs	1,072.48	10.49	81.66
JSCBs	147.18	4.22	11.21
CCBs	84.17	7.73	6.41
Rural commercial banks	5.71	6.03	0.43
Foreign banks	3.82	1.05	0.29
Total	1,313.36	8.61	100.00

Source: Based on data from www.cbrc.gov.cn.

7.1 Estimating the level of NPLs

The level of NPLs at the turn of the century is still unclear. Stakeholders and observers of the banking systems have mentioned figures that diverge quite strongly: in 1999, the then Governor of PBOC, Dai Xianglong, said that 20% of all loans were non-performing; in 2001, he revised this figure to 26.6% and in 2002 to 30% if calculated by western standards (Lardy, 1999). In the late 1990s and early 2000s, the estimates of NPLs ranged from 20 to 35% of GDP or 20 to 40% of all outstanding loans (Schmitz, 2004). Well-informed observers even put forward that 50% of all loans was non-performing by the turn of the century (Studwell, 2002). RCCs in China fared even worse: an investigation showed that in the reviewed provinces, the NPL ratio in 2001 reached on average 45% and a maximum of 67% (Xie P. *et al.*, 2005d). In December 2005, the President of ICBC disclosed the bank's NPL ratio for 1998 (based on the five-tier classification) at 47.5% (Jiang J., 2005). These divergences illustrate the lack of reliable data and the difficulty to assess the true situation, even for insiders.

Table 7.2 Non-performing loans in China

Bank name	NPL ratio (%)	Reserves coverage ratio (%)	Equity coverage ratio (%)	Reserves to portfolio (%)	Year
ICBC	4.69	54.20	27.47	2.54	2005
BoC	4.62	80.55	7.64	7.64	2005
CCB	3.84	66.78	10.91	2.57	2005
ABC	26.73	4.68	845.40	1.25	2004
Minsheng	1.30	101.44	– 0.46	1.32	2005
Merchants	2.58	111.03	– 5.44	2.86	2005
SPDB	1.97	142.07	– 20.17	2.80	2005
Huaxia	3.04	69.34	20.86	2.11	2005
Industrial	2.33	90.51	4.42	2.11	2005
SDB	10.56	37.82	198.34	3.99	2005
CITIC	3.70	83.73	10.87	3.10	2005
BoComm	2.34	69.74	6.58	1.63	2005
CCBs	7.77	23.75	77.35	1.85	2005
Bank of Shanghai	3.92	46.57	26.25	1.82	2005

Definitions: NPL ratio = amount of NPLs at the end of the year/gross loan portfolio amount at the end of the year; Reserves coverage = reserves for loan losses/amount of NPLs; Equity coverage = (amount of NPLs – reserves for loan losses)/total equity at the end of the year; Reserves to portfolio = reserves for loan losses/net loan portfolio.
Source: Own calculations based on data from banks' annual reports.

Exact NPLs figures are difficult to come by for a number of reasons:

- Poor standards for bad debt levels reporting (each branch knows how much bad debt is acceptable and the numbers are not double checked).
- Classification of loans according to the four-tier (where the classification requirements are less stringent and usually NPL levels are understated) instead of the internationally recognised five-tier classification (see below).
- A large number of loans are rolled-over even though the borrower cannot repay the principal (these are then still counted as performing).
- Existence of loans with large outstanding amounts where new loans are granted to avoid large write-offs in case of borrower bankruptcy.
- High number of inefficient SOEs and commercially unviable projects.

These issues are still unresolved and the loan classification standards are not always followed in a stringent manner (WB, 2003).

7.2 Classification standards of NPLs

Until 2004, China used a nationally devised classification for NPLs, referred to as the four-tier classification. The old classification emphasised loans over borrowers (a defaulted loan did not require that another loan from the same borrower would be treated as non-performing), principal over interest repayments, the occurrence of a default event over the true riskiness of the borrower/transaction (Huang *et al.*, 2005). Since 2004, it uses the five-tier classification, in line with international classification standards (Table 7.3).

It should be noted that international current practices with the five-tier categories classification standard still leave leeway in judging in which category a loan should fall (the difference between the categories are not laid down in hard facts). As a consequence, bank managers can still, albeit to a lower extent, report the NPL volumes that are deemed acceptable.

Regulations have also been issued to monitor and manage NPLs (References for laws 26). NPLs and assets should be regularly and systematically monitored and assessed. Special attention should be given to the largest NPL levels and volumes, to large exposures and related parties' transactions.[1] Reporting on NPLs should be made on a monthly basis to CBRC and should cover basic information and situation

Table 7.3 Four-tier and five-tier loan classification

	Before 2004		Since 2004	
Performing	Performing		Standard	
	Overdue	Missing repayment on the principal not on the interest	Special mention (SM)	Borrowers currently still able to service the debt but some factors could impede repayment
Non-performing loans	Doubtful	Within two years after payment period, still no payments	Sub-standard	Borrowers unable to cover principal and interest in full from normal operating income and losses possible (overdue >3 months)
	Unrecoverable/loss	Only in the unlikely event that the borrower is declared bankrupt or liquidated	Doubtful	Collection of principal and interest in full is improbable, significant losses certain (overdue >6 months)
	–	–	Loss	Considered uncollectible, after exhausting all collection efforts or instituting legal proceedings

Source: Marshall *et al.*, 2004a; WB 2003; own research.

on the loans (amount, maturity, trends, area, industry, etc.), write offs, concentrations, quality of newly disbursed loans, analysis of the reasons and trends in quality of new NPLs, and measures taken to improve or to resolve uncovered issues.

7.3 Reasons for the emergence of NPLs

In a speech, the PBOC governor, Zhou Xiaochuan (2004a) said,

> According to this survey [to analyse the causes of NPLs], 30% of the NPLs resulted from state planning and administrative intervention, 30% were due to defaults of state enterprises after state banks provided financing based on state policy, 10% came from structural

> adjustments as a result of state orchestrated closures, mergers and restructurings of enterprises, 10% stemmed from intervention of local governments including poor creditor protection in the judicial and enforcement process, while 20% was due to the inappropriate internal management. In addition, factors, such as poor credit culture, intentional defaults and inadequate application of accounting standards, can be found in all above categories. One striking truth is that many of these causes are related to legal, judicial and enforcement practices.

The emergence of NPLs is highly correlated with the practice of policy lending. For many banks, government interference and structures inherited from the credit plan meant lending to government projects, to politically motivated schemes, independently of creditworthiness and risks. For example, Guangdong Development Bank's loan portfolio quality is much worse in Guangdong than at its other branches (Lu Y. and Long X., 2005).

Xie Ping (2006), general manager of Central Huijin Investment Co., thinks that NPLs emerged as a result of a widespread and common collusion among banks, local authorities, their employees, regulators and asset management companies (AMCs, see Annex). Collusion entails all activities that ensure that responsible persons are not made responsible when it comes to the creation of NPLs. Collusion is useful to those who use it because the cost–benefit–risk equation is equilibrated: the risk of being discovered is low and the cost attached to it is lower than the expected benefit from collusion, the benefits depend on breadth and depth of collusion, because the deeper and broader the collusion, the lower is the risk of being caught (and the NPLs generated are more numerous). Thereby bank managers can find a position in government administration if they favour government projects and related enterprises. Another incentive is when NPLs are disposed of: because NPLs are difficult to value and the information is opaque, the chance of achieving a high price on an NPL sale is high, especially when collusion is at play. Internal collusion within banks, for example, also serves as a method to stand against always higher performance requirements set by authorities for banks.

In their internal structures, banks did not have strong internal controls and credit cultures. Loan monitoring was also ignored and there were no sanctions for bad lending decisions (no bankruptcy allowed for banks and borrowers). Sanctioning mechanisms would have increased the learning effect and strengthen responsibility and decision-making within the banks. NPLs never represented a danger to bank managers (even during an economic downturn). Because of the lack of incentives for banks to manage their risks, enterprises were also not required to reduce their leverage (and few intended to repay loans: Chen X., 2005). Furthermore some regulations hindered the development of adequate loan loss provisions (LLP) (anything above 1% of the outstanding loans in provisions is not tax-deductible) and set interest rates below the real cost of loans (Lou J., 2000).

7.4 Resolving the NPL issues

The central government's response to the NPLs issue emerged progressively. First, it created the four AMCs (for details please refer to the Annex), each one corresponding to one of the SOCBs. Then, it injected cash on more than one occasion, mainly in the SOCBs (Table 7.4). Local governments have also injected some funds into the banking system and helped create asset recovery companies. Finally, starting from 2002, the government required banks to account for their NPLs in a way that was in line with international current practices.

The other banks, mainly CCBs, only had the option to resolve NPL issues with local authorities by creating special entities which took over part of the NPLs (in 2004, local governments spent a total of CNY 23.3 bln to buy NPLs from CCBs, *Xinhua's China Economic Information Service*, 2005b), or by themselves by creating specialised loan work-out and recovery departments. These departments are more likely to deal with recent NPLs. Banks have tried to avoid outright sales of NPLs as it would mean that they need to recognise a loss. However, as the recovery value and probability of loans declines with time, it would be best to sell soon so as to recoup as much value as possible.

Higher competition and market-driven commercialisation made loan reductions necessary. These reductions were achieved mainly through disposals, sales or selective write-offs of NPLs (Table 7.5). Fresh inflows of capital have enabled the largest NPL holders (i.e. SOCBs) to write off or sell their NPLs[2] [Podpiera (2006) asserts that the NPL decreases in the first three quarters of 2005 at SOCBs can be solely explained by NPL transfers]. A large volume of NPA has technically changed hands, but is still in the system.

Table 7.4 Non-performing loans disposals at state-owned commercial banks

		Asset Management Companies				
Year	**in CNY bln**	**Huarong**	**Great Wall**	**Oriental**	**Cinda**	**Total**
1999	Volume of NPLs bought	407.7	345.8	267.2	350	1,370.7
	Loans from Central Bank	94.7	345.8	116.2	3	559.7
	Received from	ICBC	ABC	BoC	CCB, CDB	
	Debt securities from bank	313			347	660
	Financing for NPLs purchase	407.7	345.8	116.2	350	
	Average interest rate (%)	2.25				
2000–2001	Volume of NPLs bought				44.5	
	Loans from Central Bank				44.5	
	Received from the Central Bank, CCB and CDB					
2004	Volume of NPLs bought				320.1	
	Loans from Central Bank				160.5	
	Received from BoC and CCB 278.7 and from BoComm 41.4					
2005	Volume of NPLs bought					459
	Loans from Central Bank					459
	Received from ICBC and spread among all four AMCs					
	Average interest rate (%)					2.25
Total	Loans from Central Bank					1,223.7
	Volume of NPLs bought					2,194.3

Source: Based on Yu N., 2005d.

Table 7.5 Write-offs in China for selected banks

in mln CNY	2005	2004	2003
CCB	3,784	6,342	158,817
ICBC	n.a.	50,500	n.a.
BoC	4,783	186,900	0
BoComm	312	33,382	8,831
SPDB	977	509	n.a.
Minsheng	511	404	121
Merchants	745	303	468
Huaxia	800	481	378
SDB	599	835	0
Industrial	576	335	86
Total	8,304	279,991	168,701

The figures for the three SOCBs in 2003–2004 and BoComm in 2004 include transfers of NPLs to the AMCs.
Source: Based on banks' annual reports.

To decrease the level of NPLs in a sustainable manner, Xie Ping (2006) notes that banks should introduce monetary incentive mechanisms (and not government-related), truly independent check and balance mechanisms within banks (internal audit, credit controls, etc.), strengthen the role of independent external auditors, increase the level of sanctions and strengthen internal controls. However, in many cases banks have found short-term fixes to resolve their NPL issues.

A special feature of the Chinese banking system is the rolling over of loans without any clean-up practices, called "lending new to repay the old" or 借新还旧 (*China Business*, 2003a). The loans are normally for a one-year period (often also as a way to bypass administrative rules not to extend medium- or long-term loans) and are rolled over at the end of each year, without any concern for the creditworthiness of the borrower, its repayment capacity or willingness. First, the structuring of these loan facilities is done poorly. Second, the likelihood of monitoring and recognising NPLs is reduced to a minimum. This creates poor discipline on the banks' and on the borrowers' side, but at least does not increase the amount of NPLs.[3]

Banks have also employed other methods to decrease NPL levels significantly: some have in certain cases extended the maturity of NPLs or have transferred loans from the original borrower to the guaranteeing entity and so on (*China Business*, 2003b). For some observers (interviewed in the above news article) the banks' impetus for decreasing NPL levels came simply from an administrative requirement from the regulators.

For Chinese regulators, the challenge of dealing with NPLs is still very much an ongoing concern. In February 2006, Liu Mingkang stated that the gap between Chinese banking practices and international standards is still huge, especially when it comes to internal controls. The pressure is now coming from newly disbursed loans (Chien, 2006).

7.5 New loan quality

In December 2005, the President of ICBC disclosed the bank's NPL ratio for newly disbursed loans after 2000 at 1.6% (Jiang J., 2005). New loans seem to have a better quality. With the improvement of SOEs' performance as well as the increasing number of private enterprises which exhibit better efficiency and performance, the number and volume of NPLs have been decreasing (Figure 7.1). The stepped up and close supervision of NPLs in banks by CBRC has also helped raise awareness and induced efforts to reduce NPL levels.

Another reform that will surely reduce further the number and volume of NPLs in the future is linked to changed incentive mechanisms. On one side, managers are increasingly recruited in a competitive way in the job market. On the other side, banks – mainly BoC and CCB – have required officers and managers to take responsibility (Zhang X.,

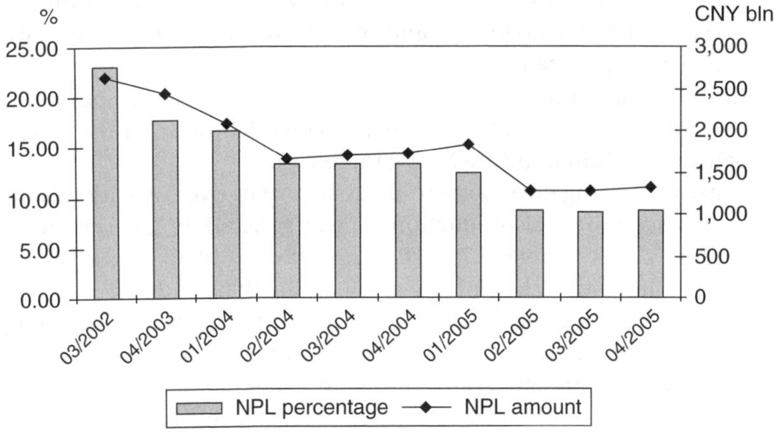

Figure 7.1 Decrease in NPLs in China.
Source: Based on data from www.cbrc.gov.cn.

2004b): large NPL ratios or volumes can become a reason for reducing remuneration or for asking a manager to step down. Further to this, banks are now required to implement due diligence guidelines from CBRC when assessing borrowers and transactions risks (References for laws 8).

However, the recent period of rapid loan growth that banks have just experienced could distort real asset quality (e.g. in real estate lending NPL ratios are said to reach 10–11% at the four SOCBs, *Caijing Magazine*, 2005b). Under high economic growth conditions, normally banks tend to be less precautious in lending and thus the amount of new NPL from these is unknown (Ling Y., 2004; Longueville and Ngo, 2004). Additionally, rapid retail loan growth also accounts for an important part of the reduction in NPLs ratios between 2001 and 2003 (*China Business*, 2003a as well as Allen *et al.*, 2004).

The *China Economic Quarterly* (CEQ) estimates that the main banks (i.e. SOCBs and JSCBs) still hold together 20% in NPLs rather than the published 13% (CEQ, 2005).[4] Although NPL ratios and notional amounts have declined over recent years, the issue is far from being resolved.

On one side, two other developments have made increases in NPLs a renewed concern. These were first the introduction of long term and thus riskier lending (which also became available to SOEs, even less concerned with risks and repayment) and second the financing of large government projects (as well as for example loans to the unemployed, etc.) from state budgets to banks' loan books (Chen X., 2005). On the other side, many banks do not yet have fully functioning credit risk management divisions, do not consistently lend based on economic principles and NPL recognition and management policies exhibit large discrepancies and data is still not reliable.[5]

The growing numbers of special mention loans (still counted as performing – see Table 7.3 for a differentiated definition of these types of loans) could hint at future NPLs (Table 7.6).

Another worrying development is the recurrent overcapacity in some industries such as steel production, power generation and cement, to name just a few (Table 7.7) (*The Economist*, 2006b). While central authorities have tried to curb investments in these industries (mostly energy and infrastructure related, as noted in April 2006, *The Economist*, 2006d), the efficiency of such administrative mechanisms is low because local governments often act against them.

Pressure is also rising on the commercial bill financing by banks (Guo Q. *et al.*, 2006a; Li Z., 2006; Yu N. and Li Z., 2006). The increase is the result of three factors: first, banks' risk management and controls have

Table 7.6 Special mention (SM) loans in Chinese banks

Bank name	2005				2004			
	Amount of SM loans in CNY mln	**% to loan portfolio**	**NPL ratio with SM loans* (%)**	**NPL ratio as published (%)**	**Amount of SM loans in CNY mln**	**% to loan portfolio**	**NPL ratio with SM loans (%)**	**NPL ratio as published (%)**
CCB	290,960	11.84	15.68	3.84	371,434	16.69	20.61	3.07
BoC	284,048	12.71	17.33	4.62	424,606	19.78	24.90	5.12
ICBC	301,283	9.16	13.85	4.69	281,267	7.59	26.58	18.99
Eight JSCBs	164,538	5.45	7.77	2.85	172,979	7.20	10.77	3.57
Bank of Shanghai	12,286	10.26	13.99	3.92	18,741	17.70	21.96	4.94

For 2005, figures do not include CITIC.
* Accounts for the special mention loans fully as if they were non-performing ones. Thus this ratio does not reflect the published NPL ratio.
Source: Own calculations based on banks' annual reports.

Table 7.7 Loan by main industries

Bank name	**Real estate and construction* (%)**	**Manufacturing (%)**	**Trade (%)**	**Consumer (%)**	
ICBC	8.82	31.95	10.09	13.28	2004
BoC	10.13	23.77	13.51	23.40	
CCB	10.40	19.43	2.83	20.36	
ABC	22.18	14.80	10.98	11.76	2004
Average SOCBs	*10.26*	*21.60*	*8.17*	*21.88*	
Minsheng	16.36	31.11	4.38	18.15	
Merchants	8.90	21.46	9.63	20.98	
SPDB	11.60	25.61	12.29	13.01	
Huaxia	12.77	26.32	9.41	8.19	
Industrial	15.72	21.77	10.29	12.62	
SDB	8.81	25.81	15.12	11.45	
CITIC	n.a.	n.a.	n.a.	n.a.	2004
BoComm	12.26	29.68	10.30	14.68	
Average JSCBs	*12.34*	*25.97*	*10.20*	*14.15*	
Average	**11.30**	**23.78**	**9.19**	**18.02**	

Data for some banks is based on year 2004, thus it is not included in the average calculations.
* For ABC it reflects only the agriculture loans.
Source: Own calculations based on data from banks' annual reports.

increased for loans but commercial bills are not under such restrictive management; second, these instruments are easier and less cumbersome than loans; and third, economic growth has boosted the use of this type of short-term financing by companies. Furthermore from the point of view of the bank, these bind less capital than usual loans. But this does not reduce the risks (Table 7.8). As shown by numerous fraud cases, problems and risks abound: Caijing (Li Z., 2006) reported that between July 2005 and March 2006 fraudulent cases amounted to a total of CNY 617 mln.

Other established lending practices have the potential to create further NPLs: the decentralised loan granting system (which decreases the oversight and control over quality, decreases consistent application of practices, increases the likelihood of outside influence, de-links lending and macroeconomic conditions), the high reliance on guarantees from related companies as collateral (greater chance of systemic risk because of inter-linked and reciprocal guarantees) and high reliance on bullet repayment loans (which disguises NPLs, reduces financial discipline

Table 7.8 Hidden risks in Chinese banks

Bank name	Bills weight (%)	Bills risk (%)	Top 10 borrowers (%)	Year
ICBC	6.09	152.55	n.a.	2005
BoC	4.39	79.36	n.a.	2005
CCB	7.26	115.80	n.a.	2005
ABC	3.64	187.07	n.a.	2004
Minsheng	26.69	961.80	43.60	2005
Merchants	30.39	904.10	42.56	2005
SPDB	28.85	1,064.72	32.48	2005
Huaxia	38.45	1,309.82	38.20	2005
Industrial	19.81	774.87	39.43	2005
SDB	53.39	2,426.49	122.22	2005
CITIC	22.12	579.21	66.74	2004
BoComm	4.28	73.22	n.a.	2005
Bank of Shanghai	7.50	184.96	49.00	2005
Average/Total	20.45	719.09	55.03	

Definitions: Bills weight = on- and off-balance sheet commercial bills/total assets; Bills risk = on- and off-balance sheet commercial bills/total equity; Top 10 borrowers = amount of loans outstanding to ten largest borrowers/total equity; Top 10 borrowers exposure is limited at 50% by CBRC prudential rules.
Source: Own calculations based on data from banks' annual reports.

with borrowers, suggests poor loan structuring and de-incentivises loan monitoring) and finally the still widespread rolling over of loans (Ramos R. *et al.*, 2005).

As long as practices and procedures on the ground do not change, what could bring about a reduction in NPLs? A bank's health is not only good because NPL ratios decrease. A bank is healthy in the long term when it is able to generate stable and sound profits from its activities and has the needed capital allocated efficiently to support these activities.

7.6 NPLs and systemic risk

Older NPLs have now been transferred away from the banks' balance sheets, but remain in the financial system. The transfer occurred towards AMCs. These still have large amounts of NPLs on their books. These represent a further challenge and a potential liability for the central authorities. FitchRatings analysts (Chu *et al.*, 2006a) estimate that the AMCs still hold around USD 197 bln in NPLs.

Table 7.9 Maturity of loan portfolios at selected banks (2005)

Bank name	Shortterm (%)	Mediumterm (%)	Longterm (%)
ICBC*	50.45	49.55	49.55
BoC	56.16	23.19	15.32
CCB	47.99	28.28	23.73
ABC*	35.70	64.30	64.30
Average SOCBs	*52.08*	*25.73*	*19.53*
Minsheng	52.04	18.84	29.12
Merchants	58.34	18.29	23.37
SPDB	65.71	15.53	18.76
Huaxia	67.02	21.47	11.50
Industrial	66.13	16.29	17.58
SDB	67.11	6.63	26.27
CITIC*	57.02	42.98	
BoComm	69.47	15.20	15.32
Average JSCBs	*63.69*	*16.04*	*20.27*
Average	**57.88**	**20.89**	**19.90**

* Figures for 2004 (not included in average calculations).
Short term means a maturity less than one year, medium term maturities between 1 and 5 years, long term maturities over 5 years.
Source: Own calculations based on data from banks' annual reports.

As long as the country continues to show strong economic fundamentals such as a dynamic private sector, a high percentage of self-financing in enterprises, capital account controls, a high propensity to save (with most savings left in financial institutions), a high level of foreign exchange reserves and low public debt (Melka and Xu, 2004), China can be assured not to feel the pinch with its NPLs.

Once economic growth cannot support such a situation, then NPL levels will be felt to their full effect. In future, the only sure way to establish a sustainable level of new NPLs is to have appropriate control mechanisms, corporate governance structures and best practices in risk management. All these need to be supported by professional and committed employees (Melka and Xu, 2004). A number of researchers agree that as long as the Chinese authorities have the financial resources to support the banking system and to pay for resolving its insolvability, then the systemic risk of the banking system remains rather low (Melka and Xu, 2004 as well as Longueville and Ngo, 2004).

Looking at the current state of NPL resolution in China, one cannot say that the NPL issue has been thoroughly resolved. Transfers have taken place, which led to large book NPL reductions. The prevention of new NPLs requires adequate credit policies and building up a strong credit culture. All such soft facts and structures are still missing in practice. No one can be sure that the next economic boom would not bring more new NPLs. The NPLs resolution schemes up to now have not created mechanisms to ensure that a build up of long-term NPLs will occur in the future.

As long as government interference impedes the development of the banks' independence and the establishment of a strong credit culture in Chinese banks, the NPL issue will remain. Most banks now have established control mechanisms on paper, but practices show that the changes have yet to happen in the mindsets and in the daily routines of credit officers: they will take time to take root.

8 Capital Adequacy and Risk Management

8.1 Capital adequacy

Chinese banks have generally been undercapitalised (Table 8.1). As shown by Brehm and Macht (2005), the ratio of capital to assets (used as a proxy for the Basel I ratio) for Chinese banks declined steadily from 12% in 1985 to its lowest level in 1997 at 2% increasing a little in 2003 to 4.3%. The Basel capital ratio has been published by banks in recent years only and is increasing as banks are more and more conscious of the necessity and the implications of the capital ratio for their business. After their second recapitalisation exercise, CCB and BoC can now boast capital ratios of 11.3 and 10% respectively at the end of 2004. Most JSCBs show capital ratios just above the regulatory required 8%. Smaller banks such as CCBs do not publish their capital ratios and many are thought to be heavily undercapitalised.

For the banking industry, strengthening their capital base is an expensive exercise (Table 8.2).

In the past, the central goal in the banking sector was the gathering of deposits. This was the single most important performance indicator: it was the fundament for paying bonuses, for developing business targets and for judging branch business effectiveness. All relied heavily on this single figure because, in the absence of an efficient money market, asset growth could only be achieved through deposit growth (Harner, 2004a). Furthermore, each branch had to be self-sufficient in terms of funding because deposit transfers between branches, across

Table 8.1 Capital ratios at selected Chinese banks

Bank name	Equity/assets (%)	Year
ICBC	3.99	2005
BoC	5.54	2005
CCB	6.27	2005
ABC	1.94	2004
Minsheng	2.77	2005
Merchants	3.36	2005
SPDB	2.71	2005
Huaxia	2.94	2005
Industrial	2.56	2005
SDB	2.20	2005
CITIC	3.49	2005
BoComm	5.84	2005
CCBs	3.41	2004
Average/Total	3.79	2005

Definition: Equity/assets = total equity at year end/total assets at year end.
Source: Own calculations based on data from banks' annual reports.

provinces were forbidden. Regulation and compliance were all based on the loan-to-deposit ratio (set at 75% in 2004) (Table 8.3). As a consequence, capital and capital adequacy were not on the mind of neither bank managers nor bank regulators and capital constraints were

Table 8.2 Recapitalisation cost of banks (2004)

	3 SOCBs	8 JSCBs	CCBs	ABC
Equity	563,078	144,211	57,700	78,063
Loan loss reserve	149,789	49,404	15,680	32,379
NPL amount	881,934	85,714	106,100	692,326
Recovery rate of NPLs (%)	20	20	20	20
Actual loan losses	705,547	68,571	84,880	553,861
Capital surplus (deficit)	*7,320*	*125,044*	*−11,500*	*−443,419*
Total loans (gross)	8,077,321	2,402,735	904,500	2,590,072
Required CAR (Basel I, 8%)	646,186	192,219	72,360	207,206
less: existing surplus capital	7,320	125,044	0	0
Required new capital	*0*	*0*	*72,360*	*207,206*
plus: existing deficit	0	0	−11,500	−443,419
Recapitalisation cost of banks	*0*	*0*	*83,860*	*650,625*

SOCBs include ICBC, BoC and CCB. JSCBs include BoComm, CITIC, Merchants, Minsheng, Shanghai Pudong, Huaxia, Shenzhen Development and Industrial Bank.
Source: Own calculations based on Hu 2002, data from banks' annual reports.

Table 8.3 Loan-to-deposits ratio at selected Chinese banks

Bank name	Loan deposit ratio (%)	Year
ICBC	55.82	2005
BoC	57.29	2005
CCB	59.79	2005
ABC	73.25	2004
Minsheng	76.24	2005
Merchants	72.15	2005
SPDB	72.68	2005
Huaxia	72.95	2005
Industrial	66.85	2005
SDB	71.65	2005
CITIC	71.81	2005
BoComm	62.15	2005
CCBs	61.98	2004
Average/Total	67.22	2005

Definitions: Loan deposit ratio = total loan amount/total deposit amount.
Source: Own calculations based on data from banks' annual reports.

unheard of. Such strong deposit growth disregarding asset quality and capital adequacy also favoured the building up of NPLs.

8.2 New capital adequacy rules

Thus when the CBRC issued in February 2004 a regulation on capital adequacy for commercial banks, it was seen as revolutionary by many observers (References for laws 28 and Marshall *et al.*, 2004a). The PBOC had previously published a minimum CAR of 8% (prescribed in the earlier *Commercial Banking Law*) but did not give any detailed calculation methods or definitions of its components, and adherence was not enforced. Thus the *Regulation governing capital adequacy of commercial banks* was in a number of respects a fundamental and "dramatic step" (Desombre and Chen, 2004). However, as in many cases in China, only enforcement will show how serious regulators are about these new rules.

The new regulations took into account Basel I and Basel II rules (see Annex) as well as the prospects of Chinese banks soon facing foreign competition (through the entry to the WTO in 2007).

Put simply, the regulations require commercial banks to get their capital ratio to above 8% by 2007.[1] The transition from a quantitative growth (based on attracting deposits or on a funds constraint system) to a qualitative growth path (reflecting the quality of the assets held or a capital constraint system) will formally take place until the end of 2006. Given the current levels of provisioning (at around 15% of NPLs according to Marshall *et al.*, 2005a) and of still high levels of NPLs, Chinese banks remain strongly undercapitalised (Table 8.4).

The main elements of the new regulation are outlined here. Capital adequacy calculations must take into account provisioning for (loan) losses (Art. 4). Capital is defined in two tiers. Tier 1 capital includes paid-up capital, reserves, capital surplus, retained earnings and minority interests. Tier 2 capital includes revaluation reserves, general loan loss reserves, preference shares, convertible bonds and long-term subordinated debt. Long-term subordinated debt shall not exceed 50% of core capital[2] and tier 2 shall not exceed the amount of tier 1 capital (Art. 12 and 13 as well as Annex 1 of the regulations).

Risk weightings promulgated by the CBRC are somewhat different from those advocated in the Basel I accord. The Chinese regulators have scrapped the Organisation for Economic Co-operation and Development (OECD) club rule and replaced it with a more Basel II like approach: claims on sovereigns and overseas banks shall be weighted according to externally available ratings from international credit rating agencies (Art. 17 and 49). A favourable risk weight will only be available

Table 8.4 Capital adequacy ratios for selected Chinese banks

Bank name	**Basel I capital ratio (%)**	**Year**
ICBC	9.89	2005
BoC	10.42	2005
CCB	13.57	2005
ABC	n.a.	2004
Minsheng	8.26	2005
Merchants	9.06	2005
SPDB	8.04	2005
Huaxia	8.23	2005
Industrial	8.13	2005
SDB	3.70	2005
CITIC	n.a.	2005
BoComm	11.20	2005
CCBs	1.4	2004
Average/Total	9.05	2005

Definitions: Basel I capital ratio = ratio as published by the banks, based on total capital.
Source: Own calculations based on data from banks' annual reports.

when the entity is rated AA- (based on the Standard & Poor's scale) or higher. Claims on the Chinese government are treated as if China was rated better than AA- (China as a sovereign is currently rated by Standard & Poor's with A-/A-1, long term and short term. The sovereign rating was upgraded from BBB+/A-2 in July 2005). Otherwise risk weights are similar to those promoted under Basel I for on-balance and off-balance sheet exposures (Art. 27, also Annexes 2 and 3). Risk mitigants are recognised in the sense of Basel II (Art. 25 and 26). A further important step taken by the regulators is the removal of the preferential treatment of SOEs (Table 8.5). They now receive the same risk weights as other enterprises (Art. 19 and 23). Furthermore, debt issued by AMCs in exchange for NPLs carries a 0% risk weight to incentivise the disposal of NPLs (Art. 22).

Market risk is also taken into account in the capital adequacy calculations. This recognises the increased level of financial market activities in China. This applies only to banks with trading positions exceeding the lesser of 10% of the bank's on- and off-balance sheet assets or CNY 8.5 bln (Art. 28, 30 and 31 as well as Annex 4). Operational risk is not taken into account in the new capital calculations, but is addressed in another document.[3]

Information disclosure and supervisory review are based on Basel II requirements. The BoD or president of the bank is responsible for capital adequacy and senior management is responsible for its implementation (Art. 33 and 34 as well as Annex 5). Supervisory review is undertaken through on-site review and off-site surveillance. Banks are categorised into three groups (Art. 38) depending on the adequacy of their capital (CAR > 8%, CAR < 8% and CAR < 4%). For each group CBRC has a range of measures at its disposal ranging from requiring

Table 8.5 Changes in loan risk weightings

in %	Until 2003	Since 2004
Loans to central-level SOEs	20	50
Loans to provincial-level SOEs	50	100
Loans to sub-provincial SOEs	70	100
Loans guaranteed by very large SOEs	50	100
Loans guaranteed by large SOEs	70	100
Loans collateralised by land rights or residential buildings	50	100
Issuance of bankers acceptance drafts	70	100

Source: References for laws 28.

management improvements to complete suspension of activities (Art. 39 and 40). Principles are basically similar to those of pillar 2 in Basel II, but they lack the rigour and level of detail of the Basel standards. Disclosure is the responsibility of the BoD and should include details on risk management policies, their scope of application, capital, capital adequacy, and credit and market risks. Disclosure to all relevant stakeholders is required within 4 months following the end of the accounting year.

By the end of 2006, all banks must publish their capital adequacy levels and ratios as well as disclose their risk management policies and strategies. Furthermore, LLP have to conform to the rules shown in (Table 8.6) (from 2006 onwards):

At the same time, general reserves remain unchanged at 1%. LLP are now fully tax-deductible, in contrast to the previously 1% LLP which were tax-deductible (only up to this level). This provided a strong incentive for not raising LLP above the 1% limit.

Capital adequacy is now the responsibility of the BoD, and stringent sanctions apply to those banks that are undercapitalised.[4] Any inadequate levels of capital should be dealt with by the BoD through a special action plan. This should make banks more efficient, more disciplined and more shareholder-oriented.[5] To comply with the above regulations, banks will have to improve asset quality, dispose of NPLs and raise fresh capital, either by looking for new shareholders (through IPOs, for example), press present ones for new capital or issue long-term subordinated debt[6] and hybrid bonds. These three alternatives are increasingly available to smaller-sized banks as well. Capital management is

Table 8.6 Mandatory special loan-loss provisions

Five-tier loan classification	**Special loan-loss provisions* (%)**
Normal	1
Watch	2
Substandard	25†
Doubtful	50†
Loss	100

* Special provisions 专项准备 are provisions raised for exposures categorised according to the loan classification. These provisions should reflect the experience of the bank and loss expectations for the future. Banks should systematically estimate provisions through a risk measurement system and standard procedures. Specific provisions 特种准备 refer to those raised for a specific industry, country, geographic area or customer (References for laws 16).
† allowed to vary by 20% below or above this level.
Source: References for laws 16.

becoming a reality and a necessity for Chinese banks. They have to consider risks and raise capital accordingly (Ba S. *et al.*, 2005b).

8.3 Chinese regulations and international standards – A comparison

Brehm and Macht (2004) analyse the degree of implementation and preparedness of Chinese regulators and the Chinese banking system with regards to Basel I and the *Core Principles for Effective Banking Supervision* (BCBS, 1997). They find that the rules on capital adequacy issued by the CBRC (References for laws 28) do reflect most of the standards advocated in Basel I, while the general rules on banking regulation and supervision (References for laws 2) do fulfil the standards issued under the *Basel Core Principles* (BCP).

With regard to BCP compliance, their findings are as follows:

- the requirements of the first principle (BCP 1) are met for most, apart from the potentially strong interference that state agencies can have in the bank's management;
- requirements for licensing and structure (BCP 2–5) are fully met;
- minimum capital and loan management requirements (BCP 6–15) are met in principle, but the Chinese regulations lack detailed and precise regulations, thus leaving room for interpretation;
- ongoing supervision requirements (BCP 16–20) are complied with strongly;
- information requirements as stated under BCP 21 have been increasingly implemented, however, but not to their full extent (quality and trustworthiness remain problematic); and
- requirements concerning remedial measures and exit as well as cross-border banking seem to be fully complied with.

The authors conclude that Chinese regulations tend to comply with most but not all internationally recognised best practices.[7] Requirements of the pillar 2 and 3 in Basel II are for most complied with or at least show broad similarities. But the devil is in the detail as some definitions and requirements in Chinese regulations lack rigour and details. This leaves much room for interpretation by regulators' regional agencies and opens the door to lax compliance on the banks' side.

A central issue is the lack of independence of banking regulators which contravenes the standards for supervision advocated by the Basel Committee. The centrality and importance of a strong and independent regulator is underlined by numerous commentators who have shown that of those countries that have experienced financial crises most had weak and inadequate legal frameworks and supervisors (e.g. see Ward, 2002).

It remains to be seen how far these rules will be implemented and enforced. The credibility of the regulators may become undermined if they show lax handling of non-compliant banks. The usefulness of the Chinese regulations will be tested on the stance taken by central and local governments. If these try to circumvent the rules, then these will be undermined as well.

8.4 Current state of risk management systems in Chinese banks

Chinese banks started to establish risk management structures and rating systems only a few years ago. This late start was the consequence of years of policy lending, of capped interest rates, of historical burdens and of poor incentives to create sound banks. The newly established risk management units are separated from sales departments. Banks have changed the incentive structures of relationship managers, started off-loading NPLs and finally have been able to share data through the PBOC credit information platform. Despite the high hurdles that Chinese banks face, more and more are moving into risk management especially that of credit risk.

The first incursions into risk management were made at the turn of the century in SOCBs (Qian X., 2004). After the end of the Credit Plan (see annex), they redesigned the decision structures for lending. First, a link was created between exposure to a client and its rating and a mechanism was created for analysing borrowers. For different loan amounts and types of loans, different authorities were recognised (e.g. working capital loans and mortgage loans can be approved at branch level, while loans for investment in fixed assets require the head office approval at ICBC). The various lending authorities were adjusted subsequently to reflect the local economic conditions as well as the performance of individual branches, or the availability of collateral. Zhang Ran and Hou Guangming (2005) report that already in 2000, Chinese banks were experimenting with rating grades. However, these were rudimentary, unstable, and lacking a mature methodology (most had only 5–6 grades, which were recently increased to 10–13 grades).

The reform process, however, has been slowed down in many institutions due to the resistance of managers. The challenge is that banks' branches are often independent and managed as mini-banks. Branches were, under the old lending processes, responsible for all lending, and authorisation was given by the branch manager. Reforms of the risk management processes and structures often challenge the authority of branch managers (Marshall *et al.*, 2005a).

The ICBC and BoC have already announced new internal rating systems (*Asia Pulse*, 2005b). Some smaller second-tier banks are also preparing the introduction of new credit risk management standards, and these include among others new Basel II compliant credit rating systems together with the appropriate documentation as well as reforming the internal organisational structure to conform to international best practices. The response of the CBRC to the Basel Committee in 2003 (CBRC, 2003) actually kicked-off the start of analyses by banks to understand the implications of Basel II (*Asia Pulse* 2005b; Zhou X., 2005). Larger banks have already embraced the new accord with internal ratings-based (IRB) approaches (see Annex) and are looking into possible implementation soon (Zhao Z., 2003).

Despite these positive developments, observers (Zhang R. and Hou G., 2005) believe that the methodology for credit risk management is not yet mature, that banks still lack a truly independent, professional and responsible risk management function. Further to these, they also see more challenges. Credit and loss data are insufficient. The capabilities of credit officers are limited. A methodology measuring credit risk to support decision-making is lacking (still often based on collateral availability, etc.).

A survey by E&Y (Hansen and Straley, 2004) showed that the eight Chinese banks interviewed have actually made strong progress towards implementing best risk management practices (e.g. in probability default modelling). However, they still remain far from Basel II credit risk management requirements. They still need to strengthen their rating methodologies or collect sufficient data. Some banks have 3 years of data, but it remains to be seen if the data is fully compliant with the new requirements.

Apart from establishing a reliable, complete and comprehensive credit loss database, Yu (2003) argues that banks will also have to focus on recruiting experienced staff for leading the measurement of credit risk, and will need the support at the highest management level. Thus he acknowledges that probably only the larger banks will have the capacity and resources to implement more complex approaches. He foresees that credit risk management will soon become the tool to create a competitive advantage in China.

The regulatory authorities have demonstrated a positive attitude towards developing better risk management processes. As stated in their letter to the Bank for International Settlements (BIS) in 2003, the authorities are committed to developing a dual approach to implementing credit risk management best practices as stated in the Basel II accord: requiring compliance with Basel I and at the same time encouraging banks to move towards Basel II (*China Urban and Rural Finance Newspaper*, 2005). Liu Mingkang advised banks to start preparations: larger ones should implement IRB approaches, while smaller ones should concentrate on improving their risk management systems first (Zhao Z., 2003). Full implementation of Basel II could take 5–10 years in China. Wang Huaqing (2006) notes that CBRC intends to follow a two-tier approach, by requiring large international banks to implement the Foundation internal ratings-based (F-IRB) approach by 2010 (standard approach for operational risks) and for all other banks leaving the choice of approach.

Despite all internal and external challenges that banks still face in China, they have embraced the new risk management requirements. Their response is commensurate to their capabilities and resources.

9
Governance and Corruption

9.1 Corruption

Another recurring challenge to the Chinese banking system is the system-wide corruption (Table 9.1). This should not be too surprising considering the low remuneration of bank officers and managers as well as the lack of effective internal controls and checks and balances.

In 2004, the CBRC uncovered 274 finance-related crimes involving some CNY 1.51 bln (*AFX Asia*, 2005). In 2005, 799 bank employees were found to be involved in frauds in 103 banks amounting to a total of CNY 588 bln (CBRC, 2005a). As a result, some 325 managers have lost their posts and in 86% of cases some form of corrective action had been taken. The on-site investigation of unlawful activities has become a central focus of CBRC's work: 15,280 investigations were carried out in 2005 (Table 9.2).

The last column shows that there is a tendency of being less compliant in entities which are more likely to be influenced by third parties in their geographic areas (for example, the lowest correction rates are found in RCCs and CCBs as well as in postal savings institutions).

Corruption is not limited to the highly visible cases of branch managers and senior managers embezzling millions of Yuan. A survey ordered by the central government on real interest rates for loans in China shows the importance of informal payments in order to obtain a loan in certain geographic areas (Xie P. and Lei L., 2005). Some 45.5% of the respondents stated that to get a loan it is necessary to bring forward some advantages to the bank officer. Of all respondents, 46% believe that people are not held responsible for loans that turn bad. Enterprises have stated that, depending on their location, they have to pay an application fee for a CNY 1 mln loan ranging from CNY 14,000 in Eastern China to

Table 9.1 Corruption in China (2005)

Country Rank	78
Corruption Perception Index (CPI) score	3.2

CPI Score on a 10 to 0 scale, 10 being the highest.
Source: Based on Transparency International 2005.

Table 9.2 Corruption investigations in 2005

Institution type	Number of investigations	Number of entities investigated	Number of consequently removed managers	Cases with corrective actions (%)
Rural FIs	6,098	26,819	222	84.39
SOCBs	5,423	20,563	81	88.39
Postal savings	1,284	12,425	n.a.	85.13
CCBs and UCCs	771	4,116	11	83.72
Policy banks	673	1,387	2	94.23
JSCBs	584	2,736	3	91.47
NBFIs	180	96	2	79.79
AMCs	172	118	1	86.36
Foreign banks	95	100	3	92.81
Total	*15,280*	*68,360*	*325*	*86.38*

Source: Based on Financial News (2006).

CNY 63,000 in Northern China. On average, Chinese companies have to pay an application fee amounting to 3.8% of the loan amount. To keep a good banking relationship, surveyed Chinese enterprises estimate that they have to pay an interest rate of 4.9% on their loans.

The number of publicised corruption cases has started a process of change at these banks. Many are now starting to review their internal controls and channels to control business processes (Ling H. and Zhang X., 2005). While banks have made efforts to reform their internal controls and credit checks, the rules are not yet being enforced at the lowest branch level (Buckley, 2005). The still high number of corruption cases is a reminder that reforms need to be more thorough and need to reach deeper in banks and culture (Wen Y., 2005). The same author suggests that corruption is anchored in the habit of cultivating separate and independent decision centres within one organisation.

Privatisation, increased effectiveness of corporate governance structures and the centralising of management decision-making have the potential to decrease the level of corruption in China.

9.2 Corporate governance

Corporate governance is hailed as the "first line of defence in managing bank risk" by McKinsey analysts (Bekier *et al.*, 2005) and one of the most crucial reform areas in China (OECD, 2005). Corporate governance structures have the potential to reduce the number of corruption cases and to improve internal controls and risk management, as well as to ultimately improve the financial intermediation capacity of banks.

Improving corporate governance structures is crucial to all banks in China. It is an inescapable part of banking reforms and will help reduce banks' riskiness (Du Y. and Xu C., 2005). Reforms have already taken place; however, we can ask how much change has there been in the governance structures of Chinese banks?

When investors invest their funds in the capital of an enterprise, they expect the firm's managers to reward them for supporting the enterprise with equity funds. Investors receive a reward in the form of dividends (and capital appreciation), when the firm generates a profit. To ensure that investors' funds are put to their most efficient use by the managers, investors or shareholders need to build in control and oversight mechanisms. These should give managers the right incentives so that they do not concentrate on higher perks, personal prestige, and dissipate the firm's resources and assets and so on. These control mechanisms form the corporate governance structure which enables the alignment of investors' and managers' interests.

A definition of corporate governance not only can be limited to the protection of shareholders but can also be extended to those of all of the firm's stakeholders (Wei W., 2005). Corporate governance mechanisms can help solve conflicts of interest that arise between shareholders and other stakeholders (especially managers), that is between agent and principals. Important in any corporate governance structure is the clear definition of lines of responsibilities, of controls and of sanctions. Otherwise, moral hazard can occur.

Corporate governance mechanisms or "checks and balances" can be subdivided into internal and external ones (Denis and McConnell, 2003; Wei W., 2005). Internally, the BoD (in some countries together with a supervisory board (SB)) and the ownership structure are the most important mechanisms.

While the board's responsibility is to hire, monitor and fire senior management, in practice the separation between board and management is not always clear since some of the management may also sit on the board. Research has shown that (Denis and McConnell, 2003) BoDs are more effective when they employ more independent directors, when the board's size is small and when turnover on the board is low. However, it could not be conclusively shown whether the board should be chaired by somebody who is not the CEO at the same time. Pay and incentives for managers should be aligned with those of shareholders, this leads to higher firm performance.

Ownership structure plays a key role in the development of sound corporate governance; however, the identity of the shareholders and the percentage of capital they hold will ultimately influence any conflicts of interests that may arise between managers and shareholders. Overall, ownership concentration (provided it is not in the hands of the state) appears to act positively on firm performance. Privatisation positively affects the performance and efficiency of firms. When the largest shareholder is the state and privatisation is incomplete, then performance is negatively affected (Clarke, 2003; Xu L. C. *et al.*, 2002). Other research has shown that foreign ownership can help align management and shareholders' interests and has a positive effect on market valuation (Bai C. *et al.*, 2003; Xu L. C. *et al.*, 2002). Listed firms can command a premium and represent higher value to their shareholders. This is also true for banks. Zheng Lujun and Cao Yanqiu (2005) show that in China, the efficiency of commercial banks is largely determined by the concentration of capital ownership and by the liveliness of shareholders (and by the size of the bank but not by the type of bank itself, such as JSCBs or CCBs). The higher concentration of ownership stakes in one or a few hands can improve efficiency up to a point: a too high or too low concentration negatively influences efficiency. The more efficient the corporate governance structures and the more active the shareholders, the more efficient the bank will become (Table 9.3).

Externally, there are also a number of mechanisms that add pressure on management to perform in the interests of shareholders, including the takeover threat and the protection of investor rights (and in more general term the legal-regulatory environment). In a competitive environment, the threat of change of control acts for management as a motivation to perform. Such pressure is, however, only meaningful and effective as long as the takeover market is lively and competitive. The lower the protection of investor rights, the more likely ownership is to be concentrated in order to compensate for the lack of protection.

Table 9.3 Profitability of Chinese banks

Bank name	ROE (%)	ROA (%)	Earning power (%)	Cost income ratio (%)	Year
ICBC	13.09	0.52	0.33	47.08	2005
BoC	12.41	0.69	0.35	45.03	2005
CCB	16.37	1.03	0.40	45.88	2005
ABC	2.57	0.05	0.15	71.40	2004
Minsheng	17.48	0.49	0.27	56.47	2005
Merchants	15.93	0.54	0.38	47.85	2005
SPDB	16.01	0.43	0.28	54.37	2005
Huaxia	12.33	0.36	0.27	53.36	2005
Industrial	20.26	0.52	0.30	48.77	2005
SDB	6.96	0.15	0.28	55.63	2005
CITIC	13.97	0.49	0.33	45.08	2005
BoComm	11.12	0.65	0.32	52.17	2005
12 CCBs	13.64	0.55	0.32	45.76	2004

Definitions: ROE = net profit for the year/total Tier 1 equity, ROA = net profit for the year/total assets at year end, Earning power = (net interest, financial and provision income – administrative expenses)/average total assets, Cost income ratio = administrative expenses/(net interest, financial and provision income). Twelve CCBs include those in Beijing, Shanghai, Chongqing, Xi'an, Dongguan, Dalian, Hangzhou, Nanjing, Ningbo, Shenzhen, Tianjin and Wuxi. All of them are located in large urban centres which are also relatively wealthy and for most located in coastal areas.
Source: Own calculations based on data from banks' annual reports.

Protection of shareholders and especially of minority ones is an important part of the effective corporate governance framework.

Banks also have a positive role to play in the corporate governance structure of firms. When firms borrow, banks monitor them in order to ensure loan repayment. This feature is especially important to smaller firms which normally do not have access to debt and capital markets (which would increase market discipline). With the additional oversight and monitoring of the debtors by banks, shareholders' position is strengthened (Ye X., 2004). First, managers will be under more pressure to manage the firm well. Second, bank loans will give a positive signal to other outsiders and investors. Third, the control exercised by banks can help level out potential conflicts between owners and managers. Raising both debt and capital enables creditors and shareholders to share the monitoring costs and responsibilities and thus to reduce the riskiness of the firm to them individually. Specialised and professional creditors can help shareholders (Ye X., 2004). To ensure that such mechanisms work and benefit shareholders, creditors' rights need to be protected, the bankruptcy threat needs to be real, and banks have to play an efficient and effective monitoring role.

Finally, the external environment in which enterprises evolve is also crucial to the establishment of corporate governance structures. Ewing (2005) also describes further institutions required for corporate governance to take root: a functioning legal-regulatory environment,[1] sound accounting standards,[2] shareholders with an oversight capacity (who take an interest in the firm's operations and understand its business), efficient financial markets as well as institutional investors (because of their large financial resources and their long-term orientation). All these preliminary conditions are in the process of being built up or are being established in China, but remain weak for now.

9.3 Corporate governance regulatory framework in China

In China, corporate governance was progressively acknowledged by the authorities (Ewing, 2005) and has been recognised as "crucial to China's development" (Zhou X., 2004c). While corporate governance is written as a high priority by Chinese regulators and authorities (CBRC, 2006b), it is still unclear how much power the authorities, acting as shareholders, are willing to yield in the process of implementing higher standards and stronger mechanisms.

The corporate governance model chosen in China is one using a BoD staffed among others with independent directors supervising senior management combined with an SB which supervises the Board. However, the scope of its functions is much more restrained and in practice it has a "rubber stamp" function (IIF, 2006).

In China, corporate governance requirements are described in the *Company Law*. The internal structure is composed of the general shareholders' meeting, the BoD, the board of supervisors and the senior managers. The general shareholders' meeting is composed of all shareholders and represents the highest authority in a company. It should decide over the business policies and investments, elect and choose directors, approve reports submitted by the two boards, approve budgets and financial accounts, decide on the registered capital, on the issuance of bonds, on the distribution of profits and losses, on the organisation of the company and its articles of association as well as on any merger, dissolution and so on. Shareholders are thus much involved in business matters of companies in China: major strategic and business decisions all require the shareholders' approval (Wei W.,

2005). In practice, however, the business steering rights are more often on the side of the BoD and not with the shareholders' meeting which has less insight into the daily business operations and thus has to rely heavily on the proposals submitted by the BoD. This role is given further importance because other means of external supervision are often weak (Yang J., 2005).

The BoD is appointed by and reports to the general shareholders' meeting (just as the SB). It is often composed of some 10 members. It controls the senior management of the company on behalf of the shareholders.[3] Its chairman is also the legal representative of the company. The SB supervises the BoD and senior management and brings any issues to the attention of the shareholders (it is composed of fewer members than the BoD, but should give appropriate representation to other stakeholders).

In the case of China, Liu Qian (2006) defines the corporate governance system as "control-based", rather than market-oriented. This is due to the fact that Chinese regulators and authorities still make much use of administrative measures to control developments in the economy. Such a system does not induce better performance within the firms and rather reduces investors' confidence.

For JSCBs, CBRC has issued specific corporate governance guidelines (References for laws 7, for SOCBs see under References for laws 34). It requires banks to establish well-defined rules and procedures, responsibilities and reporting lines, disclosure and remuneration schemes. It also makes independent directors compulsory (banks with a net worth of more than CNY 1 bln should have at least 3 independent directors). Additionally to the *Company Law*'s requirements, the guideline also introduces higher requirements for protecting minority shareholders and restricting related-parties transactions (Wei W., 2005). The nomination and appointment of senior managers cannot be the activity of a sole shareholder, so that majority shareholders cannot control the board. Furthermore independent directors are required to sit on the Board, and committees[4] should be established to introduce further check and balance mechanisms. Related-parties transactions are regulated with more detail and ensure the independence of the listed entity. In the case of commercial banks the SB has wider and deeper powers: supervision of managers' performance and activities, responsible for mandating an external auditor and should report activities to the regulatory authorities.

Zhou Xiaochuan (2004c), PBOC's governor, outlined a number of issues that remain to be resolved in China, most importantly – the clarification of ownership structures and role of senior managers, the role of the authorities and of the Communist Party as well as the protection of investor and creditor rights.

9.4 Corporate governance in Chinese banks

Corporate governance in banks can be considered as a special case compared with governance in other companies.

1. The principal–agent relations are more complex (because they also include depositors, lenders, and regulators, Cao X. and Zhao X., 2004).
2. The corporate governance structures of banks need to take the interests of other stakeholders more into account (especially those of depositors and supervisors). Because of the high level of leverage of commercial banks, the loss (in case of failure) to depositors is overall much higher than that to shareholders (Wang X. and Huang Y., 2004).
3. Because of their importance to the financial system, banks' failures are likely to have a strong impact on the financial system and banks are thus likely to be saved. As a result, internal controls, diversification activities, mechanisms to improve public scrutiny (as being the main loss carrier in case of failure), the role of various supervisory committees and profit incentives for staff, all need to be stronger (Cao X. and Zhao X., 2004; Wang X. and Huang Y., 2004). This should also be supported by a strong credit culture.
4. Information asymmetry issues run deeper because for most intermediation, quality cannot be ascertained right away (NPLs tend to be discovered in the future and not at time of disbursement, Wei W., 2005).

Chinese authorities have been active in recent years in defining and implementing a reform model for Chinese banks in terms of corporate governance (Thompson, 2005). These include the following:

- ownership structure reform (through recapitalisation, introduction of new operational and business practices, diversification of shareholders, of foreign strategic investors albeit with capped stakes)
- higher capacity and specialisation of regulators (creation of CBRC, definition of responsibilities of CBRC and PBOC, emphasis on improving banks' governance, but still regulators are lacking independence)
- strengthened the legal regulatory environment (rules-based supervision, tackling enforcement issues)

- increased information disclosure and market discipline mechanisms (capital markets development, raising of different types of capital and of debt, higher disclosure requirements)
- increased foreign entry and shareholdings (end of transition period to WTO entry, equal treatment and foreign strategic investors).

Chinese researchers (Du Y. and Xu C., 2005; Wang X. and Huang Y., 2004) see a number of issues where corporate governance of Chinese banks is still deficient which include:

- divergent operational goals of the authorities and of the banks (between the interests of society as a whole, economic development and the interests of shareholders to maximise their returns)
- inefficient corporate governance structures (the central government makes no difference in principle between directors and managers which have the same responsibilities and reporting lines) and the consequently strong control from insiders 内部人控制 (strategic development of banks is often decided by senior managers, decisions on operations and distribution of benefits are influenced by personal interests and short-term incentives)
- rigid incentives (oriented towards bureaucratic requirements rather than operations) and lack of trust between different parties
- endogenous supervision (both banks and supervisors are under the aegis of the central government)
- weak discipline mechanisms of debtors (implicitly taken as guaranteed by local governments even though this is forbidden, lack of transparency and understanding of internal events, lack of competition/ monopoly position, lack of exit mechanisms)
- inefficient organisational structure (strong power at the branch managers' level, too many hierarchical levels, separation of branching networks in many different levels, these are also more difficult to control in terms of risks incurred, lack of unified management mechanisms).

Thus for the authors the solutions lie (among other things) in the redefinition of the role of the authorities' role, the introduction of strategic investors, and the improvement of the functions of supervisors.

9.5 State ownership and corporate governance

Ewing (2005) finds that one of the strongest impediments to the sustainable establishment of corporate governance structures in Chinese enterprises is the overwhelming state ownership. One fundamental requirement of corporate governance structures is the arm's length relationship between enterprises and the state, even when it is the main controlling shareholder. However, the state still allocates to enterprises it owns a social and welfare role (generating employment, engendering economic growth, etc.). These conflicting goals result in a conflict of interests among the involved parties (Clarke, 2003).

For state-owned companies, the state acts as a principal and as an agent at the same time depending on the point of view taken (that of the people it represents or that of the bank). In China, the state draws no line between being an owner and a manager. With such large ownership stakes, the state can appoint and withdraw managers. Through the loyalty of managers to the state, it takes influence on daily operations and on strategic decisions. Furthermore with the strong involvement of shareholders required by Chinese regulations, the state is assured to be able to control management and operations at all times. The state is outsider and insider at the same time (Lu M., 2004). Thus the principal does not become the control entity it should become and interest conflicts arise between bank and state. With the control in the hands of insiders, moral hazard can flourish.

A further issue in corporate governance of all commercial banks (but especially state-owned ones) is the relationship with the relevant Party Committee (Sun M., 2005). The chairman of the BoD is often at the same time the enterprise's secretary of the Party Committee. The Party Committee nominates high-level managers and directors, it sets their remuneration and responsibilities, and it defines their reporting lines and their status in the party and state hierarchy. Wu Xiaoling (2005), PBOC's deputy governor, explains that the Communist Party is making efforts to nominate managers with professional and specialised experience and has also introduced a competitive mechanism for applying for management positions. Still many issues remain unanswered. Can the Party Committee accept the nomination of outside and independent directors, can these interfere in the Party Committee's decisions, can some of its functions be merged or transferred to other corporate governance mechanisms (such as remuneration decisions, internal controls, etc.)? Furthermore managers' incentives are designed to make them loyal to the party, so if their incentives are not market-driven, how can the old system change? Reform of corporate governance structures in Chinese banks does not address the position and responsibilities of the Party Committee. This hampers the functioning of corporate governance structures (Ling H. and Guo Q., 2006).

The ownership structures of SOCBs have changed. First the banks were turned into corporations (change of legal status, introduction of Central

Huijin as representing the state); second, strategic investors (foreign and domestic) were introduced and finally part of their capital was listed. But the introduction of the Central Huijin Investment Co. as shareholder and CBRC as empowered with nominating senior management did not increase the efficiency of corporate governance mechanisms. The state still plays its three pronged role: investor, manager and supervisor. Rights and responsibilities are all in one hand. At the same time, listings for the SOCBs require them to comply with higher corporate governance and risk management standards (as required by the stock markets on which they list and by the new international investors). Information disclosure is also likely to improve. However, the small portion of their capital which is listed does not require them to change fundamentally in the way business is done and in the scope of government interference.

Many banks have established credit management systems, separated reporting lines of risk management and customer relationships, and are lending at least in theory based on creditworthiness. Accountability is higher, but are internal controls really effective? Regulations and rules are set forth in administrative rules issued by CBRC, so enforcement and implementation remain the challenges.

Actually the Chinese authorities stand to win from sounder corporate governance practices (as well as privatisation) because these can lead to stronger enterprise performance, which in turn should generate higher returns to the state in form of taxes as well as employment. Improved bank performance can benefit economic development in the long term. Conflicts of interests between state and enterprises are short term in nature and could be aligned in the long term.

As illustrated by the first large funds embezzlement case (using 96 faked bank drafts amounting to CNY 914.6 mln, of which CNY 432.5 mln are still missing) in a Chinese bank in early 2006 (Duan H. *et al.*, 2006a), such corruption cases still happen (and it was not the single one in the first half of 2006). This sheds doubt as to whether the newly established corporate governance structures in banks have taken place. These kinds of cases remind us that restructuring should be preliminary to any further reforms and that balance sheet cosmetics (such as NPLs disposals) cannot ensure that many other types of reforms will be sustainable (Duan H. *et al.*, 2006b).

Conclusion

While reforms have taken place in a number of areas that influence the banks' operations and their long-term sustainable development, enforcement remains patchy in many cases.

Operational risk, together with credit risk, is another large (maybe the largest) risk faced by Chinese banks. This is true from the point of view of regulators, authorities, banks, creditors, customers and so on. The single, most important factor influencing operational risk is the role of the authorities. This is an issue that up to now the authorities have been reluctant to tackle. They have introduced many reforms surrounding the issue of state ownership but have never directly addressed the difficulties it poses.

Since most of the banking system's assets, financial intermediation and the regulatory authorities are in the hands of the state, market forces have had little chance to penetrate the banking system. The state has allocated to itself the main role in the banking system. Such a situation is supported by the argument that markets would not fairly allocate resources and that culturally the government has a responsibility in controlling the financial system if it is to advance rapid and orderly economic development. Put simply, the state finds it still necessary to intervene in the allocation of financial resources to ensure that its economic and social goals are reached, at least in the short term.

While such a situation does not have negative effects by itself, the fact that the banking system lacks competition, threats (including takeover, sanctions, etc.) as well as incentives to introduce sound risk management and governance practices results in less than efficient or effective financial intermediation. The role taken over by the state is not under the control of any other independent institution. This inefficiency results in distorted financial intermediation, poor service quality and a widespread short-term orientation.

The state attempts to take advantage of its dominant situation by promoting its own policies and projects through the provision of financial services by influencing the lending process at many points (choice of managers, support of banks, influence of lending decisions, etc.) with a number of methods (loyalty, corruption, co-opting, rent seeking, etc.). This is actually a rational choice of the state: who would cut the tree on which it is sitting?

The state is not committed to relinquish any of its power and control. Reforms that may reduce its power or control are compensated by an increase of influence in one way or another, mostly with an indirect or more subtle influence elsewhere. This results in influence and control becoming less visible and less formal, through channels that are less easy to monitor and measure. Thus targeting changes in these areas are even more challenging. The basic assumptions underlying the role of the state in the banking system has not changed much over recent years, and the state does not seem to be too willing to change.

While foreign funds are welcomed for the capital and the expertise they bring into the Chinese banking system, the state is still widely seen (by itself and by the domestic institutions and economic players) as the entity that is ultimately responsible for stability, both economic and social, and thus this (in itself) continues to justify the predominant position of the state in the banking system.

Part IV
Analysis of Different Bank Types

Having discussed extensively characteristics that are common to all or most banks in China concerning their environment as well as operational issues, we can now turn towards the analysis of individual banks.

While no bank is like another, Chinese banks can be grouped into different types and their specifics can be analysed. Such analysis, is not able to catch all the differences between banks, but has the advantage to give a deeper and more detailed picture of the broader banking industry in China. Each type of bank, ordered by the legal form and structure, has specific features that are important to analyse.

In the following, five main bank types will be analysed:

1. state-owned commercial banks (SOCBs)
2. joint-stock commercial banks (JSCBs)
3. city commercial banks (CCBs)
4. foreign banks and
5. rural credit cooperatives (RCCs).

The SWOT analysis for banking system is given in Table IV.1.

Table IV.1 Banking system SWOT analysis

Strengths	Weaknesses
• Large coverage, outreach	• NPL/NPA levels
• Brand names, well known	• Lack of corporate governance structures
• Cheap labour	• Interference of state with scars of socialist planning
• Highly liquid	• Lack of credit culture, risk management

Table IV.1 (Continued)

Strengths	**Weaknesses**
• First address for external enterprises financing • Financial support of the state	• Under capitalised • Lack of qualified personnel • Corruption • Related-parties transactions
Opportunities	**Threats**
• Large private sector • Consumer/consumption taking off • Strong economic environment • Reform of SOEs and stock markets underway • Building up consumer credit registries	• Opening and liberalisation through WTO entry • Basel II: loss of competitive advantage, competitive imbalances, pro-cyclicality • Consumers not bound to one bank • Weak regulators, lacking independence

Chinese banks had a successful year 2005 with profits rising to CNY 253.2 bln (compared to CNY 23.3 bln in 2001). NPL ratios fell overall from 25.4% in 2001 to 9.8% in 2005. Equity capital surged to CNY 1.1 trillion. Total assets of commercial banks amounted to CNY 37.47 trillion (an 18.6% increase since 2004) (Hooke, 2006).

10
State-Owned Commercial Banks

The four SOCBs[1] are

- Industrial and Commercial Bank of China (ICBC)
- China Construction Bank (CCB)
- Bank of China (BoC) and
- Agricultural Bank of China (ABC).

10.1 Key indicators and figures (Refer to Table 10.1)

10.2 Market share and position

The Chinese banking sector is dominated by the four SOCBs which currently hold together 52% of banking sector assets.

10.3 Ownership and enterprise forms

The banks are all under the (in)-direct control of the State Council, China's highest executive organ. The Chinese state acts as an implicit guarantor to the four SOCBs. Up to mid-2006, only the ABC had not been incorporated into a limited liability shareholding company.

The share capital of BoC, CCB and ICBC are all majority owned by the state, under the PBOC (Central Huijin Investment Co. holds directly 67%[2] in BoC's capital, 61.5%[3] of CCB's capital and 90% of ICBC's capital). The company (also called SAFE Investment) was originally created in December 2003 with an initial capital of CNY 372 bln: it will also help reform the corporate governance structure of the banks and hold shares in other banks. The company is said to look at TemasekHoldings in Singapore as a model for intervening and investing

Table 10.1 State-owned commercial banks – performance overview

	ABC		BoC		CCB		ICBC	
in mln CNY	**2005**	**2004**	**2005**	**2004**	**2005**	**2004**	**2005**	**2004**
Total assets	4,771,019	4,013,769	4,742,806	4,270,443	4,585,742	3,904,785	6,454,106	5,670,521
Net loan portfolio	2,793,266	2,557,693	2,151,893	2,071,693	2,395,313	2,171,756	3,205,861	3,684,083
Loan loss provisions	36,025	32,379	83,153	74,769	63,085	53,829	83,692	21,191
Non-performing loans	740,425	692,326	103,226	109,920	94,469	68,370	154,417	703,644
Total customer deposits	4,036,854	3,491,549	3,755,941	3,342,477	4,006,046	3,271,650	5,742,847	5,060,718
Total capital	79,607	78,063	262,620	205,351	287,677	194,744	257,481	162,983
Sub. Debt	0	0	60,179	26,070	39,907	40,000	0	0
Net interest income	67,013	69,299	100,157	86,063	117,097	103,708	141,874	113,149
Net profit	1044	2003	32,579	25,246	47,096	48,388	33,704	2,681
ROE (%)	1.31	2.57	12.41	12.29	16.37	24.85	13.09	1.64
ROA (%)	0.02	0.05	0.69	0.59	1.03	1.24	0.52	0.05
NPL ratio (%)	26.17	26.73	4.62	5.12	3.84	3.07	18.99	21.24
Basel I CAR (%)	n.a.	n.a.	10.42	10.04	13.57	11.29	9.89	n.a.

Source: Calculations and data based on the banks' annual reports.

in financial institutions (Yu N., 2005c). However, SAFE Investment comparatively lacks the capacity to attract high-level managers (Wang L., 2005a). It is thus debatable how much Central Huijin, as a state conduit for equity investments using China's foreign reserves, can push forward corporate governance best practices, how independent it could be and how it will be able to avoid conflict of interests and strategic disputes with other ministries.

10.4 Historical developments

Until 1998, banks were bound by the credit plan to lend a fixed amount to certain enterprises, sectors and regions of the economy. Only after 1998 SOCBs could slowly free themselves from such guidelines and requirements (however, it is still not possible to make a completely clear separation between policy-directed lending and commercially motivated lending, especially at ABC, Ling H., 2005b). The lenders still lack the ability to impose financial discipline on their (SOE) borrowers.

The history of policy lending has also brought the banks close to insolvency. The central government agreed to recapitalise the four state-owned banks with CNY 27 bln in August 1998 and again with USD 45 bln in CCB and BoC in December 2003 as well as with USD 15 bln in early 2005 in ICBC. Foreign investors have been invited to participate in a limited way to ICBC's, BoC's and CCB's capital. BoC Hong Kong's (July 2002), CCB's (October 2005) and BoC's (May 2006) stock market listings in Hong Kong[4] were followed in October 2006 by ICBC. The percentages listed are not large, thus leaving the state as absolute majority shareholder.

10.5 Geographic and business scope

All of the SOCBs were originally specialised in the sectors as defined through their names: CCB was specialised in construction projects, BoC in international trade and foreign exchange, ICBC in industrial and commercial lending and ABC in lending to agricultural entities. These sector specialisations have largely disappeared and each of them now targets all large enterprises in their areas. Only ABC is still focused on agriculture and rural areas.

The branch networks of the four SOCBs have decreased over the years. Most branch closures took place in rural areas, but also urban areas still witness the closure or merging of branches to make the SOCBs' networks more efficient (Table 10.2). Efficiency was also increased by shedding employees.

Table 10.2 Number of branches in Chinese SOCBs (2004)

	Number of branches	Number of employees	Assets/ branch	Assets/ employees	Total assets
ICBC	21,223	375,781	267	15	5,670,521
ABC	31,004	489,425	129	8	4,013,769
BoC	11,307	220,999	378	19	4,270,443
CCB	14,585	310,391	268	13	3,904,785
Average SOCBs	*19,530*	*349,149*	*261*	*14*	*4,464,880*
Average JSCBs	*544*	*14,171*	*1,162*	*41*	*477,021*
Average total	**10,037**	**181,660**	**711**	**28**	**2,470,950**

Source: Based on www.stats.gov.cn.

10.6 Management

Although more and more managers are being recruited competitively and their professional background is becoming more important in making a choice (Table 10.3), the senior management in these banks is appointed by the state and the Communist Party. To remedy shortages of professional managers, banks have recruited foreign executives to senior management teams.

While personnel decisions remain with the Communist Party, SBs are under the supervision of the CBRC, rights on the banks' assets remain with the Ministry of Finance and the capital is held by a SAFE investment conduit (Wei W., 2005). The high number of parties involved makes conflicts of interests inevitable and increases confusion with all remaining stakeholders (including the banks themselves).

Table 10.3 Skills and experience of Chinese SOCBs employees (2002, %)

Bank name	Employees older than 35 years	Employees with a university degree	Officers in senior/ middle management positions
ICBC	43.3	17.8	27.2
ABC	47.9	14.1	21.1
BoC	64.7	22.3	21.2
CCB	57.3	20.7	28.5
Average SOCBs	*53.3*	*18.7*	*24.5*

Source: Based on PBOC, 2003.

Finally it is important to note that internal structures are not lean. These banks have many hierarchical layers and each layer has decision powers in lending and many other business areas. Making structures leaner and less prone to outside influences is one of the strongest challenges for senior management.

10.7 Financial performance

The performance of SOCBs is highly correlated to the level of the intermediation margin they earn through loans and deposits (Zhong W *et al.*, 2004). Most of their income relies on interest from loans and for deposits. This is driven not only by the lack of depth of financial services but also by the regulations in China which reduce the possibility to earn fee income (banks only started charging fees on small accounts in 2005 and ATM fees in May 2006).

At a conference in mid-2005, PBOC's vice-president, Wu Xiaoling, set the following targets for the state-owned banks for 2005: Return on total assets should reach 0.6%, ROE 11%, NPL ratio should be between 3 and 5%. Furthermore the loan loss reserves to NPL ratio shall reach 60% for BoC and 80% for CCB (see References for laws 12 and 34). CBRC also outlined some requirements for establishing reliable risk management systems, strengthening internal auditing and improving corporate governance structures.

10.8 Challenges and opportunities

The financial performance of SOCBs has improved dramatically since 1999 (perhaps with the exception of ABC, where small progress has been made): NPLs have been transferred, capital has been freshly raised, subordinated debt has been issued, much of this thanks to the largesse of central authorities. The sustainability of the reforms will be tested among others in terms of asset quality. Repeated efforts have shown that accounting can help to clean up books in the shortterm; however, strong economic growth coupled with excessive lending could rapidly transform the banks' books into non-performing ones. It remains to be seen in the long term if the short-term successes can be maintained. For that it requires the establishment of efficient centralised credit risk management system among other things.

Following their establishment as limited liability companies, SOCBs have also established a SB, a BoD, a shareholders meeting and other specialised commissions to supervise the banks (as required in the regulations concerning corporate governance for banks). However, the scandal at CCB which came to light in late 2004 or the one at a BoC branch in early 2006, among others, questioned the efficiency of these newly established bodies. In fact, journalists reported that many functions at CCB were still held by the former president at the same time, in contradiction with corporate governance best practices (Ling H. and Li Q., 2005).

While changes are proof of the willingness to reform China's banking system and the reforms are moving in the right direction, it is still difficult to assess whether all reforms have been fully implemented and have been as thorough as required. Podpiera (2006) finds that while SOCBs have undergone years of reforms and shed NPLs, little has changed in their commercial orientation, their risk pricing ability and their lending focus (disregard of borrowers' profitability but driven by availability of funds). The reforms on the soft side, including those in areas of corporate governance, internal controls and risk management, are likely to take time until they permeate the whole organisation.

An exception among the SOCBs is the ABC, which holds the largest amount of policy loans. The situation at ABC is more challenging because of its position between commercial bank and conduit for policy loans and poverty reduction in rural areas. The ABC reform is a political challenge which could be costly.[5] It only submitted a reform plan in early 2006 and is believed to be in a much poorer state than any of the other SOCBs. According to the bank some CNY 2.8 trillion of its loan portfolio are NPLs,[6] that is a 26.3% (Yang G. and Gu A., 2006) at the end of 2005 (of the outstanding policy loans and agriculture loans, amounting to CNY 414 bln, NPLs amount to CNY 349 bln, i.e. for this part of the portfolio a NPL ratio of 84%, Ling H., 2006). Its loan portfolio is geared towards agricultural lending (39% of the portfolio and 61% of its outlets). Its operating profits amounted in 2005 to CNY 42.4 bln. Its reform should make it a prime lender in rural areas while supporting rural economic development.

The banks themselves now acknowledge the need to move away from the NPLs disposal focus which was dominant until 2005, towards a business orientation to ensure that their competitiveness is raised.

Table 10.4 SOCBs' SWOT analysis

Strengths	**Weaknesses**
• Large coverage, outreach • Brand names, well known • Cheap labour • First address for external enterprises financing • Attracting large amounts of deposits • Contributing largely to the economic growth • Preferential treatment from the authorities • Implicit state guarantee	• NPL/NPA levels • Lack of functioning corporate governance structures • Interference of state, bearing scars of socialist planning • Lack of credit culture, risk management • Under capitalised • Lack of qualified personnel Corruption • Large numbers of policy related loans • Rigid management structures • Simple products • Low level of customer service
Opportunities	**Threats**
• Large private sector • Consumer/consumption taking off, wealth management • Strong economic environment • Reform of SOEs and stock markets underway • Building up consumer credit registries • Non-interest financial services • Loosening restrictions	• Opening and liberalisation through WTO entry • Basel II: loss of competitive advantage, competitive imbalances, pro-cyclicality • Consumers not bound to one bank • Currency revaluation • Increased competition

This should be achieved by sound risk management and better products (Carew, 2006). It should be noted that while further reforms and better banking practices are on the agenda, full privatisation is not.

The SWOT analysis for SOCBs is given in Table 10.4.

11
Joint-Stock Commercial Banks

The 13 JSCBS include the Bank of Communications (BoComm), China Merchants Bank (Merchants), CITIC Industrial Bank (CITIC), Shanghai Pudong Development Bank (Pudong), China Minsheng Banking Corporation (Minsheng), Industrial Bank, formerly Fujian Industrial Bank (Industrial), China Everbright Bank (Everbright), Guangdong Development Bank (GDB), Huaxia Bank (Huaxia), Hengfeng Bank (Hengfeng), Shenzhen Development Bank (SDB) as well as the two JSCBs established at the end of 2005, Huishang Bank (from a merger of some CCBs in Anhui province) and Bohai Bank (with support from Standard Chartered).

The JSCBs have since the 1980s proven to be emerging forces in the banking system and have provided a real and lively challenge to other established entities.

11.1 Key indicators and figures

The JSCBs had at the end of 2004 a total shareholders' equity amounting to CNY 166 bln, total assets of CNY 4.8 bln and net profits of CNY 25 bln. Their average ROE was 17.79%, much higher than that in the past years (11.59% for 2003 and 13.64% for 2002) and also better by 3% points than the average RoE of all the largest 50 commercial banks. Their profits witnessed a strong growth over 2004, a 31% increase over the year (Table 11.1) (*China Finance*, 2005).

11.2 Market share and position

The joint stock commercial banks account for 14–15% of total banking assets.

Table 11.1 Selected joint-stock commercial banks – performance overview 2005

in mln CNY	BoComm	Minsheng	Merchants	Huaxia	CITIC	SPDB	Industrial	SDB
Total assets	1,423,439	557,137	733,982	356,129	611,935	573,065	473,988	229,216
Net loan portfolio	758,773	373,081	458,675	228,755	373,473	366,646	237,459	149,870
Loan loss provisions	12,601	4,994	13,510	4,932	11,938	10,577	5,111	6,233
Non-performing loans	18,068	4,923	12,168	7,113	14,257	7,445	5,647	16,480
Total customer deposits	1,220,839	489,327	635,722	313,557	520,066	504,482	355,218	209,158
Total capital	83,146	15,459	24,671	10,453	21,340	15,526	12,115	5,043
Sub. Debt	12,292	7,249	3,500	4,250	6,000	6,000	6,000	0
Net interest income	31,636	12,052	16,999	7,360	9,750	11,849	9,241	4,887
Net profit	9,243	2,703	3,930	1,289	2,980	2,486	2,455	351
ROE (%)	11.12	17.48	15.93	12.33	13.97	16.01	20.26	6.96
ROA (%)	0.65	0.49	0.54	0.36	0.49	0.43	0.52	0.15
NPL ratio (%)	2.34	1.30	2.58	3.04	3.70	1.97	2.33	10.56
Basel I CAR (%)	11.20	8.26	9.06	8.23	n.a.	8.04	8.13	3.70

For details on bank acronyms refer to the annex.

Source: Calculations and data based on the banks' annual reports.

11.3 Ownership and enterprise forms

The JSCBs' capital is partly held by the state, mainly either directly through the Ministry of Finance or Central Huijin or indirectly through SOEs. Some also have been invested by foreign entities. Finally only one is truly in private hands: China Minsheng Banking Corp. A few are partly listed on stock exchanges in Shanghai and Hong Kong: Shanghai Pudong Development Bank, Huaxia Bank, China Minsheng Banking Corporation and Merchants Bank in Shanghai and Bank of Communications in Hong Kong.

11.4 Historical developments

These banks were in most part established in the late 1980s or early 1990s to boost competition in the Chinese banking market. This relatively late establishment has enabled them to make a fresh start and thus their capital adequacy and asset quality were and are on average better than that at wholly state-owned banks.

The establishment and development of the JSCBs is an important fact and feature of the Chinese banking system, since it broke the direct state monopoly on banking assets, made the provision of banking services more efficient, customer-oriented and innovative. Labour productivity and economies of scale have, it is argued, made the banks more efficient (Chen *et al.*, 2005).

11.5 Specific regulations and authorities

The regulation of the JSCBs seems, in a number of areas, to be more stringent than that for state-owned banks (Brehm and Macht, 2005). While on one side, this may reduce the riskiness of these banks, it is also criticised as an unfair treatment of JSCBs, which constrains their competitiveness on the other side (Xiao Z., 2005). This difference in regulation may be explained by the stronger interference of the central government in the operations of SOCBs which are further away from reaching the new regulatory standards.

Furthermore, JSCBs do not enjoy the implicit guarantee of their debts that SOCBs enjoy. This creates an unequal standing. Another impediment is the bottleneck created by the lack of rules and regulations in certain areas or the restrictive regulations in other areas which stifles product and service innovation (e.g. using inventory or future assets as collateral, etc., see Xiao Z., 2006).

Licensing requirements for JSCBs have been reviewed in early 2006 (References for laws 14). The minimum capital requirement is now CNY 1 bln. Prudential requirements include having qualified management, reliable systems, sound procedures and structures for risk management and corporate governance and they are expected to comply fully with prudential indicators on capital adequacy and assert quality. Their shareholders should have sufficient financial power and strong performance. Foreign owners should additionally have capital amounting to at least CNY 10 bln and a CAR of 8%.

11.6 Geographic and business scope

The JSCBs' branch networks are much more restricted than those of the state-owned banks. Their branch networks have been built up over the last 10–15 years. The number of branches range between a few for Hengfeng Bank (which albeit having received a nationwide licence in 2003 has not yet expanded strongly) and almost 18,000 for China Merchants Bank (Table 11.2). While they have less branches overall, their product range and scope is wider. Their networks are more efficient with back office functions centralised usually in single processing centres.

11.7 Management

The performance of their management can also be viewed by their higher level of efficiency (in terms of staffing) compared to their state-owned peers (Table 11.3).

11.8 Financial performance

Compared with SOCBs, JSCBs have been able to attract more new business and customers and therefore been able to expand at a more rapid

Table 11.2 Number of branches in Chinese JSCBs (2004)

	Number of branches	Number of employees	Assets/ branch	Assets/ employees	Total assets
Average SOCBs	19,530	349,149	261	14	4,464,880
Average JSCBs	544	14,171	1,162	41	477,021
Average total	*10,037*	*181,660*	*711*	*28*	*2,470,950*

Source: Based on www.stats.gov.cn.

Table 11.3 Skills and experience of Chinese JSCBs employees (2002, %)

Bank name	Employees >35 years	Employees with a university degree	Officers in senior/middle management positions
BoComm	63.9	28.4	27.8
CITIC	84.2	44.1	27.5
Minsheng	75.8	87.6	35.1
Everbright	67.8	50.0	31.1
Huaxia	71.3	44.9	34.9
Average JSCBs	*72.6*	*51.0*	*31.3*

Source: Based on PBOC (2003).

pace (and this despite the fact that they do not enjoy the same regulatory environment as SOCBs). For example, in 2004, the assets of JSCBs grew by more than 22% quarterly (compared to the same quarter in 2003), compared with 11% on average for SOCBs.

Compared to SOCBs, JSCBs also show better asset quality. While in 2003 JSCBs had on average an NPL ratio of 6.5%, their state-owned counterparts had an average 20.8% NPLs on their books (the recent improvement in SOCBs' loan qualities is largely the result of state-induced disposal and restructuring activities). Furthermore, JSCBs only hold 11% of all NPLs, while SOCBs have an 82% share of the banking system's NPLs (at the end of 2005). Most JSCBs were never required to comply with the rules of the credit plan, did not have to lend to unprofitable SOEs and had a chance to build up more efficient structures and controls right from the start.

11.9 Challenges and opportunities

The JSCBs are, however, facing several constraints to their development (Xiao Z., 2005).

First and most importantly, their size and their market share are both small. Despite being more efficient on average than their state-owned counterparts, they only represent 16% of banking sector assets, while state-owned banks represent 52%. Each of them holds no more than 1–2% in loans or deposits in the banking system, thus reflecting their small size and market shares (one exception is BoComm which alone has a 5% market share). Furthermore they are mainly present in large urban centres and do not possess such large networks in second-tier and smaller urban centres. This is also the result of restrictions imposed by CBRC for opening new branches.

Second, their capital adequacy is relatively low. In 2004–05, most JSCBs had capital ratios just above the regulatory 8% (only Merchants had a CAR above 9%, and a few had much lower ratios: SDB with 2–3%, for example). To sustain their high growth rates, the banks need to raise more capital more often; however, capital funding channels are expensive and not well developed in China. A number of banks (Industrial, Merchants, Minsheng, CITIC, etc.) is thus looking at overseas listings (mainly in Hong Kong) to take advantage of the strong current interest of foreign investors in Chinese markets (which make market listings a less expensive alternative to external funding) and at the same time to improve their capital adequacy.

Third, JSCBs were, at the time of their establishment, targeting SMEs; however, this scope has changed and they are now targeting larger enterprises as well and thus competing head-on with the state-owned banks.

Fourth, the corporate governance structures are in place in theory, but since most of the banks' shares are state-owned ones (directly or indirectly through SOEs), conflicts of interest arise. The large and controlling presence of the state in these banks hurts the efficient functioning of the corporate governance structures. Despite being partly listed on Chinese stock markets, most of their shares remain in the hands of the state and outside investors are not yet in a position to influence positively the banks' corporate governance.

Fifth, despite being quite innovative in terms of products and services and being at the forefront of reforms regarding internal controls and risk management, JSCBs have not yet achieved a sustainable competitive advantage. This is due to three main reasons: the lack of a long-term strategic orientation, innovation happens mostly at the front office and not in the middle or back offices, and the lack of information and resources sharing among different departments (Xiao Z., 2005).

The competition with state-owned banks is likely to gather pace as these are being reformed to be able to compete with foreign banks after the end of the transition period to WTO entry. Most SOCBs have shed bad loans and staff, closed branches, installed new systems and so on. which will make them more efficient and competitive. This point can be observed as well in Internet banking. JSCBs have been traditionally strong, but the ascension of CCB in this area has challenged the position of JSCBs (Xiao Z., 2006). This will put more pressure on the smaller JSCBs which cannot rely as

Table 11.4 SWOT analysis for JSCBs

Strengths	**Weaknesses**
• Cheap labour • Highly liquid • Better quality loan portfolios • Sound management structures • Customer service levels higher • Clear ownership structures	• Under capitalised • Weaker deposit base • Smaller force de frappe • Low level of customer service
Opportunities	**Threats**
• Large private sector • Consumer/consumption growing/taking off • Strong economic environment • Reform of SOEs and stock markets underway • Building up consumer credit registries	• Opening and liberalisation through WTO entry • Basel II: loss of competitive advantage, competitive imbalances, pro-cyclicality • Consumers not bound to one bank • Weak regulators, lacking independence

much as the SOCBs on the state preference they enjoy and where they do not have the size and scope to compete.

The competition for JSCBs will not only come from better performing SOCBs in the future, but also from foreign banks which have prepared themselves for all out competition in 2007.

The SWOT analysis for JSCBs is given in Table 11.4.

12
City Commercial Banks

City commercial banks (CCBs) are local financial institutions that were set up in the reform era under the aegis of local governments. Most of them are headquartered in urban centres and their development is clearly linked to their narrow scope and environments.

12.1 Key indicators and figures

Not all CCBs do conform to the picture given by Table 12.1. Performance indicators vary widely: the largest had assets of more than CNY 200 bln while the smallest had only CNY 1 bln in total assets. Of all CCBs, 70% have assets in the range of CNY 1–10 bln. Some had NPL ratios just above 5% while others had more than 60% of their portfolio deemed non-performing. Of all CCBs, 12 had negative capital (Zhang J., 2005). The largest 34 CCBs amount to 80% of the total equity (with CNY 46 bln) and 71% of CCBs' total assets (with CNY 1.2 trillion). They also represent 80% of the net profits generated by all CCBs (with CNY 6.5 bln). They have an average ROE of 14% and an average ROA of 0.5% (*China Finance*, 2005) (Table 12.2).

12.2 Market share and position

The CCBs only account for a small proportion of the nationwide Chinese banking assets: 5.4% (in 2004 and 2005). At the same time, each of them ranks within the first four or five banks in its local area. Their local market shares varied between 1.4 and 23.25% (Zhang J., 2005). May Yan (2006) has illustrated that on average they have a banking asset market share of 8.5% in their localities and rank mostly just behind the SOCBs.

Table 12.1 Main indicators for CCBs

in CNY bln	Dec. 2005	Jun. 2005	Dec. 2004	Jun. 2004
Number of CCBs	115	113	112	112
Total assets	2037	1798	1706	1528
Total liabilities	1954	1736	1647	1475
Market share (of banking assets) (%)	5.4	5.2	5.5	5.1
Total loans	1064		904.5	
Total deposits			1434	
NPLs	84.2	103.89	106.1	119.2
NPL ratio (%)	7.73	10.43	11.7 range from 3%–50%	14.08 (four tier classification)
Provisions for loan losses	20	15.68	15.6	
Coverage ratio (%)	23.75 in some cases 100%	15.09	14.7	
Capital adequacy (%)	5.13	1.36	2.7	
Total equity	83	62.4	57.7	52.8
Total profits	12		8.2	4.8
ROE (%)	14.45		14.2	9.1
ROA (%)	0.59		0.5	0.32

Source: Based on Ba *et al.* (2005a); SinoCast China Financial Watch (2005a); China Economic Information Net (2004a,b); China Industry and Economy Information Net (2005); Financial News (2005b); Yan M. (2006); Financial News (2005c); CBRC (2004a, 2006c).

12.3 Ownership and enterprise forms

Local governments own on average 75% of the capital of CCBs (KPMG, 2005), directly and indirectly.[1] While May Yan (2006) shows that direct ownership for major CCBs is only at 23% of capital on average, one should take full account of the other government-owned enterprises which are their shareholders as well. Part of this ownership was set up in 1995 when the local Finance Bureaus were allowed to use part of their budget to invest in around 30% of CCBs' equity. Further to this, a rule had been set by the PBOC that a single enterprise cannot own more than 10% of the capital and that a single individual cannot own more than 2% (*China Industry and Economy Information Net*, 2005). The local government, as a result, often has the final say in running the bank and taking strategic decisions.

Just as for the four SOCBs (see above), the state in form of local and provincial governments has played a strong role, both as a shareholder and as a financial supporter in case of technical insolvency (Table 12.3).

Table 12.2 City commercial banks – performance overview 2004

in mln CNY	12 CCBs	All CCBs	Bank of Shanghai	Bank of Beijing	Xi'an CCB	Chongqing CCB	Shenzhen CCB	Nanjing CCB
Total assets	808,514	1,693,800	219,837	208,755	25,266	23,732	68,257	38,145
Net loan portfolio	405,963	888,820	105,880	107,270	16,657	12,700	38,548	15,556
Loan loss provisions	9,693	15,680	4,266	1,814	111	187	675	520
Non-performing loans	24,959	106,100	5,445	4,394	1,323	2,584	3,108	682
Total customer deposits	679,772	1,434,100	183,249	175,961	22,950	18,966	58,095	28,346
Total capital	32,319	57,700	7,299	7,127	1,338	1,785	2,138	1,532
Sub. Debt	3,000	3,000	3,000	0	0	0	0	0
Net interest income	17,310	n.a.	4,780	3,866	767	546	1,270	834
Net profit	4,408	8,200	1,463	336	87	78	155	215
ROE (%)	13.64	n.a.	20.04	4.71	6.50	4.37	7.25	14.03
ROA (%)	0.55	n.a.	0.67	0.16	0.34	0.33	0.23	0.56
NPL ratio (%)	6.00	11.73	4.94	4.03	7.89	20.05	7.92	4.24
Basel I CAR (%)	7.10	1.40	10.89	5.27	5.20	4.30	2.30	10.50

12 CCBs include those in Beijing, Shanghai, Chongqing, Xi'an, Dongguan, Dalian, Hangzhou, Nanjing, Ningbo, Shenzhen, Tianjin and Wuxi. All of them are located in large urban centres which are also relatively wealthy and for most located in coastal areas. NPLs and related ratios for all except Bank of Shanghai are based on the four-tier classification.

Source: Calculations and data based on the banks' annual reports as well as Yan, M. (2006).

Table 12.3 Financial support from local governments to CCBs (1994–2004)

in CNY bln	**1994–2003**	**2004**
Compensation for losses	5.14	1.99
Stripping of NPLs	7.17	5.01
Disposal of non-performing assets	23.51	16.37
Total	*35.83*	*23.36*

Source: Based on Xie D. (2005).

Table 12.4 Funds and NPL reductions for selected CCBs (2005)

Bank	**Local government funds in CNY bln**	**Reduction in NPL ratio in percentage points**
Haerbin	2.69	3.28
Mashan	2.1	49.83
Shenyang	2.0	19.87
Dalian	1.76	15.79
Chongqing	1.25	8.8
Chengdu	1.0	10.92
Qingdao	0.24	5.77

Source: Based on Xie D. (2005).

In 2004, some CCBs received funds from their respective local governments to get rid of their NPLs. In 2005, seven local governments have spent some CNY 23.3 bln for their respective CCBs (see Table 12.4).

Each of the CCBs is a limited liability entity and with a unified structure and management.

12.4 Historical developments

Most of China's CCBs were established starting from 1995 following the mergers of some 2200 UCCs and urban cooperative banks.[2] The first was Shenzhen City Cooperative Bank, established in June 1995. CCBs were created in the first place to provide financial services to SMEs, individuals and (perhaps most importantly) governments in their locality (Zhong J., 2004).

Over the 10 years since their formal establishment, one can distinguish three development phases. The first phase is characterised by the reduction of historical risks (in some cases CCBs faced payment crises) which included for most the restructuring of their capital base, the stripping-out and disposal of NPLs; the second reform and development phase, related to when they became the main finance provider of local residents and SMEs; the third entails the upgrading of systems and procedures (*China INFOBANK Limited*, 2005b). Not all CCBs are in the same development phase and some are taking longer than others.

12.5 Specific regulations and authorities

The CCBs need to comply with the same regulations as other commercial banks when it comes to asset quality, capital adequacy, information disclosure and risk management. The minimum capital required is lower at CNY 100 mln, compared with CNY 1 bln for JSCBs and CNY 50 mln for rural commercial banks.

Regulatory agencies have increased their pressure on local governments to progressively release local banks from their grip and influence. CBRC and the Chinese government have encouraged CCBs to improve their capital adequacy and their loss reserves, to establish prudential operational mechanisms, control-related parties transactions, reduce lending concentrations, and strengthen information disclosure to improve transparency, implement restructuring plans and the overall level and competitiveness of each institution (CBRC, 2004a,b). Many are also opening their doors to foreign shareholders or intending to do so as a way of diversifying ownership and improving their intermediation capacity.

The CCBs are expected to widely comply (80% of all banks) with minimum Basel I capital requirements of 8% by the end of 2006.[3] By this time, most should have effective risk management systems in place. Furthermore they should have adequate information disclosure mechanisms (already 38 CCBs are now compliant. All CCBs should publish their financial statements starting from 2005). By 2008, they should also make "appropriate" loan loss provisions.

12.6 Geographic and business scope

Historically, CCBs have been limited to expand within their locality. With the creation of Huishang Bank as a merger of a number of local CCBs and RCCs, as well as the first approved branch for Bank of Shanghai outside its own turf in 2005 (*Dow Jones Chinese Financial Wire*, 2005), regulators have taken a more opened view. Now healthier banks can apply for branches outside their localities provided they have at least CNY 50 bln in total assets, equity capital of at least CNY 1 bln, NPL ratios lower than 6% in the last 3 years, ROA of at least 0.45% and ROE of at least 10%. Eight CCBs have successfully applied for such extensions (*Asia Pulse*, 2006c).

Table 12.5 Branches of City Commercial Banks (2002)

	Number of			Average per bank	
Province	**Branches**	**Employees**	**Banks**	**Branches**	**Employees**
Total	4,855	106,199	109	44.54	974.30
Eastern	1,214	28,700	23	52.78	1247.83
North-eastern	545	19,034	17	32.06	1119.65
South-eastern	1,637	31,508	36	45.47	875.22
Central	508	10,574	13	39.08	813.38
North-western	230	3,968	4	57.50	992.00
South-western	721	12,415	16	45.06	775.94

Source: Based on PBOC, 2003.

In total, all CCBs, at the end of June 2004, had 107,000 staff and 5154 outlets or branches spread out over China. The branch network of individual CCBs ranges from 22 to 200 branches. With an average 45 branches in their locality, they can rely on a strong local visibility and presence.

While the CCBs normally market themselves as the "local economy's bank" or the "locals' bank", the structure of their loan portfolios reveals a different picture. On average, surveyed CCBs' loan portfolios were structured as follows: 17% to SOEs, 14.5% to private enterprises with more than 500 employees, 18.6% to private enterprises with between 100 and 500 employees, 6.7% to local governments, 17.8% to private enterprises with less than 100 employees and 2.2% to consumers (based on a survey of 20 CCBs: *Financial News*, 2005a as well as SCDRC, 2005). Therefore only 38.6% of their portfolio goes to SMEs or to individuals. This actually contradicts other statistics for large CCBs which show that non-state lending makes up 80% of their portfolio and that 70% of all loans go to SMEs[4] (*China Economic Information Net*, 2004a,b; Yan M., 2006). Local governments often find in CCBs strong financial support for their large infrastructure projects. The lending decision for the large credit limits is often not based on commercial grounds.

12.7 Management

Local governments do influence the CCBs not only financially, but also by choosing senior managers and directors. Most of them are chosen because of their political *couleur*, rather than their managerial and banking skills (Li Z., 2005). The human resources issue is aggravated by the fact that most CCBs' staff (98%) come from the old UCCs with low education levels (staff with specific finance educational background makes up only 30% of all staff) and performance records (Lu M., 2005). Finding good staff locally can be a challenge in second-tier cities.[5]

The CCBs co-operate with their peers in some limited areas, such as through a clearing centre, for loan syndication, funds and bonds investment management, credit card issuance and training in international banking business (*The Asian Banker*, 2005b; *Financial News*, 2005c).

12.8 Financial performance

May Yan (2006) reports that the performance and outlook for CCBs are increasingly divergent. Some of them are in good shape and well managed, while others are technically bankrupt but kept afloat by local authorities. The average figures hide some large and persistent disparities (Zhong J., 2004): some CCBs have good-quality loan portfolios, while others have NPLs as high as 60%. Some even manage to produce net profits of a few billions each year (*China Industry and Economy Information Net*, 2005). Zhou Xiaochuan, PBOC's president, gave a number of reasons explaining regional disparities: different degrees of local government intervention, different ways and standards of enforcing the same regulations, different commercial cultures, the influence until a few years ago of military entities or enterprises in some financial institutions, and the limits fixed internally by some banks for certain regions (Zhou X., 2004a).

Another important factor for the discrepancy in performance is the ownership quality of CCBs. A survey (*Financial News*, 2005a as well as SCDRC, 2005) found that it is not so much the percentage of shares held by local governments which influences banks' profitability but rather the depth of the corporate governance structures and the level of revenues of the relevant local government. Corporate governance structures are often in place (to comply with regulatory requirements) but controlled by the main shareholders and are thus more akin to puppet institutions. Where local governments can rely on abundant revenues because of strong economic development or a large economic centre, the banks tend to show lower levels of NPLs. The survey found a strong negative correlation between the level of NPLs and the per capita government revenue. This is also confirmed by another research exercise based on PBOC data (Shih *et al.*, 2005b). Overall where economic activities are supported, where private enterprises strive, where SMEs can find guaranteeing institutions for their loans, where individual incomes are higher, where local governments make efforts to protect the rights of enterprises and individuals, CCBs tend to show a healthier development and sounder financial situation. Thus the development and stability of CCBs depend to a large extent on the influence of the local authorities and their stance towards local economic development.

The results of a survey of 20 CCBs in 3 provinces in February 2005 (*Financial News*, 2005a as well as SCDRC, 2005) show that CCBs are insufficiently capitalised (capital adequacy is low overall with 2.7% in 2004 and highly volatile), carry large risk concentrations in their loan portfolios,[6] make little use of their risk management departments,[7] and pay large and larger than normal dividends to their shareholders.[8]

On the income side, 53% of operating revenues come from interest income and 71% of all expenses are management expenses. The banks lack diversified income streams. This is the result of their geographic constraints and narrow scope (*Financial News*, 2005a as well as SCDRC, 2005).

12.9 Challenges and opportunities

To reform themselves, CCBs have chosen a four-pronged approach (Yan M., 2006):

1. Financial restructuring and recapitalisation: often done with the local authorities' support which may include the creation of a separate entity to deal with bad loans. Often developed areas have demonstrated more innovative and faster ways to deal with such issues.
2. Introduction of strategic investors: potential influence of foreign investors is to be seen critically, because the 20% stakes (at most) are no larger than those of local governments. Domestic investors have also been introduced in many banks, although their visibility is much lower.
3. Expansion outside their localities: by granting licences for large geographic areas and through mergers in Jiangsu (with Jiangsu Bank which could regroup 10 CCBs in that province and have combined total assets of CNY 80 bln) and Liaoning province (*China INFOBANK Limited*, 2005b; Fang, Y. 2005), in Anhui Huishang Bank has already

opened its doors. Bank of Shanghai itself is said to be looking for acquisitions targets.).
4. IPOs: Nanjing CCB is said to be planning its IPO, for example. This can allow them to widen their business scope, diversify their earnings and balance sheets.

The CCBs all face some common issues in their future development: the improvement of their capital adequacy, of their corporate governance structures, finding ways to clean up their loan portfolios and finally orient themselves strategically towards niche areas such as SMEs in their own markets.

Capital adequacy is a strong headache for CCBs. Since their main shareholders are local governments and they should decrease their dependency towards them, increasing capital from existing shareholders is not a solution. Another possible solution would be to turn to capital markets; however, their current operating state make access to such financing problematic. Thus the only remaining option is either to attract new shareholders (foreign or domestic private investors) or to issue subordinated debt (Zhang J., 2005; Zhou W., 2005). Foreign entities are happy to enter the market at relatively lower costs (albeit with often too little shares). For local private enterprises, the incentives are lower since most CCBs have relatively low ROAs and they can find other more rewarding investment opportunities (Zhou W., 2005) and finally because they are also often borrowers in these banks. The introduction of new shareholders will drive the formation of new interests and reform current interest structures (Zhou W., 2005). This in turn can lead to significant changes internally and in risk management. In Hangzhou, Ningbo and Wenzhou, the capital has been diversified and all banks have successfully increased their profitability, capital adequacy and loan portfolio quality (Zhou W., 2005).

The Development Research Centre of the State Council recently published a report "*Research on China's City Commercial Banks 2004–2005*" which was reviewed in the *Southern Weekend* (2005). The report is said to raise three issues to be looked at in the reform process of the CCBs. The first issue concerns the external governance environment of the banks, as it heavily influences the local (private) economy. Furthermore, the credit culture is relatively stable and well developed in areas where the private economy is also strong.[9] In such environments, the costs of information gathering and risk levels are lower for the local bank. Finally, in such developed areas, the bank has a wider scope for its own development and prospects for earnings are more diversified.

Table 12.6 SWOT analysis for CCBs

Strengths	**Weaknesses**
• Cheap labour • Niche players • Improving performance • Diversified ownership structures • Better local networks and market shares	• Under capitalised • Weaker deposit base • Low level of customer service • Strong local government interference • Limited geographically • Strong reliance in interest income • Weak management capabilities
Opportunities	**Threats**
• Large private sector • Local knowledge and monitoring • Consumer/consumption growing/taking off • High SME exposure, higher margins • Less threatened by foreign banks competition • Pooling of competencies possible	• Basel II: expensive reforms • Consumers not bound to one bank • Weak regulators, lacking independence • Higher risks from SME lending

The second issue concerns the internal corporate governance structure of CCBs, which has a decisive influence on their healthy long-term development. This is supported by the evidence from the reform years. Since CCBs have been transformed into their current form, their profitability has improved, thus showing that legal ownership has had a positive influence on their results.

The last issue concerns the diversification of shareholdings. While large stakes ensure a more stable development, large shareholders can also push their own interests to the detriment of smaller or minority shareholders. Concentrated large shareholdings also favour related-parties transactions. To improve the incentives mechanisms and to balance the shareholding structure, the ownership should be more diversified and state shares should be reduced. Diversification should be accompanied with fully developed corporate governance mechanisms, the clarification of ownership rights as well as the long-term orientation of shareholders.

The SWOT analysis for CCBs is given in Table 12.6.

13
Foreign Banks

13.1 Key indicators and figures

Up to October 2005, 244 foreign banks in China came from 60 countries and had established 476 operational entities (including branches and representative offices, which represent half that figure). According to statistics published by CBRC, foreign banks had total assets of USD 84.5 bln (CBRC, 2005a). Foreign banks, at the end of 2004, held deposits amounting to CNY 64.1 bln and loans amounting to CNY 267 bln (Xu N. and Wang Z., 2005). Most foreign branches were established in Beijing (13%), Shanghai (28%) and Shenzhen (10%) at the end of the third quarter of 2005 (Xiao Z., 2006).

13.2 Market share and position

Foreign banks, at the end of October 2005, had a market share of 2% of all loans. For foreign currency loans in China, they had a market share of 20% and for settlement services they have a market share of around 40% (Yue X., 2004). At the same time, in Shanghai they hold a 12.4% share of total assets (and a 54.8% share in foreign currency loans, CBRC 2005a).

A survey by McKinsey has, however, shown how difficult it can be for foreign banks to grab market share in China: large branch networks still matter much and Chinese customers are loyal to their banks, with banking relationships lasting on average between 9 and 12 years (Bekier and Lam, 2005).

13.3 Ownership and enterprise forms

Foreign banks can only choose between four types of entities to enter the Chinese market directly: through a representative office with consulting activities, a branch with operating business, a foreign-owned bank or a joint-venture bank (whereas here it could only own 49% of the capital at most).

Indirect entry is also increasingly becoming an alternative, that is by taking an equity participation in a Chinese bank. Both entry channels have witnessed an easing of rules and the pace of their entry has quickened.

13.4 Historical developments

Foreign banks were allowed back into China starting from 1978. However, up to 2006 their business scope and geographic range has been limited due to restrictive Chinese regulations, although these have been eased over the years.

Foreign banks were attracted into China mainly because of the potential business opportunities, as shown by Leung *et al.* (2003). As the regulatory and legal environment improved, more and more have established operations. However, the prospects and the environment are not the sole aspects factored into the foreign management decision: also bank size, support and commitment to a China strategy from the head quarters and international network are important facts to take into account.

Foreign banks are smaller and concentrated in coastal areas. Above all they are well capitalised – a sound base for expansion – and enjoy the backing of their parents institutions (in terms of knowledge, strategy and systems, etc.). Luo Ping (2003) thinks that their influence on the Chinese banking system is rather small as they are (at present at least) niche players.

13.5 Specific regulations and authorities

Apart from the rules with which all banks in China have to comply, foreign banks are also regulated under specific regulations: the *Management rule regarding foreign-invested institutions* and the *Management rule regarding the entry of foreign financial institutions into Chinese financial institutions* (References for laws 36 and 19). Further to these, foreign banks need also to comply with the provisions that apply to foreign enterprises in general (Wei W., 2005). Changes in the scope of business, registered share capital, names, large shareholdings, articles of association, and appointment of senior managers must all receive CBRC's approval.

In early 2006, licensing requirements were brought more or less in line with those for Chinese institutions, and requirements for business lines and for the qualifications of directors and managers are broadly similar (see Annex). Licensing is already a level-playing field. Prudential ratios are the same for all banks.

13.6 Geographic and business scope

The business scope of foreign banks is limited in terms of products, customers and geography. Most restrictions will be lifted by the end of 2006.

In the late 1990s, foreign banks were granted licences to make CNY-denominated loans, and in 1998 they were allowed access to the inter-banking market for refinancing. By the end of 2005, foreign banks could provide both CNY- and foreign currency–denominated financial products. As of 2004, they could not offer the following: debt and securities services, insurance services, but could offer foreign currency services (investments, exchange, bills) and consulting services which were not within the business scope of Chinese banks. As of October 2005, 138 foreign banks were allowed to conduct local currency business, 15 were licensed for Internet banking, 41 for dealing with derivatives, and 5 as QFII for custodian services system[1] (Schobert and Schulte, 2005). Overall, these represented over 100 types of products and services for 12 broad types of business activities (Xiao Z., 2006). Foreign banks have established their expertise in certain areas: trade finance, money market products, foreign exchange and derivatives dealing (Metcalfe, 2005).

It is only recently that they could also reach out to all types of customers, consumers and enterprises, both foreign and Chinese. Until the late 1990s, foreign banks could only offer financial services to foreign customers, joint-ventures and foreign enterprises. Their main customers are still international companies, joint-ventures and large state-owned companies with a foreign background (Metcalfe, 2005). The industries covered range from manufacturing, automotive and electronics.

Foreign banks are, within the limits set by the regulators, located in the areas where their customers are also located. By the end of 2005, foreign banks could provide their services in 25 cities. For example, Dalian has seen a number of Korean and Japanese banks opening branches there. Most are still located in Shanghai, Beijing and Shenzhen. Even with the progressive opening of further cities, the foreign banks did not expand quickly to these areas (He L. and Fan X., 2004). Those foreign banks that have expanded recently within China are for most from bordering Asian countries (Hong Kong, Taiwan, South Korea and Japan), America and France (He L. and Fan X., 2004). Finally, foreign bank branches are concentrated in Shanghai with 30% of all institutions and 55% of the total foreign banks' business revenues generated there (*Asia Pulse*, 2006d).

Most foreign banks have only one branch. The foreign banks with more than one branch include HSBC, Standard Chartered, Citigroup, Bank of East Asia, UFJ Bank, Mizuho Bank, ABN Amro and SMBC Bank (Zhou S., 2004).

13.7 Management

Foreign banks employ expatriates as 10% on average of their workforce (Metcalfe, 2005). For non-senior positions foreign banks employ young local graduates, who often have a foreign university degree. Through the greater foreign exposure and the higher qualification levels of employees, banks aim to achieve more professional service levels and better operating results.

13.8 Financial performance

Although their market share is small, their operations are efficient, growth rates are high, and they play an important role in certain areas (such as settlement services and foreign exchange lending) and have a strong influence on the markets (CBRC, 2005a). It is also difficult to make profits in China: one-fifth of foreign banks have admitted that they have not yet fulfilled their profit targets (Hoffbauer, 2005).

Apart from the first half of 2004, the growth of foreign banks assets has been quite stable on average amounting to around 2% every quarter. In 2005, growth rates increased to 5–6%. Their loan portfolios were in much better health than those of any other Chinese bank, with NPL ratios ranging from 0.5 to 4% (Ba S., 2006a). With loans amounting to CNY 335 bln and NPLs amounting to CNY 3.3 bln, their NPL ratios reached on average only 1.15% (as of June 2005).

13.9 Challenges and opportunities

With the opening of the banking sector set for 2007 (following entry into the WTO), foreign banks can expect to grow their business bases.

Table 13.1 Foreign banks' SWOT analysis

Strengths	**Weaknesses**
• Foreign reputation • Good asset quality • Sound internal controls and risk management • Large coverage, large branch network, outreach • First address for international and foreign enterprises financing • Better quality loan portfolios • Sound management structures and incentives • Sound risk management and internal controls • High customer service levels • Clear ownership structures • Lower tax burdens • Higher profitability • No interference from governments	• Small deposit and branch base • Difficulties in finding qualified personnel • Corruption • Undiversified product and customer base • Smaller force de frappe • Limited to selected areas
Opportunities	**Threats**
• Large private sector • Consumer/consumption growing/taking off • Strong economic environment • Support from their foreign HQ • Opening with WTO full entry • Basel II competitive position	• Interference from the state, foreign banks are viewed as dangerous, as grabbing national jewels • Consumers not bound to one bank

This will increase innovation and competition. Their business is less restricted than it was, and the last restrictions should be removed with the end of the transition period and WTO entry in 2007.

The SWOT analysis for foreign banks is given in Table 13.1.

14
Rural Credit Cooperatives

Rural areas are served by a few formal financial institutions: the ABC, the RCCs, the postal savings system as well as the Agricultural Development Bank of China (ADBC),[1] a policy bank. Their main role is to provide financial services to local farmers and agricultural enterprises and to support the economic development of rural areas. The following will concentrate on RCCs (details of the postal savings system can be found in the annex) which are the most important rural financial institutions (Table 14.1).

14.1 Key indicators and figures

Table 14.1 Main indicators for rural FIs in China (in CNY)

	Dec. 2005	Dec. 2004	Dec.2003	Dec. 2002	Dec. 2001
Total assets (trillion)	3.72				
% of assets	4.4				
Total deposits (trillion)	3.26	2.78	2.40	1.993	1.726
% of banking deposits	10.8			11.07	
Total loans (trillion)	2.23		1.62	1.39	1.197
% of banking loans	10.9		10	10	
Total equity (bln)	165			– 27 (negative)	CNY 96 bln (gross)
Capital adequacy ratio (%)	8.03*			– 8.45	
NPL ratio (%)	14.8†	23.1	29.37	36.9	44

NPLs in bln[‡]	325.5	463 (Sept. 2004)		514.7	515.4 (2000)
Loans to agriculture (trillion)	1.01		0.697	0.558	
Loans to farmers	798 bln[‡‡]				
Number of RCCs			34,909	35,544	
Employees of RCCs			628,000	658,653	
Profits (bln)	18	10.5		– 5.8	–123.2

NPL and NPL ratios are according to the four-tier classification.

[*] The capital adequacy ratio of the RCCs was 8.03%, for rural cooperative banks it was 12.93% and for rural commercial banks it was 8.78% (PBOC, 2005c).

[†] With the five categories, the ratio could increase by 4–5 percentage points (Han X., 2006).

[‡] 44% of the decrease by 8.3 percentage points came from the use of special notes used in exchange, the remaining came through loan growth (Han X., 2006).

[‡‡] Funds are lent to some 70 mln farmers (estimated at making up of those farmers wanting a loan).

Source: Based on Yu N. and He Y. (2003); Liu L.and Zhu X. (2003); CBRC (2006); Han X. (2006); Dong and Featherstone (2004); PBOC (2005c) and Xiao Z. (2005).

14.2 Market share and position

The RCCs benefit from a close relationship to their target markets and are often the sole financial institutions in these under-banked rural areas. Their loan portfolios are heavily geared towards agricultural lending (with 47% in agricultural loans, and these account for 85% of all agricultural loans in the system, based on 2002 figures – CBRC, 2006b). However, they have poor operating systems and lack knowledge and experience of commercial lending. RCCs are subject to a double pressure: being commercially oriented and sustainable, and at the same time being a conduit for government rural policy.

14.3 Ownership and enterprise forms

The capital structure of RCCs is slightly different from that of other commercial banks. This is mainly due to their more or less true cooperative form. Initially the capital was held by individual farmers from the area in which they operated. Li Changyu and Jie Shuqing (2004: 83) comment, "Up to now, after 25 years of reforms towards marketisation, the 'cooperative' label of RCCs got lost somewhere early on, and the related cooperative principle has been almost entirely abandoned."

Such "cooperative" structure created highly scattered and diversified holdings which on one side guaranteed no controlling ownership but at the same time meant that individuals had little chance to take influence, so that they lost interest in truly taking up their oversight function. The benefits they could draw from such holdings were also too few to make it worth engaging in proper oversight. While the ownership structure of RCCs was originally organised around the cooperative members, it became clear over time that the power belonged to those inside the RCCs, with no oversight responsibilities taken over by the holding members (He Z., 2004). The RCCs became controlled from inside, by insiders.

The RCCs are not cooperatives by nature: this would mean that they were established voluntarily by their members, sharing risks and profits. They never met such definitional requirements (Dong and Featherstone, 2004). RCCs are collectively owned. Members of the RCCs contribute with their funds to the deposits and to the capital of these institutions. Members did not voluntarily fund the RCCs and cannot withdraw from their investments (Dong and Featherstone, 2004). The stakeholders formally also had a right to choose managers. However, the influence of local governments should not be underestimated (Schlotthauer, 2003). Furthermore it can be questionable how much participation for small farmers holding stakes in their local RCC was possible (depending on the environment, the capabilities they bring in to supervise the cooperatives, the business knowledge they possess). Around half of the generated profits were further transferred to the local authorities' public funds (10% for social security, 10% for educational purposes and the remaining 30% were distributed to the collective).

To cope with the above issues, early reforms introduced new owners, such as enterprises. These had larger stakes but in a number of cases these created controlling stakes that by no means lead to a power balance between shareholders. Still, in most cases the incentives for taking up an oversight function for holders of RCC's capital were almost inexistent due to the strong interference of central and local authorities. All these factors resulted in corporate governance structures being emptied of their usual meaning (Yang X. and Shen S., 2004). This situation is reinforced by the lack of understanding of the RCCs' business on the side of directors, thus reducing the likelihood of directors representing the interests of equity holders. Basically the relationship of directors to managers and to capital holders broke down on both sides.

A further wave of reforms brought again new structures. Most RCCs are now branches organised around a county or township level RCC union. These unions normally do not undertake any business directly but rather undertake centralised management functions on behalf of the branches (such as financial accounting, senior management, training, relationship with regulators, human resources, cash management, settlement, etc.). The member RCC branches and outlets are ordered in a hierarchy, depending on the administrative level at which they are established (county, township, village, etc.) and depending on the type of entity (branch, deposit outlet, etc.). The network of RCCs controls the county-level RCC union.[2]

In the most recent reform effort (see section on "Reform of RCCs underway"), RCCs could choose three different capital structures: a shareholding system, cooperative system or a combination of both shareholding and cooperative systems. Some RCCs have received approval for transforming themselves into rural commercial banks (i.e. shareholding companies). By the end of 2005, 72 RCCs had transformed themselves into fully fledged commercial banks, of which 12 are rural commercial banks and 60 are rural cooperative banks (CBRC, 2006b). At the same time, some 519 county-level credit unions had been established, while 200 more were awaiting approval for their formal establishment.

14.4 Historical developments

The RCCs were re-established in the early 1980s[3] to ensure financial intermediation and to direct financial funds to rural areas. They first functioned out of the ABC framework and in competition with the semi-formal RCFs (see Annex). Under the ABC leadership, RCCs suffered from a number of inefficiencies:

- Deposits were not priced well, so that the expense of managing large numbers of small accounts became prohibitive
- The RCCs were required to fund a great part of the ABC with their own funds (20–30% of their deposits)
- Loans-to-deposit ratios were lower than that for the rest of the financial institutions because of large deposit requirements at the ABC
- High operating costs were the result of inefficiency and large branch networks
- The operating model of RCCs did reflect that of ABC (geared towards large agricultural clients) rather than the needs of their own customers (smaller enterprises and farmers) (Watson, 2003).

The ABC played diverse and conflicting roles with the RCCs: depositor and drawer of funds, supervisor and leader, the ABC and not their own customers were given preferential treatment by RCCs.

In the mid-1990s, the rural financial system was overhauled: ABC and RCCs were made independent from each other and RCFs were closed (Zheng Y., 2003). The newly won independence of RCCs (their supervision was directly orchestrated by PBOC) brought higher efficiency and even profits in some cases.

14.5 Specific regulations and authorities

The RCCs were previously regulated by the ABC (between 1983 and 1996), then by PBOC (before 1983 and between 1996 and 2003) and are now under the supervision of CBRC. RCCs do not have an effective independent and specialised control institution (as, for example, the one that overviews and checks the accounts of Genossenschaftsbanken in Germany, Liu M., 2004).

In 2003 and 2006, the regulatory authorities issued rules with regard to the management and licensing of RCCs and other rural financial institutions (References for laws 14, 23, 24 and 25). According to these rules, rural financial institutions (just as any other banks in China) are responsible for their risks, gains and losses and should conduct their business free from any interference, especially that of local authorities. Rural financial institutions are also required to establish proper corporate governance structures (see Annex).

14.6 Geographic and business scope

Nowadays, their customers include rural farmers, rural enterprises, as well as local authorities. Products and services are reduced to the simplest ones and innovation is not supported by the authorities. RCCs do not orient their lending specifically towards their members. Statistics show that while the deposits of farmers have increased, the loans to them has continuously decreased over the same period of time (in 1984 the percentage of loans to farmers was 41% and in 2000 it was 19%). This is due to the fact that RCCs are not willing to lend without collateral and because collateral often cannot be provided by members (He Z., 2004).

The RCCs lend in most cases short-term facilities (most of them under 1 year and none of them over 3 years): supply is not adapted to the requirements of farmers who would prefer longer maturities loans with different repayment schemes (Xie P. *et al.*, 2005a).

The network of RCCs reaches out to the lowest administrative level in China: branches and outlets can be found in urban centres, townships and villages. In their operations, RCCs are limited to their localities. The geographic restrictions have had negative effects: first, it made local authorities' interference in the daily operations of RCCs easier (especially since the 1980s when local governments depended on tax revenues from local enterprises for their economic development); second, it hindered the establishment of a market discipline mechanism and created a strong monopoly (which created "too important to fail"-institutions); third, it destroyed the opportunity to achieve economies of scale (due to the scattered and small size of each individual RCC); and fourth, it weakened the RCCs' risk withstanding ability (because of a small capital base and undiversified activities). The removal of such constraints could increase competition in rural areas (Liu M. *et al.*, 2005).

14.7 Management

The RCCs' hierarchies and structures are modelled on the same administrative hierarchies found in local authorities. This ensures a quick and easy channel for influencing decisions and helping resolve the financing difficulties of farmers, a central point of concern in the eyes of the authorities. This is reinforced by the fact that managers are nominated by the authorities (Yang X. and Shen S., 2004). The higher the management quality in RCCs, the lower the likelihood of interference by the authorities.

As a part of the management system reform, RCCs had to choose between management through a provincial level centralised entity or a two-level approach with provincial and county entities (in form of either a commercial bank or a credit union). Most chose a provincial level entity, but such scheme has limits: this did not hinder influence by local authorities (provincial ones this time), management did not change and the emergence of the provincial level union increased even more the number of interested parties in the financial system (Xiao Z., 2006).

14.8 Financial performance

Even as a monopolist in most rural areas, the RCCs are still not in a position to produce high net profits. Most are weighted down by NPLs, interest rates controls and poor efficiency. In many cases, the value of assets is lower than that of the liabilities and insufficient to repay debts (资不抵债).

Asset quality is a challenge for RCCs. The NPL ratio at RCCs was on average 14.8% when using the four loan categories (by the end of 2005, CBRC 2006b). While recent decreases in NPLs are a welcome signal, the decreases follow mainly the strong growth in lending experienced by RCCs (Xiao Z., 2006), thus not hinting at a sustainable and long-term change in lending practices and controls.

Interest rates are an important factor and incentive mechanism for generating profits. Shen and Cheng (2004) estimate that RCCs would need, depending on their location, to charge between 8 and 16% p.a. to be fully sustainable. In practice the interest rates charged currently range from 4.5 to 8% p.a. (Xie P. *et al.*, 2005d). Territorial restrictions in moving funds from one RCC to another aggravate the lending distortions in rural areas.

14.9 Reform of RCCs underway

In 2001, reforms obviously became an absolute necessity: of all RCCs, 46% were losing money and the remaining RCCs were insolvent (Shen M. and Cheng E., 2004). Thus central and local authorities as well as regulators set out for yet another wave of reforms. The aims of the latest reforms are "to transform the RCCs into local rural financial institutions servicing agriculture [projects and enterprises], rural areas [in terms of economic and social development] and farmers, to turn RCCs into the main financing force and link in rural areas, in order to improve the harmonised economic development of rural areas" (Li C. and Jie S., 2004: 84).

In the words of PBOC's governor, Zhou Xiaochuan, the reforms would "spend money to buy a mechanism" (花钱买机制), meaning that the central authorities would help resolve the historical burdens (i.e. NPLs), provide incentive mechanisms for reforms, and would give priority to prevent any forms of moral hazard (Xie P. *et al.*, 2005d). The wording seems to imply a short-term fix for the most indebted institutions in the banking system, so it remains to be seen if this has created the basis for sustainable rural finance.

The reforms concentrated on ownership structure (including corporate governance) and management (the transfer of management responsibilities of RCCs to provincial authorities and under the supervision of CBRC), supported by the transfer of financial funds to cover up historical losses (estimated at around CNY 38 bln) and tax subsidies (tax burdens reduced to 3% on operations). In total the costs could be around CNY 165 bln (Shen M. and Cheng E., 2004). At the end of 2005, special commercial notes amounting to CNY 159.9 bln (with interest of 1.89% p.a., limited to 8 years) from the government had been issued to finance the reform process of RCCs (*China Economic News Net*, 2006). According to Zhou Xiaochuan, these were necessary in order to reduce NPA and to create the correct incentive mechanisms (Xie P. *et al.*, 2005b).

Reforms were first approved for seven provinces (Jiangsu, Shandong, Zhejiang, Guizhou, Jilin, Shaanxi and Jiangxi) and one municipality (Chongqing) in August 2003 by the State Council. The reforms were widened to all of China in August 2004. Those RCCs that show poor financials and high risks would be merged, closed or restructured (Xiao Z., 2005).

The reform efforts yielded some fruits and these were summarised in a preliminary investigation of 49 RCCs in 8 provinces (Xie P. *et al.*, 2005b). RCCs from the first batch of reforms had on average some 52,169 shareholders each in 2002. This figure has been reduced to 27,898 by 2004. Meanwhile the average total capital of each cooperative increased from CNY 26 mln in 2002 to CNY 131 mln in 2004. RCCs in the second batch of reforms increased their average number of shareholders from 17,812 to 19,263 and increased their individual total capital from CNY 7 mln to CNY 12 mln. The percentage of shares in the hands of individuals is above 97. The dividend payout ratios for those paying dividends are around 6% on average. For most managers, the reforms were kicked off by the provincial governments. In 75% of the cases, they have chosen to establish provincial level credit unions to manage the restructured entities. In 81% of the cases, managers believe that any further losses (not including NPLs) will not be taken over by local authorities. Of the respondents, 70% believe that the resolution of NPA was only averagely affective; 59% also believe that the local authorities will not be available for further resolution of NPLs after the end of the reforms. On the corporate governance side, efforts have not been as successful: 57% of RCCs managers responded that the power was in the hands of the provincial level RCCs and not in the hands of shareholders. While responsibility lines have been redrawn, most managers are still accountable to the same institutions and entities.

The reforms have already been hailed as a success in view of the already good financials, especially in comparison with the previous 10 years of continuous losses, high debt levels and negative capital. At the end of 2005, the CAR reached on average 4%, the industry showed profitable accounts for the first time ever. The reforms provided a real financial effort to reduce historical burdens and in most cases real reform of the capital structure was implemented. All these improved the level of operational management in RCCs (Xie P. *et al.*, 2005c).

14.10 Challenges and opportunities

The most important and strongest challenge for RCCs is now to clearly and unequivocally choose between development and commercial goals. As such profit orientation does not necessarily to clash with their development focus. Microfinance experiences elsewhere have shown that sustainable performance is possible. But in such cases banks need to be fully responsible for decisions and for losses. The authorities still expect the RCCs to take over part of the rural development goal, by requiring them to set a percentage of their loan portfolio that should go to rural borrowers and agricultural activities (the regulations require the shareholders' meeting to set such percentages, at least). Although RCCs have a definite lending advantage in rural areas because of their knowledge of local markets and borrowers, they typically, however, do not capitalise on this.

The RCCs, like many other financial institutions in China, are plagued by government interference and poor internal structures. Their corporate governance structures have for most part yet to be established, and internal controls are in most places inexistent. Staff quality is poor and capacity is underdeveloped. RCCs and their related RCC unions are still managed by insiders without external control or oversight. Shareholders have been little involved in the reform processes.

Another challenge that still needs to be addressed is the creation of real competition in rural areas. Competition is already growing in gathering deposits, but for lending RCCs are the sole providers. Competition should be more widespread not only in terms of areas covered, but also in terms of products and services and of customers served. The monopolistic position of RCCs has some negative effects (Liu M. *et al.*, 2005):

1. while in the short term the effects are mainly positive because RCCs have access to needed deposits without incurring costs from higher competition; however, in the long term this creates low efficiency in operations and in services
2. because RCCs are the only providers in rural areas, they are also employed by the authorities as a conduit for policy lending
3. since they are the only providers, there is no risk to be eliminated because of poor performance (and thus the incentives for reform are few)
4. because RCCs cannot be closed (cross-subsidisation of bad and good RCCs takes place in mergers)
5. because RCCs will not be allowed to fail, shareholders do not need to worry about potential losses arising from mismanagement and thus have no incentives to supervise and control the entity
6. the same applies to depositors which know for sure that debts will be repaid and do not need to oversee the depositing institution.

The creation of greater competition could be achieved with the removal of geographic constraints to the highly segmented RCCs. However, in practice it remains to be seen if costs for expansion are not too high thus constraining expansion. Furthermore another argument against this type of competition is that adverse selection is not avoided: low capacity managers might make the wrong choices and expand to subsidise already loss-making activities in other localities (Liu M. *et al.*, 2005).

As Xiao Z. (2006) points out, the reforms have been led up to now by the authorities and official policy, RCCs have yet to de-link themselves from the official grip. Apart from these main challenges, others include the:

- lack of sufficient funds and capital to support the development of rural areas (large amounts of NPLs and small capital bases cannot ensure proper supply of financial funds to rural areas, capital shortage is increased by the difficulties in attracting sufficient deposits, sources of funding are scarce and capital outflows are greater than inflows into rural areas, competition for savings with the postal system)
- the higher risk of rural lending linked to climatic factors (e.g. bad harvest) and natural catastrophes cannot be appropriately rewarded under the current pricing mechanism (Xiao Z., 2005)
- lack of exit mechanisms (collateral and property laws, bankruptcy proceedings)
- interest rates controls (rendering finance more affordable but less accessible, because prices do not reflect risk)
- the higher likelihood of the county-level authorities taking the opportunity to interfere in daily operations and decisions (for example, county-level authorities retain a right to propose and nominate directors)
- the effectiveness of mergers (because the consolidation of RCCs under the union's umbrella was based on administrative regions, the better-managed RCC's have no incentive to show better performance, while the worst ones also have no incentive to improve, both are merged anyway without recompenses or sanctions)
- the possible emergence of a free rider problem (poor performing RCC's lack the incentive to improve and draw resources from other RCCs in their union) (Liu M. *et al.*, 2005).

The SWOT analysis for RCCs is given in Table 14.2.

Table 14.2 SWOT analysis for RCCs

Strengths	**Weaknesses**
• Cheap labour • Monopolistic position • Niche players and strong local knowledge • Slowly removing financial obstacles to better performance • Diversified ownership structures • Strong deposit bases	• Under capitalised • Low level of customer service • Strong local government interference • Limited geographically • Weak management capabilities
Opportunities	**Threats**
• Large rural sector • Local knowledge • Less threatened by foreign banks competition • Pooling of competencies possible	• Basel II: expensive reforms • Weak regulators, lacking independence • Higher risks from SME lending • Mixing up development and commercial goals

Conclusion

Performance has improved over recent years. This is true for all types of banks. Profitability as well as asset quality is better, but still a number of risks remain. Risks include governance structures and incentives mechanisms as well as disclosure standards.

Reforms have changed a number of aspects of the Chinese banking sector already; however, the changes are more superficial and targeting obvious issues such as NPLs and undercapitalisation. Progress has been fast and results already start to be seen on balance sheets; however, deeper-rooted changes, targeting more profound issues in the Chinese banking sector (such as risk management and corporate governance structures), remain far from being fully integrated in the reform agenda. Finally the issue of government interference remains a major reform challenge.

In the future, to develop a profitable system, China will need an infrastructure and an environment that is conducive to sound banking practices. Despite the large number of reforms that have taken place in many cases, their impact has been superficial – governance issues remain a serious drawback to creating a competitive banking system. This situation, however, is likely to be challenged in the future with the new capital accord and the WTO entry.

Conclusion

Part V
Future Challenges

The environment in which banks in China are evolving is changing quickly. As a consequence banks are also required to change the way they do their business and how they serve their customers. These strategic questions are embedded in three important changes already underway or upcoming in China: developments in the retail lending market, the New Basel Capital accord (Basel II) and full WTO membership.

15 Retail Banking

Since the liberalisation process began in 1978, Chinese banks have already widened the scope of their financial products. While they traditionally lent mainly to relatively large enterprises, target customers have been widened to include smaller and private enterprises as well as consumers. The changing product focus has meant that banks nowadays offer a wider range of loan and investment services. One of the main growth areas in the Chinese banking system is retail banking.

Retail banking is relatively new to China and has been recently growing at a strong pace. During the period 2000–2004, Fitch researchers (Marshall *et al.*, 2006) estimated that growth overall amounted to 40% annually. In 2000, retail loans accounted for 5% of GDP and in 2004 they had increased to 13%. As a result, retail loans make up around 12% of all loans for the 2000–2004 period, but 15% for 2004. At the end of 2004, retail loans amounted to CNY 2.2 trillion. Most of these loans are residential mortgages (77%), followed by other consumer loans (16%, including credit cards lending with only 3% of the total, Yan M., 2005) and automobile loans (6%). Holding the lion's share of retail lending, mortgage lending also experienced the strongest growth. Despite such developments, however, mortgages still only accounted for 11.7% of GDP (end 2004). For now, banks claim that their NPL ratios in retail lending are low (around 1.5%).

The market for retail lending is dominated (as in the case of other types of lending) by the four SOCBs and to a lesser extent by the JSCBs. The SOCBs accounted for 77% of the retail lending market at the end of 2004 (Table 15.1) (Marshall *et al.*, 2006).

McKinsey (von Emloh and Wang, 2004) estimates that, within the next 10 years, the highest growth area in the banking sector will continue to be retail banking. This area will definitely increase its share

Table 15.1 Loan to consumers and in real estate at selected Chinese banks (2005)

Bank name	**Real estate and construction* (%)**	**Consumer (%)**
ICBC**	8.82	13.28
BoC	10.13	23.40
CCB	10.40	20.36
ABC**	n.a.	11.76
Average SOCBs	*10.26*	*21.88*
Minsheng	16.36	18.15
Merchants	8.90	20.98
SPDB	11.60	13.01
Huaxia	12.77	8.19
Industrial	15.72	12.62
SDB	8.81	11.45
CITIC	n.a.	n.a.
BoComm	12.26	14.68
Average JSCBs	*12.34*	*14.15*
Average	**11.37**	**17.26**

Expressed as a percentage of the total outstanding loans for each bank (based on 2005 figures only).
* For ABC it reflects only the agriculture loans.
** Figures for 2004.
Source: Own calculations based on data from banks' annual reports.

of banks' operating profits from the mere current 4%. Analysts see three reasons behind such development:

1. the more consumption-driven economic growth in China
2. the tightening of cash management in Chinese corporates (thus requiring less loans)
3. the deregulation of interest rates (which will enable banks to price their products closer to the real risks).

According to von Emloh and Wang (2004), however, not all consumer segments are profitable: the more affluent customers account for 18% of customers and generate 40–50% of profits, but the less affluent 80% are unprofitable. The affluent customers are concentrated in coastal areas and have higher requirements in terms of level of financial services. This is an area where foreign banks can distinguish themselves.

According to McKinsey analysts, a mere 2% of Chinese households control over half of the banking system's deposits (Pitsilis *et al.*, 2004). In fact, if these had more investment opportunities, for example abroad, they could provide a strong control mechanism for banks to force them to allocate adequately their deposits.

Fitch analysts (Marshall *et al.*, 2005a) have added a word of caution with regard to the development of consumer lending. Its growth pace is strong but lending is likely to be falling in quality as creditworthiness is poorly assessed, as there is still little experience with such loans in China (from the monitoring and collateral point of view) and as the supporting infrastructure is under-developed (only recently established credit bureau, difficulties in realising collateral).

15.1 Credit card lending

Bank cards are now widespread in China and the market is growing quickly (Yan M., 2005). There are some 663 mln bank cards[1] in issue in China as of the end of 2005 (Marshall *et al.*, 2006). For foreign banks, credit cards represent a great potential to reach out to high net worth individuals and urban consumers without having a widespread branch network similar to that of SOCBs. The cards also offer substantial data gathering opportunities to study consuming spending patterns and behaviour.

Cards in China come into three versions: ATM cards, debit cards and credit cards. Most of the cards issued are debit cards which enable the holder to withdraw money at ATMs and make payments that are debited automatically from current accounts. By the end of 2002, there were 500 mln cards in circulation and the transaction value amounted to CNY 11,560 bln (Worthington, 2005). While the number is large, the penetration of debit cards is small, covering only 3.96% of retail sales (in 2003, Jing X., 2005). In 2001, a new type of debit card was introduced, called 银联 (yinlian), which enables the holder to withdraw and pay at all points of sales terminals and ATMs in the country (at a cost, but at least the linking of all institutions was thus possible). At the turn of the century, the largest issuers were the SOCBs, with a market share of 90% (Worthington, 2003; Yan M., 2005).

Credit cards account for 15% of all plastic cards (i.e. 98 mln) – which is a relatively low figure. The first credit cards were introduced in 1979 by BoC as an agent for large foreign international banks. In 1985, BoC proceeded to introduce its own domestic credit card. In 1987–1988 it signed agreements with MasterCard and Visa. Ten years later, the bank could boost 30 mln card holders, a network of over 61,000 merchants and access to 26,000 point of sale machines (Worthington, 2003). At the end of the 1980s, the other SOCBs had followed suit with their own cards. In 1996, PBOC promulgated regulations with regard to credit card management. Credit limits are granted often as a percentage of income for individuals in full-time employment.

China's credit card market lags behind the country's economic development. On one side, this can be explained by the high propensity to save in China (the gross domestic saving rate was 40% in 2001 and 48% in 2004 – one of the highest worldwide). On the other side, this can also be explained by the high cash dependency of the Chinese economy and the limited acceptance of such cards. Spending per card and per month was, at the end of 2004, only between CNY 300 and CNY 650 (Marshall *et al.*, 2006). Only around 5% of the population hold credit cards (Jing X., 2005). Further to this, most cards in circulation are not being used at all or only sparsely (around 2/3 of all cards). Only half of all true credit cards are estimated to be usable internationally (some of the credit cards also allow dual currency payments).

Due to their growth stage and potential, credit cards are still a lucrative business in China. Margins are high (with interest rates at 18% and deposits remunerated at 3.6%) and for now, delinquency is low (Yan M., 2005). Credit card fees are relatively low with an average annual fee of CNY 100. Marketing credit cards has been successful mainly through employers marketing (Robinson, 2006).

Credit card lending is also an area which will be strongly influenced by the full membership to the WTO. However, various challenges remain to the establishment of a well-developed retail banking market:

- retail risk management systems and procedures are underdeveloped (e.g. limited credit bureau information, lack of local market knowledge, limited access to accurate centralised data, technology challenges)
- limited nationwide network/delivery systems for sales (interoperability is only recent, mostly used are debit cards, low credit card service fees averaging 1%)
- high consumer savings rates (credit cards as most often used for international travel payments, but not for other forms of consumer credit due to the high rates charged, the bulk of current users repay their bills every month).

A number of foreign banks have chosen to enter the credit card market through strategic partnerships with Chinese banks (such as the partnership between HSBC and Bank of Shanghai). This enables them to use the network and pool of customers of their Chinese counterparts, while the Chinese bank can access the knowledge and experience that foreign investors bring to the partnerships. Chinese banks lack experience and knowledge in structuring consumer products, in analysing the repayment capacity, using the data collected to increase profitability and so on. The foreign entity can manage the daily operations of the credit card activities while the Chinese bank remains the face of the credit card business to Chinese customers (van Emloh and Wang, 2004).

15.2 Automobile finance

Automobile lending is also a growing area of consumer lending. Automobile loans amounted to CNY 200 mln in 2003. To date there are only six foreign providers in China. The quality of these assets is much lower than for credit cards with NPL ratios averaging 5% (Allen *et al.*, 2004). A recent article mentioned a NPL ratio closer to 10% in commercial banks (*South China Morning Post*, 2006c). Only 10% of car buyers are said to use automobile financing. Buyers are now required to provide 20% of the car price to receive a loan.

According to Moody's (Yan M., 2005), the auto lending business is suffering a number of challenges:

- over-supply of cars
- prices declining rapidly in China and in the export business (some 30% of all cars are financed by loans – Allen *et al.*, 2004)
- the withdrawal of insurers from this type of business.

15.3 Real estate lending

Property loans amounted at the end of 2005 to CNY 3.07 trillion with an NPL ratio of 3.56%. The SOCBs hold in this market a share of 73.7% and their non-performing property loans level stands at 4.6% (*South China Morning Post*, 2006b).

Residential mortgages accounted for CNY 1.8 trillion, some 11.7% of GDP at the end of 2004 (Marshall *et al.*, 2006). These have seen strong growth rates, with an average of 30% p.a. The loan to mortgage value ratio is capped nationwide at 70% by regulators (for larger apartments, Xiao Z., 2006). Furthermore the monthly repayments should not exceed 50% of a borrower's monthly income (in reality this is difficult to assess because banks have relatively few means for checking borrowers' true incomes). Finally the preferential interest rates for property lending were removed as a means of cooling down developments in the property markets.

The growth of real estate lending was concurrent to the growth in real estate prices. This development worried the authorities which intervened with administrative measures. In April 2005, to curb real estate lending, 16 Shanghai lenders were ordered to stop short-term consumer real estate lending business, preferential interest rates were removed (i.e. for first-time buyers, the 10% reduction on the base rate was removed and the base rate for second time and other buyers was 6.12% and only higher rates were allowed), and lenders could only finance up to 70% of their mortgages (PBOC, 2005a). This had the effect that deals and loans became scarcer. Further cooling measures such as taxation (increasing the tax burden when reselling property within 5 years) and prudential requirements (including increasing the risk weight for some real estate loans in the capital adequacy calculation) were also introduced in May 2006 (Yu N. *et al.*, 2006).

Part of the growth in real estate lending is also related to the active role local governments tend to play in the local economic development (*The Economist*, 2006h). For many local governments, land sales represent an important source of revenues and thus they tend to keep prices high and lending on this side high as well. Cooling this market down would have to involve broadening investment opportunities for idle funds of enterprises and individuals, because real estate is often the sole financial investment available to them.

Retail lending in general (as including credit card, automobile and mortgage lending) is a growth area for Chinese banking. It is still in its infancy and experiences as well as reliable data are few. Retail lending could also become an area showing poor quality, if sound banking structures and systems are not introduced. Another related area is wealth management; it is the area of choice for foreign banks in China. They will compete for the 300,000 potential high net worth individuals said to be living in China (*SinoCast China Financial Watch*, 2006b). Potential business was opened with the relaxing of capital movement controls, allowing private individuals, through banks, to invest overseas in fixed-income securities.

Forays into retail banking can be acknowledged as the first steps towards wealth management. In this area, China is one of the markets with the highest potential: the financial wealth held by China's high net worth individuals was estimated at USD 0.9 trillion in 2004 and could reach USD 1.7 trillion in 2009 (Maude, 2006).

16
Impact of the New Capital Accord

Another major event which could potentially have a strong impact on Chinese banks and their environment is the new capital accord (Basel II). This is mainly due to the fact that Basel II and the whole risk management framework are at a stark contrast to the current Chinese banking reality.

Ba Shusong[1] (Ba S., 2005b) sees challenges for China with Basel II, ranging from capital and risk management to data and disclosure, as well as organisational structures, incentive compatibility (between banks and regulators), market-oriented supervision and the fostering of financial innovation.

It is necessary to differentiate among three ways in which the impact will be felt: first, the new capital rules will influence bank's activity when they have to comply with the new standards; secondly, relationships between Chinese banks and other international banks through which they have inter-bank business will also be affected; and finally, the adoption of the new rules will impact on Chinese regulators (Marshall *et al.*, 2005b).

At the level of the bank's operating environment, a number of challenges appear. The authorities (especially local authorities) will certainly have different incentives from those of the regulators in implementing these reforms. Since social stability is a priority, it is questionable how far reforms can go. It is by no means certain that Basel II will represent a final departure from the usual use of administrative controls rather than laws and regulations. In addition, Basel II could guarantee the end of local authorities' influence in choosing the banks' local management. Finally, the recently established CBRC still lacks the human and financial resources as well as sufficient knowledge and experience in bank supervision to fully enforce all the new capital adequacy standards.

The CBRC has clearly stated that it will first concentrate on implementing Basel I requirements and will thus not require Chinese banks to comply with the new Basel II rules for now. "结合国情，积极参照" is the motto (i.e. "according to the national situation, participate actively", CBRC, 2006a). But because other banks will implement Basel II standards from 2007 onwards and the costs of implementation are expected to be higher in China, CBRC has demanded that Chinese banks slowly edge towards the new rules and start preparing (Ba S., 2005a). Regulators and banks will need to work together in order to spur financial innovation, increase information and transparency, and finally create an effective supervision in credit risk management, where banks have the right incentives to comply with (Ba S., 2005a). If credit risk measurement is set to remain based on Basel I for the time being, pillar 2 on supervisory review and pillar 3 on market discipline (see Annex) will be implemented more quickly in China. The CBRC has received the BIS approval for proceeding in this way.

16.1 Rationale and incentives behind the current implementation schedule

In view of the above mentioned challenges, it is important to review the choices that are available to Chinese regulators and which approach would take into account the current conditions in China. What are their incentives in implementing Basel II and what are the choices?

Because Basel II has no legal force, Chinese regulators can choose whether to implement the standards of the accord. They must decide whether it makes sense and is possible to implement the standards in China. Their decision will also depend on the banks' external and internal environments.

Liu Mingkang, the Chairman of CBRC, was quoted as saying that Basel II represents "extremely crucial and formidable novel reform practices" (*The Asian Banker*, 2004b). In his letter to Jaime Caruana (CBRC, 2003), Liu recognises the importance of the new accord and shows his full support for the new developments (CBRC had always closely followed the latest developments and integrated them into new regulations). The position of CBRC is clear: a better risk and capital management in banks would promote economic growth and the stability of the financial system. But Basel II is "both an opportunity and a challenge for the Chinese banking industry" (CBRC, 2003). Thus, in view of the current situation of the banking industry in China, Liu proposes not to officially implement the new accord in full for at least a few more years after 2007. The lack of preparation in Chinese banks is not the only reason for delaying implementation. Another reason may be the uncertainties remaining in terms of impact of the new standards on capital levels and other issues such as competitiveness and pro-cyclicality.[2] Consequently, the CBRC has chosen to implement only parts of the Basel II accord and in other parts to remain on Basel I for now. A timetable for future implementation still has to be published.

Regulators' incentives

Through the new Basel capital accord, regulators will be able to have a better and more accurate view and understanding of banks' risks and potential losses which will enable them to react in a timelier manner. The focus of this incentive is on prevention. The implementation, especially at larger banks, will raise their capacity to withstand crises in the financial system as a whole. The more accurate measurement of risks will also lead to a more accurate measurement of the potentially lacking capital to fully meet the requirements. Thus problems can be recognised in a timely manner and solved with appropriate mechanisms more efficiently. It will also increase the efficiency of regulators by promoting more advanced methods of risk controls and measurements.

In their wish to protect depositors (for fear of social unrest), and at the same time, to protect the financial system[3] (thought this is more a second-tier priority, behind social stability), Chinese regulators might find it difficult to achieve the right balance. The drawing of funds from the state by the state banks could be reduced or even come to a halt once the authorities have established a fully functioning, stable and sound banking system. Such funds could be used for other tasks. Thus, despite the fear of social unrest, there is an incentive for the Chinese authorities to implement international risk management best practices. It would also protect them from being used as a "cash machine" for failed banks.

A final incentive for regulatory agencies to push ahead with Basel II implementation is the recent fact that asset-backed securities and derivatives have been used more frequently in the banking system. Remaining on Basel I would mean that Chinese banks may start using these financing techniques for regulatory arbitrage.[4]

Ba Shusong (2005a) points to the possible "incentive incompatibility", arising between regulators and banks because their incentives differ: it is necessary for regulators to take into account banks' incentives to comply with as well as to understand the potential costs.

Banks' incentives

As argued by Ward (2002), banks' incentives are one of the most important factors to take into account when analysing the likelihood of implementing Basel II. Their incentives are not driven only by the potential for lower capital requirements. Short-term incentives under the current conditions are different from long-term incentives (assuming a reformed environment).

The *current* incentives for banks to comply with, apart from the sanctions that could be imposed on them, are few. In fact, Chen J. (2003) observes that Chinese banks have always enjoyed strong deposit growth rates despite low capital adequacy levels. Banks do not have in theory a strong incentive to implement costly international practices because they can be expected to continue to amass deposits. With the increased importance of capital adequacy and the removal of the loan-to-deposit ratio as a main performance benchmark, this situation is likely to change. Further to this is the fact that bankruptcy mechanisms are not functioning and thus the incentives to introduce sound risk management practices is low. The threat of failure is currently rather small and the oversight of depositors almost non-existent. Moral hazard is a potential threat to the banking system.

Banks have some clear *long-term* incentives to comply with. One incentive is the competitive pressure stemming from foreign banks and other local banks (Yu Y., 2003). A stronger risk management and a more risk-sensitive approach could give banks a competitive advantage in enterprises financing. A second incentive is to increase investors' confidence, their reputation and international credibility (the cost related to non-compliance might be much higher than that of implementation). This incentive is especially strong for those looking at a possible stock market listing in the near term (Zhao R., 2005). A third incentive (for internationally active banks) is to be able to enter international markets once recognised as a creditworthy and sound bank (by multinationals and by other banks for business and by foreign regulators for expanding abroad). Finally, it is important to note that Chinese banks will discover over time one incentive to comply with: the wealth of information they can derive from a risk management system. It will also enable them to efficiently raise capital and provisions, to derive loan and product pricing, to measure the efficiency of the risk management process and so on.

The investments that banks have already made show that incentives for compliance weigh in the balance. The incentives should be based on market mechanisms and a positive and supportive environment.

16.2 Further implementation of Basel II

Assuming that current incentives to apply Basel I lie in the balance, is it really feasible for China to move in a few years to Basel II?

Some authors (Mrak, 2003; Ward, 2002) argue that emerging market economies need to meet various pre-conditions before going ahead with implementation.[5] Unmet requirements (Table 16.1) could put a whole industry or country at risk (given the large influence and role that banks play in financing emerging markets enterprises). Markets need to have functioning capital markets and show sufficient competition. Implementation of Basel II in China is rated as highly risky in terms of industry risk by Standard & Poor's (*Xinhua Financial Network [XFN] News*, 2005a). Challenges include, in the agency's view, dealing with large levels of NPLs and lack of adequate and reliable data.

Furthermore regulators will need to take into account the level of readiness in banks, their own preparedness, the structure of the banking system (international orientation, scope, depth, etc.), as well as the sophistication of banks (stage of development of internal systems,

Table 16.1 Current situation in China in terms of Basel II implementation

Area: macro level	**Current situation in China**
Baseline supervisory system	Broadly in line with the requirements of Basel II, but lack of regulators independence.
Legal-regulatory infrastructure	Issues include: embryonic development of the external rating industry, lack of recognition of creditors' rights and absence of bankruptcy proceedings.
Human resources	Few bankers and regulators have sufficient banking and modelling experience. However, the learning process has started.[6]
Disclosure regime	Broadly in line with the standards of Basel II.
Corporate governance	In place, are not (sufficiently) used.
Accounting/provisioning practices	Most obstacles have been removed.
Availability of loss data	Moving early towards Basel II will enable the banks do collect necessary data and experience.
Incentives for implementation	More on the long-term side.

Source: Based on BCBS (2004c) and own research.

product range, etc.). To adapt to the current situation, national regulators have certain discretion (such as mentioned by Liu Mingkang which can relate to: various risk weightings, OECD club deals under Basel I, operational risk weights, domestic currency ratings, treatment of SMEs, CBRC, 2003). They can also reduce the scope of application (by using different approaches depending on the bank type, or with different implementation timetables for various types of banks – this requires them to fully understand the impact of each factor, variable and estimate in the Basel II accord). The shift towards Basel II will also require some legislative changes and adjustments to the way supervision is conducted (shifting to an assessment of the quality of risk management).

For Chinese regulators, as for other emerging markets regulators, the choice of a quantitative credit risk management approach is challenging. Regulators can choose to move towards Basel II and implement the complete set of standards, implement only part of these or remain on Basel I.

Although Basel II is complex, costly, requires a high amount of historical data, gives much autonomy to banks and is calibrated to G-10 countries (Balzarotti *et al.*, 2004), implementing only the standardised approach (SA) across the Chinese banking industry means little difference to the (relatively) risk-insensitive Basel I. Most conditions required for the full implementation of the SA in China are not yet fully realised: credit rating agencies are under-developed, externally rated borrowers are few and unlikely to turn to banks for financing, corporate bonds data is poor, and finally credit bureaus are under-developed. Further problems linked to the SA include the potential growth in retail lending (because of lower charges), thus increasing the concentration of portfolios, as well as the lower capital charge for commercial real estate lending which might be unreasonable for Asia, and for China (Marshall *et al.*, 2005b).

While the SA does not seem feasible, challenges with IRB approaches (F-IRB and A-IRB, see Annex) definitely exist. Issues outstanding with regard to the implementation of IRB approaches in emerging markets include the following:

- Rating system design and data quality are underdeveloped and less reliable.
- Greater volatility in business cycles might make the use of historical data a poor tool for assessing credit risk (Marshall *et al.*, 2005b).
- Consequently, stress testing and calibration might be impossible.

- Recovery rates might be much lower than the proposed 65% (i.e. loss given default (LGD) of 45%) as shown by the recovery rates achieved by China's AMCs.
- The implementation of IRB approaches in some banks might lead high risk borrowers to turn to SA-banks for financing.

Thus the IRB is too complex for Chinese banks to be implemented straight away. To overcome the above challenges inherent to all approaches, researchers have proposed two possible responses: one encourages temporal flexibility, and the other introduces a compromise approach (between SA and IRB).

Wu J. (2005) proposes a phased approach to implement the new Basel accord. Until 2009 the larger SOCBs could be required to comply with the F-IRB approach, with the aim of complying with the advanced internal ratings-based (A-IRB) approach by 2012. This would also entail the exchange of experiences among more advanced banks and those in other groups. For a second group of banks, a unified approach should be chosen and the F-IRB should be implemented by 2012 and the A-IRB by 2015. For the last group of banks, which are weaker in terms of sophistication (including the smaller JSCBs and CCBs), they should only be encouraged to comply with and if possible follow the second group.

Such a phased approach is problematic however. First, it does not create a level-playing field for banks and the weaker ones would face even stronger competition from larger banks, without being able to use any competitive advantage. Another argument against this is that it does not sufficiently create incentives for smaller banks to implement new best practices for risk management in general. In many cases these banks are already thinking about the IRB approaches and ways to implement them, thus putting them back at a lower stage would derail the change processes in these banks. Third, implementing different approaches across the industry could hurt smaller banks (Hakenes and Schnabel, 2005). It would make sense to implement the IRB approach on an industry-wide basis rather than choosing a phased approach, because where small banks have a choice among ranges of Basel approaches, they are likely to choose the less costly and less complex one. This would put them at a competitive disadvantage compared with larger banks which have the resources to implement more complex and thus less capital-intensive approaches. Fourth, if the choice of approach is left to the banks and the smaller ones choose the less expensive but less risk sensitive approaches, then a two-tiered approach might increase the instability of the financial system (Rime, 2005). Thus it would be a sensitive choice to implement only one approach to risk management and for all banks at the same time.

Some authors (Balzarotti *et al.*, 2004) thus argue that emerging markets should implement a "centralised IRB approach" which would be more closely adapted to the realities in emerging markets (higher loan given default, less diversification possible in portfolios, contagion more likely, etc.), restrain banks' autonomy and facilitate control and validation. In a unified approach, banks would get the same measurement framework, but each would be individually responsible for setting ratings for any borrower or transaction. The parameter estimates would be defined by the regulators, based on a wide pool of data gathered at all participating banks. Such a database would provide more stable, complete, comprehensive and reliable data sets (because it is more closely calibrated to the Chinese reality). Such an approach would require in China the building of a fully fledged credit registry, a structure that could already become reality soon.

Where compliance with Basel I and sound risk management practices are partly achieved, capital requirements should be increased for banks, and where rating penetration is low – as is the case in China – Powel (2004) argues that such a "centralised IRB approach" would be sensible. This will enable China to increase its capacity while allowing the more widespread use of more risk-sensitive practices and measurements in banks, thus making the system more stable and more reliable as a whole. Finally, this would enable banks to edge progressively towards the full implementation of Basel II.

While this approach would require some preparatory work for regulators (to invest time and resources in designing a rating scale that reflects conditions in China), some advantages stand out. Comparability and ease of checks would be easier and more forward-looking (Majnoni *et al.*, 2004). It would also give way to a more cost-efficient monitoring of banks from the regulators' point of view. It would favour the progressive development of credit risk measurement techniques in the banks and allow for an observation time to understand the workings and impact of the new accord and to make necessary adjustments if required. It would create an even-playing field and spread implementation costs over time and banks. The disadvantage with such model is that it would create a uniform rating system and will not reflect the specific situation of each bank. This could be mitigated by introducing rating scales and specific loss data for several types of banks (e.g. CCBs, JSCBs, credit cooperatives, etc.).

However, Chinese regulators seem to be moving more towards a phased approach (as proposed by Wu J., 2005). CBRC is preparing a guideline for IRB implementation and established a working group with the main lenders (SOCBs and JSCBs) to discuss approaches to IRB implementation (*China Economic News Net*, 2005). In April 2006, CBRC announced that major internationally active banks could be required to implement Basel II rules from 2010 (with a transition period from 2010 to 2012, *Reuters News*, 2006).

16.3 Quantitative impact of Basel II on Chinese banks

All other things being equal, higher core capital and supplementary capital, lower NPL levels and lower risk-weighted assets (RWA), higher ROAs and lower tax rates will lead to a higher CAR (Table 16.2).

Impact on capital requirements

Researchers and surveys (BCBS, 2003; EU, 2003; PwC, 2004b) have shown that for most types of banks and for more complex approaches, the capital requirements should be lower than they are presently. The

Table 16.2 Selected key data and ratios for selected banks (2004)

in CNY mln, %	SOCBs	CCB	JSCBs	Merchants	CCBs	Xi'an CCB
Total assets	13,845,749	3,904,785	3,990,100	586,571	1,693,800	25,266
Total Tier 1 equity	563,078	194,744	144,211	20,881	57,700	1,338
Total loans net	7,927,532	2,171,756	2,353,331	363,097	888,820	16,657
Loan loss provisions	149,789	53,829	49,404	10,920	15,680	111
NPLs	881,934	68,370	85,714	10,774	106,100	1,323
Published CAR (total capital) (%)	10.67	11.29	7.62	9.55	1.40	5.20
Capital/assets (%)	4.07	4.99	3.61	3.56	3.41	5.30
NPL ratio (%)	10.92	3.07	3.57	2.88	11.73	7.89
RWA	5,279,681	1,724,925	1,893,465	218,649	4,121,429	25,731
RoA (%)	0.63	1.24	0.52	0.54	n.a.	0.34

SOCBs include ICBC, BoC and CCB. JSCBs include BoComm, CITIC, Merchants, Minsheng, Shanghai Pudong, Huaxia, Shenzhen Development and Industrial Bank.
Risk-weighted assets (RWA) = total tier 1 equity/published CAR.
Source: Based on data from the banks' annual reports, own calculations.

more complex approaches, all other things being equal, are said to have a positive impact on reduction of capital charges. The amount by which capital could be reduced following the implementation of any of the Basel II approaches is closely correlated to the structure and composition of a bank's loan portfolio, with its operating environment (bankruptcy codes impact recovery rates: Davydenko and Franks, 2005), its internal structure and strategy and so on.

Results from the QIS3 for Chinese banks (five banks representing 48% of the banking assets) have shown that the impact of Basel II in China would broadly be in line with the impact on banks worldwide (CBRC, 2003; Fan S., 2003). The five participating Chinese banks showed RWA increasing by 9.02% (credit risk by 5.19% and operational risk by 3.83%).

Table 16.3 shows for the main banks or types of banks the estimated likely impact of Basel II implementation on capital requirements (assumptions are discussed in the Annex). The CAR is calculated under the assumptions for Basel I, Basel II (SA) and Basel II (IRB centralised approach). Then, the bottom part of the table shows the amount of capital (in money terms and as a percentage) that would be required to reach an 8% ratio under Basel II. This additional level of capital is thus compared to total assets to enable a comparison across banks (RWA did not include operational and market risks nor off-balance sheet exposures, thus the real-life RWA are likely to be higher, consequently commanding a lower capital ratio, closer to the required 8%).

If banks would implement the new capital accord under the current circumstances, they would need even more capital. The present calculations show that banks would face much higher RWA under IRB approaches as assumed through the QIS3. The higher RWA are the result of influences from probability of default (PD) and loss given default (LGD) estimates (for explanation and definition on these, see annex).

Overall Table 16.4 shows that banks in China are likely to see, just as discovered in the quantitative impact studies (QIS) exercises in other countries, reductions in regulatory capital ratios.[7] In some cases the reductions could be very large. While the capital reductions seem large for IRB approaches, one should be reminded that other assumptions could yield different results. Important here is the reduction that banks are likely to enjoy. This is a consistent result, independent of bank size and independent of the banks' creditworthiness and asset quality. However, those with a better asset quality and more capital are likely to need in the future less capital to reach the 8% CAR. The results should,

Table 16.3 Capital requirements for Chinese banks for credit risk (not operational or market risks), based on 2004 figures

in CNY mln, %		SOCBs	CCB	JSCBs	Merchants	CCBs	Xi'an CCB
General Information	Total assets	13,845,749	3,904,785	3,990,100	586,571	1,693,800	25,266
	Total Tier 1 equity	563,078	194,744	144,211	20,881	57,700	1,338
	Total loans net	7,927,532	2,171,756	2,353,331	363,097	888,820	16,657
	Loan loss provisions	149,789	53,829	49,404	10,920	15,680	111
	NPLs	881,934	68,370	85,714	10,774	106,100	1,323
	Published CAR (total capital) (%)	10.67	11.29	7.62	9.55	1.40	5.20
Portfolio weights	% to corporates	60.8	49.7	72.9	68.8	49.7	75.6
	% to SMEs	10.0	36.4	10.0	10.0	36.4	10.0
	% to retail	18.3	18.5	13.5	18.3	2.2	6.5
CAR	*Basel I (for reference)* (%)	8.52	9.76	6.59	6.21	7.30	8.91
	Basel II-SA	6.95	9.24	6.26	5.89	6.09	7.86
	Basel II-IRB	2.33	4.47	2.69	3.13	1.63	2.33

Table 16.3 (Continued)

	in CNY mln, %	SOCBs	CCB	JSCBs	Merchants	CCBs	Xi'an CCB
Additional capital required	Current situation						
	(a) Capital available (+)/required (–) at 8%	140,704	56,750	– 7,266	3,389	– 272,014	– 720
	(b) Representing possible RWA growth (%)	33.31	41.13	n.a.	19.38	n.a.	n.a.
	(c) Required capital increase in %	0.00	0.00	5.04	0.00	471.43	53.85
	CAR decrease Basel I-Basel II SA (%)	22.48	5.64	5.25	5.38	19.92	13.41
	CAR decrease Basel I-Basel II IRB (%)	265.16	118.26	144.73	98.52	346.63	282.95
	Capital required to reach calculated Basel I CAR						
	(d) under Basel II-SA	82,523	8,993	6,223	693	49,961	271
	(e) under Basel II-IRB	326,460	91,254	73,780	6,740	233,463	1,694
	resulting capital increase under Basel II-SA (%)	14.66	4.62	4.32	3.32	86.59	20.26
	resulting capital increase under Basel II-IRB (%)	57.98	46.86	51.16	32.28	404.62	126.62

Source: Own calculations based on published 2004 figures (banks' annual reports, in some cases Yan, 2006 and PBOC, 2006)
Calculations for the capital adequacy ratios are based on the following assumptions and the calculations methods given by the BIS (BCBS, 2004a,c, 2005). SOCBs include ICBC, BoC and CCB. JSCBs include BoComm, CITIC, Merchants, Minsheng, Shanghai Pudong, Huaxia, Shenzhen Development and Industrial Bank. Assumptions were as follows: LGD = 80%, M = 2.5 years, EAD as loan volume and PD for corporate, SME and retail borrowers as 2.04, 2.69 and 0.78% (see annex for details). (a) Capital available to the bank for growth until it reaches a CAR of 8% or capital required by the bank in order to reach an 8% CAR. (b) Growth in RWA rendered possible by the additional capital available. (c) Increase of capital required in order to reach an 8% CAR. (d) By comparing the CARs calculated for Basel I (as reference) and for Basel II-SA, amount of additional capital required by the bank if it uses the Basel II-SA and needs to reach to previous Basel I CAR (as calculated for reference). (e) By comparing the CARs calculated for Basel I (as reference) and for Basel II-IRB, amount of additional capital requried by the bank if it uses the Basel II-IRB and needs to reach to previous Basel I CAR (as calculated for reference).

Table 16.4 Risk-weighted assets under the above assumptions Basel I, Basel II (Standardised and IRB centralised approach)

in CNY mln, %	SOCBs	CCB	JSCBs	Merchants	CCBs	Xi'an CCB
RWA						
under Basel I	6,612,581	1,994,580	2,188,727	336,191	790,540	15,014
under Basel II-SA	8,099,249	2,107,096	2,303,641	354,267	947,986	17,028
under Basel II-IRB	16,305,109	4,104,687	4,616,192	689,183	1,961,817	35,358
Percentage increase compared to Basel I						
Basel II-SA (%)	22.48	5.64	5.25	5.38	19.92	13.41
Basel II-IRB (%)	146.58	105.79	110.91	105.00	148.16	135.49

Source: Own calculations.

however, be observed with caution, because they analyse the situation in 2004 with only part of the required data and based on simplifying assumptions.

The calculations show that in comparison to the ratio found under the current Basel I accord,[8] Chinese banks are likely to find that their capital is not sufficient to implement the Basel II accord. Banks will need less capital to support their lending to customers, but to reach the 8% required minimum capital ratio, they will need to raise more capital. Better quality banks show a smaller amount by which additional capital would be required. It makes sense for banks to first recapitalise themselves, to clean their books to make themselves more creditworthy and sound, because they can then enjoy better terms when implementing Basel II's more complex approaches.

Impact on costs structures in Chinese banks

Not only will the change in capital requirements drive the choice of Basel II approach and its impact, banks will also see their borrowing costs, cost of capital and the interest rates they charge to customers change (calculations and assumptions can be found in the Annex). Finally, the expenses of implementation will also drive banks' considerations.

When international banks lent to Chinese banks under Basel I, they took into account the maturity and the type of exposure. For most Chinese banks, these were short-term claims often with a trade finance background (e.g. letters of credit), thus the capital requirements were much lower (see annex for details). Under the new capital accord, the cost of borrowing will be largely influenced by the creditworthiness of the Chinese bank and the recovery on these exposures. The higher rated Chinese banks, that is the larger ones, are likely to win from the implementation of more complex approaches at internationally active banks and the smaller ones would benefit more by turning to less risk-sensitive banks for borrowings (see Annex for detailed calculations). For banks with the worst ratings among Chinese banks, the costs could increase substantially by 26–57%.

The cost of borrowing for Chinese banks will influence the overall cost of capital to them (defined as the weighted average cost of capital). At internationally active banks where Chinese banks also enjoy financial support, the interest rates will be adapted to their creditworthiness. With Basel II, the banks will be required to hold more capital, that is its weight in the calculation will be higher. This means a 20–22% increase in the weighted average cost of capital for the average Chinese bank. The additional cost is around 51–55 basis points.

As a consequence of higher weighted average cost of capital and of higher capital requirements for Chinese banks, the rates for lending to Chinese borrowers will be higher, all other things being equal, as banks transfer their higher costs to their customers. These are likely to be adjusted then for the creditworthiness of the borrower and recovery on each exposure. Compared with the simpler approach of Basel I and under the SA, the borrowers are likely to win on average. Only risk weights of at least 100% would require higher interest rates.

Based on estimates from international researchers (Intrater and Garside, 2003a,b; PwC, 2004b), the ranges given for implementation costs vary widely: anything between 0.05 and 1% of a bank's assets or anything between USD 50 and USD 150 mln is possible. For China, two papers estimate (Deloitte & Touche, 2005a; Zhao R., 2005) that the cost of implementation could be USD 50 mln per bank. Due to their size, the four SOCBs are likely to have the financial resources to implement costly Basel II solutions. For smaller banks, such as CCBs with assets of CNY 15 bln on average, the costs could reach CNY 150 mln, which could be far too expensive for each of them individually. Most of these costs will be divided between IT-related costs (40–80% of these) and personnel costs. One study (*The Banker*, 2004) estimated that Asian banks needed some 24 full-time staff for implementation (while this is the figure currently stated by banks in Asia, the number is more likely in practice to be raised to 60, the figure currently stated by banks in Europe). The costs will also include expenses for better communication and disclosure as well as the costs for professionalised supervision.

Above these, one has to take into account the costs that are only indirectly related to Basel II implementation. These are costs for restructuring internal processes, systems and procedures. These are costs for bringing the risk management and control functions up to date. These depend on the size of the bank and its current condition, but apply to all Chinese banks, albeit to varying extents.

Set against all these costs are the gains that banks can expect from implementation. The gains in terms of higher productivity and efficiency are difficult to assess. Profitability could potentially be raised by 10 bp of total assets for each bank (*The Banker*, 2004).

This analysis has clearly shown that in quantitative terms, Basel II is going to be expensive for Chinese banks. The potentially high costs could become a strong argument against Basel II implementation especially at smaller banks. First, higher required levels of capital are going to be a major weight in banks' calculations. Raising fresh capital might be costly in the current environment, thus some lending might be reviewed with regards to its effectiveness and return rates. NPLs management will also be given more strategic meaning in Chinese board rooms. Second, higher costs of capital are going to influence banks and are likely to drive them either to search for cheaper funding alternatives, encourage them to use their resources more efficiently and to enhance their creditworthiness in the long term. Third, the high implementation expenses will also be a strong argument for looking at ways to spread these over an as long as possible period or to share them within strategic alliances or mergers. Taking Basel II as a new goal is going to be expensive in monetary terms, but is also likely to help reshape the banking industry profoundly.

16.4 Qualitative impact of the Basel II accord

Apart from the quantitative impact as analysed above, the implementation of the Basel II accord will also have a qualitative impact on Chinese banks. Tactical implications[9] for implementing Basel II can be divided into 12 categories:

1. human resources and management issues
2. corporate governance and organisational structure
3. transparency and disclosure
4. higher credibility
5. IT systems and databases
6. decision-making

7. credit culture
8. comprehensive view of the bank
9. active risk management
10. internal controls
11. treatment of NPLs
12. use of risk mitigation instruments.

In terms of human resources, the implementation of the new accord will lead to a shift in incentives chosen to reward officers and managers. When the risk-return equation becomes the basis for analysing a transaction, then the personnel incentives will need to be adjusted from the current loan-to-deposit metrics. Managers will have more closely defined areas of responsibilities and will be fully responsible for what happens under their leadership. Finally, the new rules will also force banks to introduce lending limits (by industry, borrower, authority, etc.) and keep these limits enforced.

As a result of Basel II, Chinese banks are likely to be internally remodelled in order to fully comply with best practices. This will include the separation of lending and risk management departments and the creation of new reporting lines. At the same time such changes will also improve corporate governance. At some point the corporate governance institutions will not only be promoted on paper, but become fully part of the reality of each bank.

The Basel II accord calls directly for better information disclosure and more transparency, thus this can also be expected in Chinese banks. At the same time the higher disclosure standards will encourage the markets and other banks' stakeholders to get a greater interest in and to analyse the information. This will thus raise the awareness for banking outside banks. It will also raise the level of scrutiny in banks. A direct consequence of higher transparency and awareness is likely to be the establishment of better reputation for those banks which comply with the standards. This will have an impact on banks' operations, as customers are likely to become more choosy when depositing money or looking for a lender.

The Basel II impact is most likely to be felt on the wealth of data produced by the newly introduced systems. It will mean a radical shift from managing an institution with no timely and comprehensive information to making decisions based on real data. With more accurate data, the banks are then also in a position to take more informed decisions. The decision-making process is likely to be based more on exact numbers and quantitative measures than it was ever in the past. Risk pricing will be made possible, as well as managing banks based on risk-adjusted return on capital (RAROC) and economic value added ® (EVA) metrics, for example. Overall risk management will be fully integrated in the overall bank strategy and resources allocation (such as use of capital and human resources).

One of the most profound implications of the new Basel II accord is the creation and the establishment of a credit culture. It is clear that this process has already started in many banks, but it is important to note that the new accord would further strengthen the importance and centrality of a sound credit culture in the eyes of all stakeholders. This will also raise the awareness and understanding of mechanisms beyond the analysis of borrowers and transactions. In terms of analysis, the newly developed tools are likely to shift the focus of credit analysis from collateral-based towards cash flow-based analyses.

Along with the introduction of more information and new tools, the risk management function is likely to be strengthened, as people recognise its centrality and as it enables a comprehensive view of the institution (as opposed to the current individual loan view). With a full view of the risks incurred, managers can turn towards a more active portfolio management (provided financial markets become efficient and supportive). The implementation of Basel II will also strengthen internal control functions, such as internal audit, accounting departments, loan review departments and loan monitoring.

With regard to NPLs, the treatment of NPLs under Basel II approaches will make the sale of NPLs more desirable. Sales are likely to take place more often and more quickly, or banks will choose to write off loans more quickly to avoid higher charges. The new rules would improve the management of NPLs as well. Banks will be more likely to look for ways to avoid making bad loans in the first place and put more pressure and incentives on loan officers for monitoring, as well as taking measures to deal with bad quality credits more swiftly (by establishing specialised departments or outsourcing the debt collection services).

The treatment of risk mitigants is likely to influence the range of forms of collateral accepted in Chinese banks as well as widen the range of derivatives used for mitigating credit risks. The newly developed asset securitisations law is the first step towards a new market for securitisation in which banks are likely to find growing interest (especially as long as they remain Basel I compliant).[10]

All these implications, being directly or indirectly the result of Basel II implementation, are impossible to quantify in monetary terms, but are likely to result in higher profitability and efficiency. The influence of best practices in risk management will require banks to move towards a more market-driven and incentive-compatible approach to lending and banking business in general. Business will be integrated more closely with risk-return considerations.

Despite the high costs associated with Basel II implementation in China, it will require banks to adopt international standards and best practices and challenge established thinking and current practices (Peng J. *et al.*, 2005).

However, Basel II could also have a negative impact on some aspects for Chinese banks: banks implementing Basel II are likely to find insufficient opportunities for diversifying their portfolios (when banks are limited in their expansion in some way), and banks might choose to concentrate on lower risk weight banking activities or those receiving a more favourable treatment, in order to reduce capital costs.

An area of future challenges, whether or not Basel II is fully implemented, will be operational risk. Moody's sees operational risk as the largest single risk faced by Chinese banks (Yan M., 2005). Banks will need to collect data, to understand the drivers and triggers of operational risks and ways to lower these. A first step in that direction will be the implementation of structures that enforce controls and create a reliable and sound credit culture.

16.5 Impact of Basel II on the Chinese banking system

The impact of Basel II is likely to be felt at the level of the banking system in terms of systemic safety and soundness. Stephanou and Mendoza (2005) find that the last two pillars of the Basel II accord will contribute to establishing a well-functioning and stable financial system, something that is often lacking in emerging markets. However, they also note that the impact on the domestic banking system is not fully understood (redistribution of capital requirements within and across banks, competitive disadvantages, refocus exposures to some products), and that in emerging markets, pillar 3 could be seen as inefficient (market discipline is mostly inefficient in emerging markets because creditors have few incentives to monitor banks – because of the central and supportive role of the state, and due to inadequate bankruptcy laws, etc.).

Lack of data on credit risk to construct internal rating models and inappropriate calibration of models may lead to improper capital requirements (the BIS impact studies were calibrated on data based on developed markets and this may lead to distortions in the calculation of capital requirements, Stephanou and Mendoza, 2005). Consequently implementing the spirit of the accord (Helbekkmo *et al.*, 2005) by concentrating on the last two pillars could be a safer choice.

For Chinese banks as for other emerging markets, the Basel II capital requirements are likely to require capital charges that are closely linked to economic cycles. It would mean that in an upward swing, for example, Chinese banks would favour the Basel II accord because it offers them the possibility of requiring less capital, even if they remain highly undercapitalised. In a growth period, it would thus lead to the dangerous situation of banks being even less capitalised, and in a recession, it could possibly restrain the amount of lending in order to keep the regulatory minimum capital requirements. Such swings will depend on the economy's ability to withstand crises (Segoviano and Lowe, 2002; Griffith-Jones *et al.*, 2002), and also on the ability of markets and of regulators to discipline banks. (Zhang Z. [2004] thinks that regulators and bankers may not find it easy to carry out their responsibilities as required by best practices, and that Chinese regulators and markets, as required in the last two pillars, may face difficulties in disciplining market participants.) At the same time it will also depend on asset correlations in emerging markets: usually assets that are more dependent on idiosyncratic factors than to systemic ones, thus an economic downturn would not spread equally among a portfolio. Thus it cannot be concluded whether Basel II could make the Chinese environment more pro-cyclical.

Overall, Chinese researchers (Zhao S., 2004; Jing X., 2005; Zhang M., 2005) welcome the implementation of the Basel II accord in the long term because they expect the banking system to become safer. The level of management capabilities and the management resources as well as in terms of software development and staff knowledge are likely to improve (Chen Y., 2002; Wu J., 2005). Its increased risk management capacity and resources should also enable enterprises to access more bank finance.

The financial intermediation function of banks is likely to improve. The better capacity to understand the risks incurred will also have an impact on the use of inter-bank lending by the Chinese banks themselves. This will increase the level of exchange with foreign and international banks as well as increase the level of integration of the Chinese banking system. Credit infrastructure and the lending environment will be pushed to be reformed. Already signs appear that banks are pressuring authorities into adopting more lending-friendly measures (creditors' rights reforms, use of other collateral in coastal areas).

If the banks are given the right incentives for complying with and have less incentives to drive themselves towards failure (in the expectation that the government would step in), then the financial system as a whole will benefit. However, some other deficiencies in the financial infrastructure will need to be addressed at the same time.

Regulators and banks need to take a gradual and prudent approach to ensure that the environment is ready for Basel II and that they themselves are fully compliant. Regulators need to support banks through their supervisory role and not to control them with straight jackets which would take away the flexibility and vitality of the banking institutions (once they have been given the right incentives to use sound banking practices). Self-regulation should become progressively more widespread (under the conditions of a favourable and supportive environment and supervision). Finally, changed regulatory capital requirements will enable supervisory authorities to develop more specialised functions which will lead to a greater capacity to prevent financial crises.

In view of the costs that banks are likely to face when implementing the new Basel accord, both in terms of implementation costs and of capital adequacy requirements, it may be advisable for Chinese banks to choose a more progressive and comprehensive view of the accord. It may be too early for them to think in terms of full implementation. But, and this is the most important thing, it is never too early to prepare, gather data, reform structures, create the right incentives and put in place basically a whole infrastructure that will support future implementation.

From the point of view of the regulators which will have to make a choice between Basel I and II, among a number of possible approaches and with regard to the timing of the implementation, the discussions by international researchers and experts have shown that in the light of the current stage of development of the Chinese banking industry, it is probably preferable to strengthen the implementation of the current accord and put the emphasis on what banks currently lack most: corporate governance and structures that support the development of risk management and of a risk culture. Furthermore, it should be the final goal to move at some point towards a full implementation of the new accord, perhaps only once the legal and economic environments are more supportive and reforms have had a more thorough impact. Implementation should also then take into account the pitfalls discovered in other countries and learn from other experiences abroad. A feasible approach may be to allow at first only one approach, a type of centralised IRB approach, to allow for greater risk-sensitivity while keeping a level-playing field and ensuring a broad common basis from which to start.

17
Entry to the World Trade Organisation

入世 is the Chinese abbreviation for China's accession to the World Trade Organisation or WTO (the expression in full being 加入世界贸易组织). Taken to the individual meaning of each character, this abbreviation could also mean "enter the world". What will be the impact of Chinese banks entering the world? Or is the world finding access to Chinese markets through its accession to the WTO?

The banking sector is one of the sectors of the Chinese economy to open last and at the slowest pace. This certainly reflects the fact that it represents the weakest link in the Chinese economy, despite being one of its most crucial components. The full entry to the WTO in 2007 will make the need for Chinese banks to increase their competitiveness in front of foreign entrants inescapable. Will this push Chinese banks to improve their performance and further integrate into the international banking system? Will competitiveness and intermediation capacity of the Chinese banking system increase? Will it be safer and induced to use sounder banking practices?

China is currently witnessing the internationalisation of its banking industry (Liu L., 2006a). First, in terms of the internationalisation of the banking system: the system is moving from a national monopolistic market to a more competitive market. Second, in terms of the internationalisation of supervisors: their professional scope has changed from a focus on protection to anti-monopolistic supervisory activities. Third, in terms of the spreading of risks incurred by Chinese banks over diverse international markets.

17.1 Chinese commitments

After some 15 years of negotiation, in December 2001, China finally became a member of the WTO. Part of the obligations to WTO entry includes commitments in the area of financial services and specifically banking. By 2007, when the transition period to accession ends, China's banking sector should be fully open to foreign competition. The removal of restrictions will increase the degree of competition in China because it should give the same business conditions to foreign and domestic banks.

Foreign banks are not new to the Chinese banking industry. As showed earlier, they started entering directly the Chinese banking markets in the 1990s, albeit in a limited manner (through representative offices, branches, etc.). They also started at the beginning of this century to participate indirectly in Chinese banking as shareholders.

Chang G. C. (2003) argues that the Chinese leadership had no choice but to open and reform its banking system in time for full WTO accession in 2007. For him the WTO entry was a strong wake up call. Chinese authorities had to make their banks more resilient to the international financial and economic system before a full opening (this was stressed by Liu Mingkang, CBRC's chairman, when he acknowledged the need for the banks to stand on their own feet, without the financial backing of the authorities, *Agence France Presse*, 2005).

For China, the decision to enter the WTO challenged by itself the way it treats foreign entities. With the accession, national treatment should be granted to all entities, regardless of their origin. This challenged the protectionist approach to the treatment of banks. The legal framework, the business restrictions as well as the strong administrative and unpredictable handling of these issues by the Chinese authorities placed foreign entities in China at a strong disadvantage (Jing X., 2005).

To close the gap between foreign and Chinese banks, the Chinese authorities allowed themselves to have a transition period of 5 years (between 2002 and 2007), before fully opening the country's banking sector. The restrictions in force against foreign banks in terms of target customers, scope of business and geographic presence were phased out progressively. New licensing requirements were also introduced to ensure equality among foreign and Chinese financial institutions.

With regard to banking services (excluding insurance and securities), the commitments China made are given in Table 17.1.

Compliance progress in the banking sector

To ensure compliance with its WTO commitments, China progressively removed regulatory obstacles. Jing X. (2005) reports that up to 2003, in the finance sector, the authorities had abolished 68 regulations, 69 had

Table 17.1 China's WTO commitments for the banking sector

Scope of banking services: • Deposit taking; • All lending activities; • Financial leasing; • Payment and money transfer services; • Guarantees and commitments; • Trading in foreign exchange.	1. Excluded are the provision and transfer of financial information; and advisory, intermediation and other auxiliary financial services in cross border supply and international consumption. But can be provided by Chinese branches of foreign banks. 2. No consumption abroad for these services. 3. Geographic and client coverage of commercial presence: restrictions will be removed for foreign currency businesses upon accession, and will be progressively phased out during the 5-year transition period for all other terms. In 2007, there will be no geographic restrictions at all (foreign banks will also be able to provide services to clients located out of the geographical presence of that bank) on the provision of local currency business.* No limitations on national treatment.
Licensing	After the end of the transition period licensing criteria should be only prudential. Non-prudential ones such as ownership, operational and juridical ones will be removed. Exceptions: 1. Foreign financial institutions with total assets of at least USD 10 bln can establish a subsidiary or finance company. 2. Foreign financial institutions with total assets of at least USD 20 bln can establish a bank branch. 3. Foreign financial institutions with total assets of at least USD 10 bln can establish a Sino-foreign bank or finance company. No limitations on national treatment.
Automobile finance by NBFIs	Scope of services is limited in the same way as above (see first line).

* To this there is only one limitation: for the provision of local currency services, foreign banks must have been profitable in the last two consecutive years and have operated at least 3 years in China prior to their application for a local currency business licence.
Source: Based on WTO (2001c) and Jing X. (2005).

lost effectiveness and a further 47 have been changed to accommodate the new WTO rules.

During the transition period, China scrapped the regulation stating that the State Council could decide where foreign banks would be allowed to set up. It also scrapped the entry requirements for foreign banks for accessing the CNY currency market (although limits in terms of currency amounts remained). The requirements for foreign banks willing to form a joint-venture were eased by removing the constraint of choosing a Chinese bank as a partner (Jing X., 2005).

The restrictions on geographic presence were, up until mid-2006, removed as progressively as originally committed. All cities where China had promised to allow foreign bank entry have been opened. It only remains to be seen if all of China becomes open to all foreign banks by the end of 2006. Restrictions on local currency business and on customer segments were also fully removed.

Since December 2001, foreign banks were allowed to conduct foreign currency business with all kinds of customers (Chinese and foreign enterprises and individuals) in all of China. For local currency business, the opening was more gradual and started in 1996. By December 2001, foreign banks were only able to conduct such business with foreign enterprises and individuals and were restricted to Dalian, Shanghai, Shenzhen and Tianjin. Guangzhou, Nanjing, Qingdao, Wuhan and Zhuhai were added by December 2002 as further possible cities for business. In December 2003, the scope was further enlarged to Chengdu, Ji'nan, Chongqing and Fuzhou and to all Chinese enterprises. A year later, Beijing, Kunming and Xiamen were added to the list of opened cities. In December 2005, finally Ningbo, Shantou, Shenyang and Xi'an were also opened. Starting from December 2006, as promised under the WTO agreement, foreign banks will have access to all types of customers in all of China for both local and foreign currency businesses.

In terms of licensing requirements, the progress has also been positive. The minimum capital requirements for both foreign and Chinese banks are now similar, if not identical. Apart from the exceptions that were granted on the time of entry (requirement for foreign entities to have total assets amounting to either USD 10 or 20 bln, depending on whether they establish a subsidiary or a branch), the other requirements are solely prudential 审慎性条件 (such as sound banking practices, risk management, corporate governance, etc.). These are, when considering the same licensing areas (i.e. licensing for same new products or establishment of same legal entities), the same for Chinese and for foreign banks (Table 17.2).

Due to the relatively lower profitability, capital adequacy, and asset quality of Chinese banks overall, new requirements could be said to put foreign banks even at an advantage (because, all other

Table 17.2 Comparison between licensing requirements

Institution type	Minimum registered capital	Minimum operating capital for branches
JSCBs	CNY 1 bln	CNY 100 mln (and SOCBs)
CCBs	CNY 100 mln	
Foreign invested bank	CNY 300 mln	CNY 100 mln
Sino-foreign bank	CNY 300 mln	CNY 100 mln
Foreign finance company	CNY 200 mln	
Sino-foreign finance company	CNY 200 mln	
Foreign banks' branches		CNY 100 mln
Further outlets in same city		CNY 10 mln

Source: Based References for laws 14.

being equal, they are more likely to be able to comply with the prudential requirements).

Based on the above-described commitments and recent developments, we can ascertain that

- within the 5-year transition period, foreign banks have been given (full) access to the Chinese market, and
- within the 5-year transition period, foreign banks were given access to all types of customers with foreign and local currency services.

Furthermore, foreign banks are not required anymore to hold certain amount of assets to cover deposits (for foreign and local currency). The previously enforced ratios (first, 30% of the foreign currency or local currency operating capital shall be maintained in interest-bearing assets in that currency; second, the percentage of CNY-denominated assets shall not be less than 80% of its risk assets; third, the percentage of CNY-denominated assets shall be at least 8% of its operating capital; and fourth, the percentage of foreign exchange deposits shall not exceed 70% of the total foreign exchange assets of that bank) have now been removed (Zhou S., 2004). All requirements set out in Articles 24, 25, 26, 28 and 30 of the *Management rule regarding foreign-invested institutions* (Reference for laws 36) will be removed.

Finally, during the transition period, in terms of openness and transparency, the Chinese regulatory framework has undergone profound changes. It is now moving ahead towards a risk-based supervision, away from an administrative regulation (for example, supervision is now being based on the CAMELS system). The separation of duties and responsibilities between PBOC and CBRC has enabled the regulatory authorities to achieve a higher degree of specialisation and expertise. Laws and regulations are published in advance, for discussion with relevant parties and stakeholders, and are accessible to all (the new regulation on risk indicators supervision, for example, was already published for trial implementation on January 2006 before becoming fully compulsory in early 2007. In the mean time, banks have the opportunity to comment and discuss the regulation). However, foreign banks still complain about the unpredictability and unreliability of changes in regulations and laws (Metcalfe, 2005).

In conclusion, we can say that in most aspects, China is already compliant with its WTO commitments for the banking sector, and the remaining commitment to open up all of China to foreign banks at the end of 2006 is likely to be fulfilled in time.

Other barriers to foreign banks' entry

Compliance has been positive, but does this amount to a full opening? Constraints and barriers still remain, making establishment and development of foreign competition difficult (Metcalfe, 2005). Such barriers were not part of the banking sector commitments.

In terms of equity participation in Chinese banks, the entry of foreign banks is still strongly constrained. These were actually not part of any specific agreement under the WTO. At the moment the equity stakes, foreign banks can buy of the Chinese banks' capital, are limited to 20% (individually, or 25% together). Regulators have even added further conditions that need to be fulfilled by foreign investors to make their strategic investment in China (see Part II).

Barriers still exist in the provision of financial services by foreign banks. Foreign banks' scope of financial services were defined in the WTO agreement and these are allowed, but for any other types of services or activities foreign banks still face the restrictions that were stated in previous regulations (References for laws 18, 19, 30). For example, issuance of subordinated debt or of bonds, participation in the issuance of government bonds (as agent, arranger), act as an insurance agent, trust management or management of enterprises, or pensions fund business are not mentioned in the new licensing rules (Tang H., 2004). For investments in securities, the QFII regulations still apply. For the issuance of forex credit cards, foreign banks are, for example, required to have 5 years of operations in RMB-denominated cards before making an application.

Some requirements are still making it more difficult for foreign banks to establish themselves in the market and to conduct their activities (Wei W., 2005; EIU, 2006a):

- Reserve requirements in domestic currency are the same, but those for foreign currency are higher for foreign banks (reserve rate of 5% for less than 3 months and 3% for more than 3 months, compared to 2% for Chinese banks).
- Foreign banks have to pay higher interest rates on borrowings on the inter-bank market.
- Furthermore, borrowings on the inter-bank market are limited to 40% of a bank's CNY-denominated liabilities (something that is not a constraint to highly liquid domestic banks).
- Capital ratio requirements are the same for foreign and domestic banks; however, foreign banks must provide domestic currency capital for domestic currency assets.
- Exposure to the largest client should not be more than 25% of the capital of a foreign bank or 10% of the capital of a Chinese bank. Largest client, however, refers in the case of foreign banks also to companies associated to that largest client, which is not the case for domestic banks.
- The foreign banks' CNY liabilities cannot exceed 50% of their liabilities in foreign currency.
- Foreign banks are required to lend no more than 50% of the value of their foreign currency deposits.

Cultural barriers, an under-developed inter-bank market, a weak credit culture, the shortage of experienced human resources, as well as the preferential treatment of the Chinese state towards large Chinese banks (in terms of financial support and implicit guarantee) also influence the standpoint of foreign banks trying to take hold of market share in China.

Regulations are seen as being one of the most crucial and most difficult issues in China (Metcalfe, 2005). While progress has been made in some aspects, the Chinese banking system is still over-regulated. Other challenging aspects of regulations are the arbitrary enforcement and leeway in interpretation left to local regulators (Longueville and Ngo, 2004). This stifles innovation and transparency and promotes the protection of domestic banks compared to foreign ones. Legal risk is often perceived by foreign banks as a major risk by foreign banks (Metcalfe, 2005).

Foreign banks could be required to incorporate their branches in China in order to be part of the deposit insurance system which is due to start in the near future (Areddy, 2006a,b). Foreign banks would have to register corporations in China following the same licensing requirements as for JSCBs (*Asia Pulse*, 2006d). This could potentially create a new hurdle to expansion in Chinese markets (in terms of the licensing process) by putting foreign deposit-taking institutions at a disadvantage. At the same time, it could allow them to circumvent regulations that apply only to foreign banks' branches.

Finally, while conditions for operating a foreign bank have become more equal over time, historical legacies still create disparities in the system and make foreign bank activity in China still rather cumbersome, restricted and costly.

National treatment for all

Foreign banks enjoyed, before the accession to the WTO, a preferential treatment in some limited areas. Such preferences (albeit few) are likely to be removed by the end of 2006.

Until now, foreign banks have enjoyed one strong advantage compared to their Chinese peers: in terms of taxation. Up to now, the corporate tax for domestic banks is 33% of profits, while it is 15% for foreign banks. Business tax paid by domestic banks is 5% on revenues, a tax not paid by foreign banks (Yusuf *et al.*, 2006). Following the WTO principles, foreign banks could lose their favourable tax treatment (Xiao Z., 2005). Thus the widening of the national treatment to all banks would mean a cut into the actual and potential profitability of foreign banks.

Furthermore, to comply with the equal treatment of foreign and domestic banks, foreign banks could also be subject to controls and restrictions in lending as for domestic banks (Xiao Z., 2005). For example, under the *Loan principles* (Reference for laws 15), Art. 59, Chinese banks' branches receiving deposits or lending to entities outside their geographic scope are required to seek PBOC's approval for such activities in general. Foreign banks, however, can extend loans to and collect deposits from entities which are headquartered outside the areas for which they have received a licence (Tang H., 2004).

Finally, foreign banks can provide investment-banking services (including the sale and purchase of securities, bonds of enterprises and government, etc.), whereas these types of services are off limits for Chinese banks and must be conducted through securities firms (Tang H., 2004). Here regulators have tended more towards a liberalisation of rules for Chinese banks by recently allowing banks to do mutual funds business.

For these national treatment issues, it is unclear which way new regulations (required through the WTO entry) might go: levelling rules either towards foreign banks or towards Chinese ones. In view of the protective stance of Chinese regulators, it is more than likely that rules will tilt towards those that apply to Chinese banks.

17.2 Impact of foreign entry on emerging markets

There has not been any rigorous study (as far as we are aware) to understand the effect of foreign entry or the impact of the WTO accession on the banking sector in China. A number of papers study the effect of foreign bank entry on emerging markets, especially those in Latin America.

As studied by Claessens *et al.* (2001) for many countries around the world, the financial performance of domestic banks will be below those of the foreign entrants. In the long term, foreign entry benefits banks' customers (of domestic and foreign banks). Furthermore the authors found that the number of new foreign entrants has more impact than their overall share of the market: the greater impact is felt at the time of entry, not after foreign entrants have gained substantial market shares. The authors finally warn of the necessity of the timing of foreign entry as well as supporting it through efficient and prudent rules and regulations.

Crystal *et al.* (2001) find that the improvement in banking practices in domestic banks is only slight for those that are not fully state-owned. Foreign banks' higher performance (which is often due to the fact that they have more diversified funding sources, show stronger loan growth, high provisioning for bad assets, while interest margins are similar) influences positively the banking systems in which they are established. However, these results should be considered carefully, as influences from the banking environment or differences in individual banks (according to their size, markets, etc.) were not taken into account.

Clarke *et al.* (2002) show, using borrower surveys from diverse countries (not including China), that foreign banks' entry in emerging markets improves the local enterprises' access to credit. Their improved access to credit influences their development and thus their employment creating ability, which in turn affects positively a country's economic stability and long-term development. This result holds for all sizes of enterprises (albeit the positive impact is more significant for larger ones). Thus the fear of a number of national authorities that foreign bank entry might negatively affect economic performance is not well funded. The researchers also find that efficiency increases as a result of foreign bank entry: first, lower margins and administrative expenses often are the result; and second, domestic banks are observed to change their behaviour (by seeking new markets, new lines of business).

Findings of La Porta *et al.* (2000), which show that government ownership has a negative impact on banking systems (in terms of lower pace of development and lower growth of per capita income) around the world, suggest that Chinese banks would benefit greatly from diversification of shareholdings and from the relaxation of foreign banks' entry restrictions. Barth *et al.* (2000) have shown that strong restrictions upon the scope of businesses that banks can undertake (such as, for example, excluding banks from securities transactions) have a negative effect on the banks' performance and thus on banking system stability. Dages *et al.* (2000) conclude from Argentina's and Mexico's experiences with foreign banks' entry that ownership diversification and bank performance are key to the stable development of a banking system.

17.3 Impact of banking industry players

According to the above research, it can be expected that in China greater foreign bank entry will have an impact on: the performance of Chinese banks (lower margins, higher efficiency), banking practices (although this is also strongly influenced by ownership) and the overall financial intermediation capacity of the system (diversification into segments and products that were previously not in the banks' scope).

The end of the transition period (starting from 2007) could have a three-pronged impact on players in the Chinese banking system:

1. among banks themselves (creating an even level-playing field where all can participate and make useful partnerships or cooperation)
2. between banks and authorities (in terms of finally respecting the requirements of the banking regulations whereas banks should be independent and fully responsible for lending decisions and losses, etc.)
3. between banks and customers (Wang Y., 2004).

Likely response of foreign banks

Foreign banks have a strong expertise, and in some limited areas and services have a clear leadership. The competitive advantages of foreign banks lie in the provision of good services (by putting the customer at the centre of their reflections), their expertise (by encouraging innovation and new products) and experienced management (by ensuring sound systems and procedures in managing liabilities and assets, risks, internal controls, etc.) as well as diverse products and an international presence (most foreign banks are linked in one way or another to an internationally active bank, Li Z., 2004). To add to these strengths, foreign banks will now enjoy a larger scope of business: they will be able to expand from foreign to local currency, from wholesale to retail services, from foreign to Chinese customers, as well as into other products and geographic areas.

Based on the above and earlier observations, one could conclude that full membership to the WTO would result in a run on Chinese banks – Chinese individuals withdrawing funds from domestic banks and shifting these to foreign institutions (Langlois, 2001). Such fears, however, seem totally unfounded. Chinese banks have a strong customer and branch base, with high visibility and remain implicitly guaranteed by the state. Thus Chinese customers are unlikely to move away from such secure institutions. In addition, foreign banks are starting from such a small base, that their share of banking assets is unlikely to grow to substantial levels in the next few years.

Table 17.3 shows that to reach the market share of 30% after 10 years as predicted by Jing (Jing X., 2005: 47), foreign banks would have to grow by 62% annually (that would be double the growth figure that foreign banks expect for themselves in the near future, Metcalfe, 2005). While foreign banks have been able to increase their assets by 41% in 2005, it is rather unlikely that on a nationwide basis and over a time span of 10 years, they will be able to sustain such growth in assets (unless the regulators relax foreign ownership caps). OECD researchers estimate that foreign banks will probably stabilise their market share at around 10% of banking assets, similar to their situation in other Asian countries (OECD, 2005).

Foreign banks, even after the easing of most regulations in 2007, will still face a challenging existence. The survey conducted by Pricewaterhouse-Coopers (PwC) (Metcalfe, 2005) reveals that foreign banks at the time of interview saw five different types of risks to their expansion in China: regulatory (due to the rudimentary nature of the legal environment), credit, reputational, legal and operational risk. In addition, building a branch network remains hugely expensive. Finally, the environment is growing more and more critical of foreign banks (as seen in Chapter 5).

Some researchers (Leung M. K. and Chan R., 2006) think that foreign banks in China can choose between two strategies depending on their

Table 17.3 Growth of foreign banks to match Chinese banks

	Total assets (2003)		In ten years time		Growth assumptions (%)
	in bln CNY	Market share (%)	in bln CNY	Market share (%)	
State-owned commercial banks	15,194	60	49,505	30	12.54
Joint-stock commercial banks	3,817	15	34,186	21	24.51
City commercial banks	1,462	6	8,283	5	18.94
Foreign-invested banks	397	1.6	49,225	**30**	**61.94**
Other financial institutions	4,645	18	23,423	14	17.56
Total for all commercial FIs	25,515	100	164,622	100	20.50

The growth assumptions are based on average quarterly growth for the individual types of banks in 2004 and 2005.
Source: Based on PBOC (2003) data and CBRC (2005a) data for the average growth assumptions.

asset base and expertise: a niche strategy or a market challenging strategy. The former is basically available to all banks that have branches in China and they can choose the niche depending on their expertise. For those few with a strong force de frappe, both in terms of financial resources and local knowledge, the latter can also be an option by competing with domestic banks in all mainstream banking areas. In both cases these are selective approaches, the strategic choice of foreign banks in China.

Traditional Chinese banking markets (such as lending) are already only marginally profitable for foreign banks, thus it is unlikely that they will expand in these areas (Metcalfe, 2005). Foreign banks are unlikely to provide all types of services, as Chinese banks do. Rather they are likely to target only those customers or business areas that promise sufficient returns to cover the expenses. Only profitable channels are going to be chased. Thus these will only include a small number out of a wide range of possible activities.

The customers they are going to target are most likely going to be foreign-invested or Sino-foreign ventures, large Chinese corporations and local governments. However, some banks, such as Standard Chartered and DBS Bank, intend to target SMEs as well (*SinoCast China*

Financial Watch, 2006c). This area, which was traditionally the focus of CCBs, is likely to become the setting for a direct challenge to Chinese banks. On the retail side, foreign banks are likely to concentrate on wealthy clients with international needs. The foreign banks appetite for chasing Chinese domestic deposits will also be limited (Langlois, 2001). New products could include credit cards, mortgages and investment plans for individuals as well as derivative products, debt capital markets products and risk management products (Metcalfe, 2005).

Faster growth for foreign banks could be achieved through a strategic partnership with a commercial bank in China (although most likely are those with others than the SOCBs). Joint ventures are not preferred options anymore because of the challenges resulting from the lack of clear ownership and control structures (Metcalfe, 2005). A range of products interesting to foreign banks can also be dealt with through strategic partnerships (e.g., credit cards), to enhance market participation of the foreign bank. As a consequence of such strategic choices, the likely changes following the entry to the WTO could concentrate in the area of product and markets development.

Likely response of Chinese banks

Chinese banks show lower efficiency and lower profitability, poor asset quality, and rely on traditional banking business for most of their revenues (Yue X., 2005). The competitive strengths of Chinese banks, relative to foreign banks, do not lie in products knowledge and customer service, or in management expertise. In these, Chinese banks on average are weaker. Their strengths lie in the broad customer base and the large networks that enable reaching out to many clients, albeit in an undifferentiated manner. Furthermore they possess local market knowledge, which foreign banks would have to build up first in many cases. Last but not least, Chinese banks, especially state-owned ones, all enjoy some degree of implicit guarantee from the state (even though JSCBs or CCBs are not implicitly guaranteed by the state, it cannot be denied that any of the larger ones would be supported in case of difficulties), which gives them a strong argument in front of customers depositing their savings.

A number of Chinese authors, such as, for example, Jiang Xuecheng (2005), think that it is highly likely that more informed and wealthier customers will turn to better-run foreign banks away from Chinese banks. However, an exodus as he foresees may be exaggerated. For one reason, Chinese banks are not all bad service providers. Many JSCBs are competitive. For another reason, many clients are not interested in foreign banks and are out of reach for them. Finally, foreign banks cannot, from their small base, attend to large numbers of clients. These arguments are also mentioned by Shi Jiliang, one of CBRC's vice-chairman (Zhang D., 2006b). For him an exodus is unlikely despite the better services provision of foreign banks. This is due to their customer target focus. In lending, however, competition could increase in serving large corporations and those with a better creditworthiness, leaving the large majority of enterprises with their local bank.

The WTO entry will surely expose the weak points of the Chinese banking sector, especially in large urban centres, where competition will be stronger. In view of their current situation and standing, Chinese banks are likely to find challenges in a number of areas: customer targeting, governance structures and geographic focus. Overall, Chinese banks have a much broader approach than the highly specialised foreign banks. Chinese banks are beginning to realise the advantages of targeting and segmenting customers with specific products. While the broad scope provides Chinese banks with an important source of resources, the customer specialisation of foreign banks brings them a source of profits (Xi H., 2004). For Chinese banks it will be necessary to target customers and thus to understand their needs and behaviour. It will require the re-orientation of organisational structures around the customer as the centre. It will also require the diversification of distribution channels and of products which are more adapted to the needs of customers. It will finally involve the more focused customer segmentation strategies – abandoning some while chasing others (Xi H., 2004).

The banking landscape could also witness a change of geographic focus. In recent years, Chinese banks have been seen as withdrawing from less developed areas and concentrating in larger urban centres where profits are easier to be made. However, with foreign banks' entry this trend could be reversed. Because foreign banks are likely to target only large economic urban centres, Chinese banks could be pushed towards less developed areas and cities (He L. and Fan X., 2004).

Also important is the fact that governance structures in Chinese banks are, at present, much weaker than in foreign banks. This results in better risk management and controls and thus in higher performance at foreign banks. To increase their force de frappe, Chinese banks will need to match the foreign banks' management capacity. Thus they may have to enter into mergers or strategic partnerships with other banks, foreign or Chinese. In the words of Zhou Shaoyang (2004) the strategic equity stakes serve the interests and goals of both sides, they represent a "short cut 捷径" for both: Chinese banks provided access to foreign best practices and technology and foreign banks access to Chinese market knowledge and experience. Domestic banks may have to team up with each other in order to withstand foreign entry.

Impact of WTO entry on authorities

Regulators are also likely to feel the impact of the WTO entry. As a consequence of the entry, regulators could find themselves increasingly under pressure to consolidate their regulatory and supervisory power into one entity (CBRC) and to increase the importance of international cooperation (including adherence of Chinese regulations to create similar rules across countries for internationally active banks, Liu X. and Liu S., 2004).

The WTO commitments did not include any required reform of the ownership structure of banks. But in theory the Chinese authorities, through the WTO entry, have, as any other country in the WTO, sealed the end of hidden government support and subsidies. Thus a question remains: will the authorities still be in a position to act as bank saviours in the future? A recapitalisation effort for individual banks or the whole banking system would come nothing short of a government subsidy to domestic banks – but this may be a necessity if crisis looms. Xu Ying (2006) thinks that the full WTO membership means that to provide for an equal playing field, the Chinese authorities will have to withdraw from their financial supporting role of the past. For smaller banks, there may be an argument against the subsidies, but for a large bank, where financial stability could be endangered, the situation would probably not change with full WTO membership. Thus large banks with direct or indirect state majority ownership could still enjoy preferential treatment.

Finally, new regulations will be required for a deposit insurance scheme, for bankruptcy proceedings for banks, for exit mechanisms and for mergers and restructurings of banks (Tang H., 2004). The current lack of such regulations will become even clearer with full WTO membership. Such regulations are required to create an even playing field between foreign and Chinese banks in the long term.

17.4 Impact of WTO entry on the banking system

The expectation is that overall WTO membership will lead (and has already done so) to higher efficiency in the provision of financial services in Chinese banks. Shen Liming and Hua Jinhui (2005) think that the entry of foreign banks will be useful in raising the efficiency of the banking system. This is because the technology level will be raised and operations will gain in quality at domestic banks. It should spur financial innovation, increase the role of technology and information systems, promote the use of sound risk management systems and the disposal of bad assets, and will also require the nurturing of human resources and expertise. This in turn will ensure a more effective use of funds and of capital, thus raising overall efficiency.

For Shen Liming and Hua Jinhui (2005), a second positive aspect of the foreign banks' entry will be the increased stability of the whole banking system. Their entry is likely to raise the resistance of Chinese banks to shocks and external negative influences. This is due partly to the foreign banks' arrival accompanied by higher information disclosure standards as well as alternative deposit opportunities if one bank fails. This is also due to the fact that it will require the system overall gather pace in reforms, to improve management levels and corporate governance, to increase the level of asset quality and financial management as well as capital efficiency (He L. and Fan X., 2004; Wang Y., 2004).

Xu Nan and Wang Zhongsheng (2005) also see the impact of foreign banks on the Chinese banking system as positive. For them the impact will be felt by the ending of the SOCBs' monopoly (and thus the quickening pace of reforms), the stronger development and training of the Chinese financial markets as well as the expansion of Chinese banks abroad. They also think that the WTO entry process will benefit customers. This is due to the fact that higher levels of competition will help bring down management costs (by as much as 20%) and will be transferred to customers through lower transaction prices. Finally, as other commentators have noted, the allocation of funds and capital will become more efficient (and this may also improve the quality of assets). The direct impact on capital allocation will be felt in the number of new products catering more closely to the needs of customers. The indirect impact of foreign banks' presence will be felt in the increased confidence of foreign investors in China and in the decreased transactions costs for multinationals operating in the country.

The WTO entry has the potential to increase the speed of reform of Chinese SOEs and their profitability is likely to improve as a result (Yusuf *et al.*, 2006). The changes are actually just conforming to an already long-established reality: micro-economically China has changed (now private and TVEs enterprises do produce more output than SOEs and are more profitable). The entry of foreign banks is one step within the overall reform of the banking system. It distributes the burden of financial intermediation over many banks and withdraws the full responsibility for finance from the four SOCBs. It will also stop SOCBs from further abusing the system by having an indefinite support for their lack of management incentives. Finally, WTO entry is expected to reduce the level of concentration in the banking system (Yue X., 2004).

The WTO entry will increase the internationalisation and the integration of the Chinese banks into the world financial system. To be able to withstand the challenges, they will have to greatly increase the depth and breadth of their intermediation capacity, in terms of both product strength and customer focus. The impact of the WTO entry will be more like a wake up call rather than an earthquake or a tsunami.

Conclusion

Chinese banks face three main upcoming challenges: the development of retail lending, the implementation of Basel II and the full accession to the WTO. These challenges each target different areas of the Chinese banking system: products and segments, and risk management. These developments are expected to result in stronger competition and a sounder banking system overall – Chinese banks could also win in the long term, if they change the ways they have done business up to now. If they put the customer at the centre of their preoccupations, build up strong and stable systems and procedures to manage risks incurred, raise their efficiency and widen their scope of activity, then they are likely to transform the above challenges into profitable opportunities.

Part VI
Conclusion

As shown in this book, Chinese banks have successfully gathered large volumes of deposits, but have not yet been able to redistribute these efficiently, as illustrated by the distorted financial intermediation process, poor risk management capabilities and interference of government (at both the state and local levels). The single most important and highest risks China and its banks are facing are operational and credit risks (some also add legal risks). As we have seen, the financial infrastructure and especially the ownership and governance features of banks also impacts bank behaviour. It influences the performance and the healthiness of banks as well as their future prospects. Ownership features also influence their operating environment as well as customer expectations. As long as metrics in the economy remain positive and healthy, the banks are likely to do reasonably well. But what happens when the economy goes into recession?

Central and local government are powerful forces in the Chinese banking system. Through the influence they have on personnel, business, strategic and lending decisions, through the stakes they hold indirectly or directly in banks' capital, and through the powerful financial resources they have at their disposal to rescue any failed bank, they are able to control the entire banking system and to steer it in the desired direction. Thus they are able to control the flow of financial resources from banks to enterprises. This enables them to control the growth path and speed of the entire economy.

Because such control and power ensures that governance structures and ownership features between different players are blurred, this has given rise to a number of serious problems that still need to be resolved:

very high levels of NPLs, inefficient financial intermediation, corruption and so on. A growing sense of emergency has helped the authorities realise the extent of the problem. As a first step, central and local authorities have provided funds to clean up balance sheets. This, after several trials, has been successful overall. At the same time, regulators (which are also part of the state apparatus) have been given the task to enforce new regulations and punish misbehaviour in the banks. New regulations commanding a new management culture have been widely published. They further promote market discipline, credit controls and the establishment of various risk management procedures, to name just a few developments. All are steps in the right direction, but how much has this permeated the banking system at the lowest levels?

Despite these developments, central and local authorities still use much of their power to influence banks. Relinquishing some of this power is an issue that has been discussed extensively and still little progress has been made in this area. To the dismay of many commentators, most reform has not been in this particular area. The authorities can profit from the financial resources gained during the strong economic growth periods (and thus the potential insolvency of the banking system does not, for the moment at least, represent a systemic threat to China's economic health; also banks are awash with excess liquidity collected, thanks to other artificial restrictions, only awaiting to be disbursed to any project). They still have the means to save banks from failure and have levers to put pressure on bankers to protect their interests (although this should not be considered solely a one-way relation: banks, in many cases, willingly receive state support). The authorities thus ensure that the banking system in China remains the weakest link and remains under their control. Is this a strategy that the authorities deem necessary? This may be the case despite overriding evidence showing that in most countries less state influence results in a sounder financial system. Is this a strategy to maintain their legitimacy? Authorities do not have an earnest interest in changing the status quo, because for now, it allows them to protect their economic and political interests.

Two tests will be brought to China through the opening and the integration in the international banking system: the application of Basel II standards and the entry to WTO. Both will surely have only a measured impact on such a complex and interwoven banking system and will not be any kind of panacea for the current ills of Chinese banking. Still these are likely to add pressure for reforms on the system and on the authorities. More and more, decisions within Chinese banks will become independent. Observers of the Chinese banking system can hope for a more stable and more resilient banking system in the future. But this war on reform has not yet been won and foreign influence can still be counted as small.

As said earlier, most reforms have been cosmetic in nature and have encouraged the first steps towards true reforms: removing all historical burdens from many battered balance sheets. Now banks are given a fresh start. So what does it need to really make reforms a sustainable success? Only the right incentives can push banks into a sustainable long-term development model. They could become a more decisive force in China's overall economic development. McKinsey (MGI, 2006) has calculated that a thorough reform of the Chinese banking system could boost China's GDP by USD 62 bln annually. And this could be achieved mostly by increasing bank (lending) efficiency and financial intermediation. Ira Kalish (2006) also agrees that a more efficient use of financial funds would have probably enabled China to grow faster.

The right incentives and mechanisms could be provided, for example, by modern bankruptcy proceedings, by reliable legal enforcement, by extending the scope of available collateral, by strengthening independent regulators and by further opening the banking system to full competition (under the condition that the incentives are real ones and not artificially created by authorities on paper). Each of these elements individually is unlikely to have a strong impact, but taken together they might foster the right financial infrastructure. The single most powerful incentive would be a full privatisation and the full retreat of the authorities outside the banking system; however, this is only a distant possibility. With such deep-rooted changes, a different risk culture is likely to emerge only gradually.

It should be clear from above that tougher reforms lie ahead, and this will test the authorities' and banks' commitment to reforms. As noted by some analysts (Ramos R. *et al.*, 2005), China has sufficient growth and financial resources (and also the political will) to "fix" the banking system. And as long as these metrics remain, a banking crisis is unlikely. Now that China has the instruments in its hands to make a deep reform of the banking system, will it have the foresight and strength to make the appropriate changes?

The resistance from the authorities with regard to privatisation cannot simply be explained by fears of large lay-offs or economic difficulties. It rather seems that the authorities are interested in maintaining political and economic supremacy – and ceding these rather slowly. Economic prowess helps sustain political power and strengthens the case for continued support from the authorities. Instead of privatisation, another factor that could help transfer the attention of the authorities to banks would be if the banks lost their supremacy in financing (i.e. when alternative financing intermediation channels fell into private hands). But is this realistic? Is the government trying to use economic prowess to bolster its political legitimacy? This would explain to a great extent why it refuses to yield any power and control over financial flows because these support the economic development process.

At the same time, the increasingly widespread view that recapitalising banks is a costly exercise could ultimately lead the authorities to prefer further gradual privatisations so as to wind down their involvement in the banking sector at a slow pace and to establish arms' length relationships with strong banks in the future. This seems the most likely scenario although only time will tell what the future holds!

Annexes

List of the main players in the Chinese banking industry

Regulatory authorities

People's Bank of China (PBOC)
China Banking Regulatory Commission (CBRC)
China Securities Regulatory Commission (CSRC)
China Insurance Regulatory Commission (CIRC)

State-owned commercial banks (SOCBs), ranked by assets

Industrial and Commercial Bank of China (ICBC)
Bank of China (BoC)
Agricultural Bank of China (ABC)
China Construction Bank (CCB)

Asset Management Companies (AMCs), ranked in parallel to the related SOCBs

Huarong Asset Management Company (Huarong AMC)
Orient Asset Management Company (Orient AMC)
Great Wall Asset Management Company (Great Wall AMC)
Cinda Asset Management Company (Cinda AMC)
Huida Asset Management Company (Huida AMC)

Policy-lending banks

Export–Import Bank of China (Exim Bank)
China Development Bank, formerly State Development Bank (CDB)
Agricultural Development Bank of China (ADBC)

Joint-stock commercial banks (JSCBs), ranked by assets

Bank of Communications (BoComm)
China Merchants Bank (Merchants)
CITIC Industrial Bank (CITIC)
Shanghai Pudong Development Bank (Pudong)
China Minsheng Banking Corp. (Minsheng)
China Everbright Bank (Everbright)
Industrial Bank, formerly Fujian Industrial Bank (Industrial)
Guangdong Development Bank (GDB)
Huaxia Bank (Huaxia)
Shenzhen Development Bank (SDB)
Hengfeng Bank (Hengfeng)

Newly established banks (JSCBs)

Huishang Bank
Bohai Bank

The credit plan

The credit plan was designed to control financial flows from banks to enterprises. The credit plan included the 4 SOCBs as well as, between 1988 and 1995, some of the JSCBs, that is Bank of Communications, CITIC and China Everbright Bank. For other institutions, financial flows controls were operated through the loan-to-deposit ratio requirements. The credit plan was prepared jointly by the Ministry of Finance, the NDRC and PBOC. The setting was based on GDP, investments and inflation indicators goals as well as (local) industry financing requirements and needs (Grimm, 2005). Under the credit plan, each bank was given a limit for loans which was then broken down to individual branches and provided loans for specific purposes and terms. SOCBs could refinance themselves through PBOC. Enforcement was always an issue because as soon as limits were surpassed, new funds flowed in. The credit plan was abolished in 1998 and thereafter PBOC used a window guidance scheme for selected projects. Only in 2004, with the publication of the new capital adequacy regulations, did the loan-to-deposit ratio loose as well its importance.

The negative effects of the credit plan by far surpass the positive ones and its effects are still felt now. Because the constraints put on banks were soft, and because the interest rates were fixed at that time, the credit plan actually created an excessive credit creation (Girardin, 1997). It encouraged expansion with no concern for viability or sustainability. Accountability was not on the agenda in banks. There were thus no incentives for internal controls, for risk management and for financial intermediation. The credit plan transformed banks into passive fund transfer machines (Montes-Negret, 1995). It also created competition and conflicts of interests between banks and authorities (interference in lending decisions and allocations) as well as between different authorities (it was also an instrument of the central authorities to control flows into provinces).

CAMELS bank assessment system

Table A.1 CAMELS bank assessment system

	Factor	Pts	Indicator and comments	Pts
Capital adequacy	Quantity	60	CAR	30
			Tier 1 CAR	30
	Quality	40	Components and quality of bank capital: stability, fully paid in or not	6
			Overall financial status of the bank and its impact on capital: profitability, competitive position, adverse factors	8
			Asset quality and its influence on capital (comparing trends in NPLs/provisions)	8

			Ability of banks to raise capital in markets or other channels	8
			Management of capital: plans, strategy, forecasting, profits distribution	10
Asset safety	Quantity	60	NPL ratio	15
			Estimated loan loss ratio	10
			Lending ratio of the biggest single customer or customer group	10
			Reserve coverage ratio	20
			Non-credit asset loss ratio	5
	Quality*	40	Tendency of NPLs changes and other non-performing assets and their influences on the bank's asset safety situation	5
			Loan industry concentration and its impact on bank's asset safety	5
			Procedure and effectiveness of credit risk management	10
			Completeness and effectiveness of loan risk classification system	10
			Management of guaranteed loans and mortgages (pledges)	5
			Risk management status of non-credit assets	5
Management administration	Bank management	50	Fundamental structure of the bank's management: structure, institutions in place and responsibilities	10
			Decision-making system of banking corporate governance: shareholders, directors qualifications	10
			Execution system of the bank's corporate governance	10
			Supervision system of the bank's corporate governance	10
			Encouragement, restriction and responsibility specification system of the bank's corporate governance	10
	Internal controls	50	Internal control environment and culture (mechanisms, structures, culture)	10
			Risk identification and assessment: Risk management procedures and systems	10
			Controlling behaviour and responsibilities (business policies, responsibilities, control mechanisms, emergency systems)	10
			Information communications: information sharing, integrity of information	10
			Supervision and correction	10
Profitability	Quantity	60	ROA	15
			ROE	15
			Interest income recovery rate	15
			Asset expense ratio	15
	Quality	40	Cost and income status as well as profitability level and development tendency	15

Table A.1 (Continued)

	Factor	Pts	Indicator and comments	Pts
			Quality of the bank's profitability and its influences on the bank's business development and asset loss provisions	15
			Financial budget and settlement system, completeness and effectiveness of its financial management	10
Liquidity	Quantity	60	Liquidity Ratio	20
			RMB Excessive Reserve Ratio: RMB Excessive reserves means RMB reserves after deduction of required reserves	10
			Foreign Currency Excessive Reserve Ratio	5
			Loans Deposits Ratio: Combination of RMB and Foreign Currency	10
			Loans Deposits Ratio: Foreign Currency	5
			Net Interbank Borrowing Ratio	10
	Quality	40	Composites, development tendency and stability of the bank's capital sources	5
			Assets and liabilities management policy and the capital distribution situation	5
			Management over liquidity	20
			Ability of the bank to meet its liquidity demands through methods of voluntary liabilities .	5
Market Risk	Ability of the bank's Board of Directors and senior management to identify, measure, supervise and control its market risk exposure. Character and complexity of interest rate risk exposure originated from (non-)trade position. No market risk assessment for now due to the lack of capacity and expertise in Chinese banks in using relevant products.			

Definitions: NPLs defined as last three categories (Section 7.2). Estimated loan loss ratio = (normal loans × 1% + precautionary loans × 2% + substandard loans × 20% + doubtful loans × 40% + loss loans × 100%)/total loans. Reserve coverage ratio = (general reserves + specific reserves + special reserves)/(substandard loans + doubtful loans + loss loans). Non-credit asset loss ratio = Non-credit asset losses/Total non-credit assets. Asset Expense Ratio = Operation Expense/Total Assets. Net interbank borrowing ratio = interbank borrowing ratio – interbank lending ratio.

* Each type of procedure will be marked with a set number of points.

Source: Based on References for laws 30.

Main licensing requirements for establishing Chinese commercial banks

General requirements

Comply with relevant rules and regulations regarding professional directors and senior managers, sound organisational structure and management system, business premises and security system, sound corporate governance, risk management, internal controls, no investments by local governments, investors also to include good foreign ones, good HR management system, adequate capital.

Requirements for banks' investors

If commercial bank: CAR 8% (otherwise 10% risk-based capital ratio): equity investments not exceeding 50% of own capital, profitable in last 3 years, good corporate governance and internal controls, compliant with prudential indicators of supervisors.

If foreign investor (financial institution), additionally

Total assets at least USD 10 bln, good international credit rating in last 2 years, profitable in last 2 years, sound supervision at home and sound economic environment at home.

Table A.2 Licensing requirements for Chinese banks

Type of institution	Capital required (CNY mln)	Further requirements for the applicant
JSCBs	1000	
CCBs	100	CAR 8%, core capital 4%, NPL under 10%*.
UCCs	50	
Branches of SOCBs and JSCBs	100	Sound corporate governance, risk management, internal controls, MIS, capital adequacy, asset quality, profitability, no unlawful activities in last two years, good CAMELS rating, compliance with prudential indicators.
Branches abroad		CAR 8%, equity investments less than 50% of own capital, profitable in last 3 years, CNY 100 bln in total assets, have foreign currency funds, sound corporate governance and internal controls, comply with prudential indicators.
Foreign exchange business		Sound performance and risk management, CAR 8%, core capital 4%, professional staff and relevant policies, comply with prudential indicators.
Issuance of subordinated debt		Using five-tier loan classification, core capital not less than 4%, adequate LLP, good corporate governance, no unlawful activities in last 3 years.

* if applicant is established as the result of merged RCCs, then CAR 6%, core capital 6%, NPL 15% (18% for UCC), total assets at least CNY 6 mln (CNY 5 mln for UCC), 2 years without risk management problems, good operating performance, ROA at least 0.2%, ROE at least 8% (4% for UCC).

Source: Based on References for laws 14.

Changes to be approved by CBRC

Changes in shareholders or shareholding (above 10%), operational capital, statutes of the institution, business premises, name.

Main licensing requirements for establishing rural financial institutions

General requirements

Have professional and qualified board and senior management, at least a director and a vice-director, at least 80% of employees have 1 year of relevant finance experience, sound organisational structure and management system, business premises and security system, sound risk management and internal controls, effective HR management system, mechanism for replenishing capital, local government does not hold any capital.
Requirements for branches and other outlets: Respond to a service need in area, strong internal controls (no unlawful activities in last 2 years), good asset quality, at least 80% of employees have 1 year of relevant finance experience, business premises and security system, professional and qualified directors board and senior management, at least a director and a vice-director.

Table A.3 Licensing requirements for rural financial institutions

Rural financial institutions	Minimum number of issuers	Capital required (CNY mln)	Further requirements
RCCs* 农村信用合作社	500 people	1	Natural persons cannot hold more than 2% alone.
Union of RCCs 农村信用合作社联合社	8 RCCs	1	Employees cannot hold more than 25% together or 2% alone of the capital, other unions cannot invest, issuers should be local RCCs with equity investments should not be more than 50% of net assets. An individual RCC shall not hold more than 50,000 shares or 20% of the capital.
Rural credit unions (RCUs) 农村信用合作联社	1000 people	10	Natural persons cannot hold more than 0.5% alone; other credit unions or RCCs cannot invest. Core capital no less than 2%. Min. capital may be adjusted by CBRC but no less than CNY 5 mln.

Union of RCUs 农村信用社联合社	–	5	Issuer can be local rural FIs. Issuer must have no more than 50% of its capital invested in equity, hold no more than 10% of shares or 30% of capital.
Rural Commercial Bank*, ** 农村合作银行	1000 people	20	Established on the basis of RCUs or RCCs. Natural persons cannot hold more than 0.5% alone of the capital. Unions cannot invest.
Rural Commercial Bank*, ** 农村商业银行	–	50	Natural persons cannot hold more than 0.5% alone of the capital. Unions cannot invest.

* Requirements for issuers: Issuers can be natural persons, non-FIs and FIs (also foreign). *Natural persons* must have good records and be living in area at least for 3 years. All employees together cannot hold more than 25%. *Non-FIs* must have also good records and reputation, at least profitable in last 2 years, have strong profitability ability, net assets of no less than 30% of total assets, equity investments should not be more than 50% of enterprise capital, registered in local area of RCC, should not hold alone more than 10% of the RCC capital. *FIs* (excluding unions) should have CAR of 8% at least (NBFI 10%), equity investments should not be more than 50% of net assets, at least profitable in last 2 years, sound corporate governance and structures, should not hold alone more than 20% of the RCC capital (for foreign financial institutions additionally: total assets no less than USD 1 bln, 2 years of good international rating, together do not hold more than 25% of the capital).
** Higher merger requirements: Merger should be made on own will of participating entities, have a strong management ability, consolidated accounts, NPLs no more than 15% (five-tier), core capital no less than 4%, CAR 8%, investment shares no less than 60% of all shares, set percentage of agricultural lending set by shareholders meeting.
Source: Based on References for laws 23, 24 and 25.

Table A.4 Licensing requirements for branches of rural financial institutions

	Operating capital* (CNY mln)	**Further requirements for the applicant**
RCCs	0.3	CAR no less than 2%
RCUs	1	CAR no less than 4%, min. capital can be adjusted by CBRC to CNY 0.5 mln
Rural cooperative or commercial bank branch	1	CAR no less than 4%, NPLs less than 15%
Rural cooperative or commercial bank outlet	0.5	CAR no less than 4%, NPLs less than 15
Cooperative FIs' savings branch	none	none

* making up no more than 60% of HQ capital.
Source: Based on References for laws 14.

Main licensing requirements for establishing foreign-invested banks

Table A.5 Main licensing requirements for foreign banks until 2005

In CNY mln	Branch	Joint-venture	Foreign bank	Foreign finance company
Foreign exchange business with all types of foreign entities		100	300	200
Foreign exchange business with all types of customers	200	100	400	300
Foreign exchange and RMB business with all types of foreign entities	200*	200*	400*	300*
RMB business with all types of foreign entities and foreign exchange with all kinds of customers	300*	200*	600*	500*
RMB business with all types of foreign entities and foreign exchange with all kinds of customers and prescribed RMB business (inward and outward export settlements) with non-foreign invested enterprises	300*	200*	500**	400**
RMB and foreign exchange with all kinds of customers	400†	200†	1,000†	700†

* Of this amount at least 100 mln should be in RMB.
** Of this amount at least 200 mln should be in RMB.
† Of this amount at least 300, 200, 600, 400 mln respectively should be in RMB.
Source: Based on References for laws 14.

General requirements for shareholders (since 2005)

Investors must be financial institutions.

For sole or largest shareholder

Must be a commercial bank (or a finance company for Sino-foreign entity), CAR 8%, must have established a presence in China in last 2 years (no time limit for Sino-foreign banks' investors, no previous presence required if coming from HK), have no less than USD 10 bln total assets (if coming from HK: USD 6 bln, and if establishing a branch: USD 20 bln), be under a sound supervisory authority in home country.

Table A.6 Main licensing requirements for foreign banks (since 2005)

Type of institution	Capital required (CNY mln)	Further requirements for the applicant
Foreign bank Sino-foreign bank Foreign FC Sino-foreign FC	300 300 200 200	Sound corporate governance structure, good continuous financial performance, audited financial statements of last 3 years are unqualified, no bad records, good reputation, complying with other prudential indicators.
Foreign banks' branches	100	If applicant has other branches in China: these must have sound risk management system, internal controls, MIS, professional managers,* good financial performance and asset quality, no bad records, no money laundering problems, compliant with any other prudential indicators.
Branch of (Sino)-foreign bank	100	Operating in China for at least 3 years; be profitable in the last 2 years, CAR of at least 8%.
Further outlets in same city	10	One year operational in that city already, no unlawful activities in last year, operational capital should not account for more of 60% of the branch/bank's own capital, have professional managers, business premises and security systems, already have branch in that city.
Representative office		Be under a sound supervisory authority in home country, no unlawful activities, have anti-money laundering procedures, compliant with prudential indicators.
For CNY business**		Have operations in China for last 3 years (in HK 2 years), profitable in last two consecutive years and branches must have sound risk management system, internal controls, MIS, professional managers, continuous good financial performance and asset quality, no bad records, no money laundering problems.
For e-banking**		Have operations in China, sound risk management system, internal controls, MIS, and no major operational problems in last year, security procedures.

Table A.6 (Continued)

Type of institution	Capital required (CNY mln)	Further requirements for the applicant
For derivative transactions**		Sound risk management and internal controls, separation of front and back office, managers with 5 years professional experience, no negative records in last two years, appropriate systems and premises.
For private wealth management**		Plan for guaranteeing returns, relevant products, sound risk management and internal controls, professional management, market risk management, no major negative events.

* Directors and managers need to show sufficient experience: 10–15 years of relevant experience for directors and CEOs and at least 4–6 years for other most senior positions. Further, they need to comply with all rules and have no bad records.
** For first time or expansion application.
Changes to be approved by CBRC: changes in shareholders or shareholding (above 10%), operational capital, statutes of the institution, business premises, name.
Source: Based on References for laws 14.

Legal bankruptcy proceedings in China

Bankruptcy is relatively new to China. In China, the term *bankruptcy* is used when "winding-up insolvent enterprises" (Ng, 2002: 364). The term *liquidation* is used for solvent enterprises which are being winded up or dissolved. The Chinese system is based on civil law principles. The *Bankruptcy Law* (for trial implementation) was enacted in December 1986 after years of reviews and discussion. It became effective in 1988. The number of declared insolvencies has grown significantly in the 1990s, but still remains with some 25,000 cases relatively low (Wormuth, 2004). Institutional weaknesses have largely influenced the number of bankruptcies: the lack of independent courts, the lack of valuation expertise and lack of secondary market for asset sales, and the asset depletion (in many cases debtors have used the time between the opening and the recognition of insolvency to sell out their assets).

Bankruptcy proceedings currently apply only to SOEs and could be extended to other enterprises, but only to juridical persons (Art. 3). Insolvency is simply defined as the "inability to pay debts due to severe losses because of poor management" (Art. 4, 3). Shenzhen and Guangdong have received approval to introduce their own bankruptcy regulations which are much more precise than the national law, but the scope of these examples has always remained local. Further to these precedents, a national working group, the National Bankruptcy Liaison Group, has been established in March 1997 to coordinate and organise bankruptcy proceedings in certain geographic areas (Ng, 2002).

A *bankruptcy proceeding* can be opened by both creditors and debtors, but in the case of SOEs these need the approval of the responsible ministry (Art. 10–12 and Art. 179). Secured claims are not part of the bankruptcy proceedings and must be settled outside the proceedings (Wormuth, 2004). In practice, most trade creditors are fully ignored (WB, 2000). Administration of the bankrupt entity is done by a group chosen from ministries and government departments. If the remaining assets are not sufficient to ensure full repayment, then repayment is made according to a percentage. In many cases, China has preferred to use other instruments (such as mergers, restructurings or relocations in other provinces) rather than bankruptcy.

For *commercial banks* insolvency proceedings can only be opened once insolvency has been declared and once PBOC has approved of the proceedings (*Commercial Banking Law*). In those cases, seniority is as follows: first come salaries and social insurance, then deposits of private persons and interest payments to lenders (Art. 71). Apart from the rules above, China has issued the *Rules on dissolution of banks*. Dissolution can be ordered for a number of reasons including unlawful activities, mismanagement, and not only inability to repay debts. The rules describe the process of dissolution and management of the dissolved entity, but do not actually regulate debts issues. Because authorities have in the past always preferred, in the sake of social peace, to use other instruments, Wormuth (2004) speaks of "asset shifting".

The promulgation of a *new bankruptcy law* which has been in gestation since 1996 has been mainly delayed by the lack of a social security system and the unresolved issue of SOEs' treatment. In October 2004 it was reviewed in a second reading by the NPC, and was expected to become reality within 2005, but has been delayed again. Nonetheless the new law appears highly promising because it widens the scope of applicability to any type of legal person (only private persons are not included). The insolvency should be declared based on a simple cash flow test: cession of debt payments is a signal of the inability to repay debts. The institutional position of all creditors (also for those minority creditors) has been strengthened by giving them the possibility to cease the debtor's business. Finally the new law emphasises methods and means for restructuring entities that can be rescued: reorganisation (rehabilitation plan for the business), conciliation (compromise proposal to settle debts) can all be proposed by the creditors and/or the debtor (PwC, 2004d).

Asset management companies

In 1999, after the Asian crisis, the Chinese regime established four[1] Asset Management Companies (AMCs) to deal with NPLs in state-owned banks (one AMC for each SOCB). Such schemes were initially not available to other banks. The purpose of these AMCs was to help restore the originating bank's loan portfolio quality, to clean up the banks' balance sheets, to centralise the disposal of NLPs, to opt for faster methods in resolving the NPL issue and to sell out some NPLs in open auctions.

The state-owned banks have transferred in 1999 an initial CNY 1.4 trln of NPLs to the AMCs. For loans originated before 1996, the AMCs purchased NPLs at face value from SOCBs supported by central bank cash. In return, banks received notes issued by the AMCs to the PBOC (carrying interest) and consequently the PBOC funds the losses incurred on the NPLs (Griffiths, 2005). The four SOCBs sold further NPLs to the four AMCs in the following years. In total, between 1999 and 2005, the banks sold CNY 2.2 trln in NPLs (Yu N., 2005d). The latest string of NPL sales to AMCs (prior to the listing of BoC and CCB) has used a simpler scheme: PBOC paid 50% of the face value in cash and the bidding AMC transferred the recovered amount to PBOC later (Yan M., 2005).

The AMCs have a range of other possible means to deal with non-performing assets: legal disposal, sales of collateral, debt restructuring, debt for equity swaps, sales of asset bundles, disposal by a trust or liquidation. Initially, most loans were sold through auctions and securitisations. NPLs sales that have occurred in the past were sales of loan bundles to a small number of investors (including foreigners) in private bidding processes. The disposals of NPLs (through sales and securitisations) have been largely restricted, despite the large amounts of NPLs in the banking sector and despite the willingness of foreign investors to participate in the distressed debt market (PwC, 2004c; Shih V. *et al.*, 2005a; PwC, 2006). Restrictions, such as lack of open sales and high minimum prices set by the authorities, have made further deals more difficult. A strong impediment to NPL sales is the requirement that they should not be sold below their net book value. Thus SOCBs do not have strong incentives to sell large amounts of NPLs (Rodman and Chan, 2004).

The recovery rates were initially 32.5% for Huarong, 24% for Great Wall and 35.1% for Cinda. In 2001, these were reported to be on average 20.9% (Gaenssmantel, 2003). Up to March 2005, AMCs had resolved on average 49.4% of all NPLs they had taken over (Huarong 52.6%, Great Wall 61.8%, Orient 39.9%, Cinda 41.2% – as calculated by Yan M., 2005). The better loans have now been sold out, thus begins a difficult period where recovery rates will decrease and where new ways will have to be found. At the end of 2005, there remained an estimated USD 105 bln on the AMCs' books, that is 6% of GDP (PwC, 2006).

The AMCs enjoy favourable taxation, fees structures and support in the courts and can thus dispose more efficiently of bad assets. However, they are still facing a number of basic challenges:

- Inadequate legal environment: lack of a law specific to the AMCs (there are only administrative rules), thus their status is not fully clear[2] (Li D., 2006); uncertain collateral realisation (Shih V. *et al.*, 2005a).
- Strong local government interference (Li D., 2006): no separating line drawn; AMCs require approval[3] for each foreign sale (a cumbersome and lengthy process where the outcome is uncertain, Shih V. *et al.*, 2005a).
- Questionable asset valuations in China (Li D., 2006).
- Lack of a defined future: these should be dissolved in 2009, thus the employees have little incentives to work towards their end (Shih V. *et al.*, 2005a).
- Little rights in managing the companies they have to restructure and take over: they lack voting rights and rights for intervening in enterprises' restructurings (Li D., 2006). The AMCs did not take over their owner responsibilities, thus the ownership mechanism and pressure did not have any effect (owners were neither interested nor allowed to take any influence or control on management, on operations and on assets) (Steinfeld, 2005).

- Lack of differentiation between often conflicting commercial and governmental goals and measures (Li D., 2006).
- Lack of incentive to introduce deeper reforms to ward off NPLs: often cash is used to resolve NPLs, rather than using long-term means (Shih V. *et al.*, 2005).

Markets are not well established and do not provide useful instruments: the primary market is dominated by the four AMCs, while the secondary market lacks transparency, liquidity, discipline and intermediaries (Li D., 2006).

Finally, debt–equity swaps have had a perverse effect: they restored the SOEs' balance sheets, reduced their indebtedness to normal levels and stripped the pressure from interest repayments (Steinfeld, 2005). Thus the SOEs were actually able to seek loans from SOCBs, which had previously sold their old debts with these companies to the AMCs (the SOEs are then meeting the required financial ratio standards, they have shown that they receive the state's support and finally the banks help AMCs out, by providing cash to the SOEs taken over by AMCs).

The future of the AMCs is still being discussed. Originally it was clear that once they would have sold off their non-performing assets, the companies would be dissolved. However, over the years they have proved to be doing a job that would still make sense in the future. Thus the closing down of the AMCs is an option, but an unlikely one. Other options for the future could be to transform them into fully commercial entities or to regroup them into one commercial company while another separate entity would still keep its policy focus (the focus could be to specialise in NPL disposal, to establish an entity similar to an investment bank, or to become a debt and corporate restructurer or servicer, Li D., 2006).

The strengthening of bankruptcy proceedings, the establishment of a claim prioritisation from which AMCs can benefit and the establishment of clear practices for AMCs (McIver, 2005) would enhance AMCs' prospects. Local authorities have also chosen in some cases similar schemes which used asset prices reflecting closer the reality and achieved better results (such as in the case of Yufu Asset Operation Company in Chongqing, see Zhang Y. and Li Z., 2006).

Corporate governance principles (OECD)

The principles were first developed in 1998 together with national governments and international institutions. Subsequently these have been accepted as the basis for corporate governance initiatives and have also been recognised as standards for financial institutions. The aim is to help governments in any country to "[...] evaluate and improve the legal, institutional and regulatory framework for corporate governance [...]". While the focus is on all types of listed companies, these can also be applied to private or state-owned ones. The principles define corporate governance as "... one key element in improving economic efficiency and growth as well as enhancing investor confidence. Corporate governance involves a set of relationships between a company's management, its board, its shareholders and other stakeholders. Corporate governance also provides the structure through which the objectives of the company are set, and the means of attaining those objectives and monitoring performance are determined" (OECD, 2004a: 11). Corporate governance involves choosing the right incentives and with respect of interests of all stakeholders. While the stress of the term *stakeholders* lies in management team and shareholders, the other stakeholders (minority shareholders, employees, etc.) are also important players. For stakeholders it should be the goal to achieve a fair treatment as well as exercising their rights. The principles, which are not binding, intend to cover different existing models of corporate governance.

Principles:

- Promotion of market transparency and efficiency, fully in accordance with the rule of law, establishment of a supportive legal infrastructure (drafting of laws should include consultation with concerned parties, ensure that a long-term view is taken for assessing impact, effective enforcement), clear division of responsibilities among authorities (avoid conflicts of interests and over-regulation, ensure professionalism and expertise).
- Ensure that shareholders can exercise their rights (including ownership and property rights (through representation), share transfers, information disclosure, participation in decisions, share profits, monitor the accountability of management).
- Equal treatment of all shareholders, independently of their shareholdings, geographic origin and location or legal status; ensure respect of creditor rights.
- Encourage participation and cooperation to create efficient and sound enterprises (through ex ante and ex post actions).
- Information disclosure timeliness and accurateness (for material issues such as financial statements, managers' incentives and remuneration, strategic changes and decisions, related parties transactions, operational changes, ownership structures, management involvement and loyalties, and any other risk factors; establishing a continuous dialogue, supporting informed decisions, ensure transparency).
- Ensure steering and monitoring of the company and its management (observing the rights of all parties, duty of care and duty of loyalty of the board of directors, standards for the board of directors including strategic guidance and decisions, monitoring their implementation and the progress of the company, overseeing management, aligning stakeholders' interests, monitoring the compliance with the above standards).

These standards stress the importance of independent control mechanisms (such as outsiders on the board, of auditors, etc.), the importance of information disclosure, the importance of designing efficient incentives structures to all stakeholders.

Source: Based on OECD, 2004a.

Corporate governance standards for banks (BIS)

The standards are guidance tools for banks and regulators worldwide and are based on OECD principles and have been adapted to the specificities of banks. The governance structure is defined as composed of a board of director and senior management, which should stand in general for oversight and management functions. The documents take the same definition for corporate governance as the OECD. Corporate governance influences a bank's operations, strategy, accountability, activities and behaviours, and ensures the protection of depositors. "Effective corporate governance practices are essential to achieving and maintaining public trust and confidence in the banking system, which are critical to the proper functioning of the banking sector and economy as a whole" (BIS, 2006: 4).

Transparency and checks and balances are central to a functioning corporate governance structure. It involves the independence of risk management and the oversight and supervision of the board.

Sound corporate governance principles:

1. Qualification and professionalism of board members (may require the establishment of specialised committees to advise and support the board's decisions), responsibilities include the oversight of the company strategy and operations, avoidance of conflicts of interests, promote safety and soundness, avoid involvement in day to day operations.
2. Board approves and oversees strategic goals and corporate values to be infused throughout the bank (should pay special attention to conflict of interests within the bank, related parties transactions, preferential treatment terms, and dealing with such issues within the bank, ensure independence within the bank, and ensure information disclosure).
3. Board designs responsibilities and reporting structures, ensuring accountability.
4. Board oversees management and ensures that there is no contradiction between board decisions and likelihood of implementing these, ensure professionalism at management level.
5. Use independent reports and audits to review the bank and identify issues and problems, ensuring also that auditors have a favourable work environment, maintain sound control functions, direct reporting of internal audit department.
6. Design remuneration and incentives policies that are in accord with company goals and objectives (based on policy, oriented towards the long term, avoid unnecessary risk taking).
7. Transparency (incl. adequate, timely and accurate disclosures that are proportionate to the bank and the materiality of changes). Information (apart from financial information) disclosed should include board composition, ownership structure, organisational structure, incentives structures, code of conduct, conflicts of interests.
8. Understanding of bank's operations and risks (arising from legal structures where operations are undertaken, from type of products offered, should ensure appropriate policies and procedures, supported by efficient structures), regularly oversee and evaluate the operations, ensure implementation of procedures, etc.

Role of supervisors:

- Bank guidance in implementing corporate governance structures
- Consider the interests of stakeholders other than the shareholders
- Judge whether banks have sound corporate governance structures

- Assess bank auditing functions
- Assess the integration of a bank within another group of companies or banks
- Bring to the attention of the board issues that necessitate their intervention
- Promote an environment that encourages sound practices.

Source: Based on BIS, 2006.

Postal savings

The postal savings system is intrinsically linked to the Chinese post office. At the end of June 2005 the postal system sat on savings deposits amounting to CNY 1.2 trillion, that is 9.25% of all savings deposits in China. It had a network of around 36,000 branches in 2468 counties in 31 provinces. This represented a large chunk of financial institutions in rural areas and served some 250 mln individuals with 7000 bank cards (*Southern Daily*, 2006). It is the largest deposit institution in rural areas and its deposits collected come to 90% from rural areas (Yan M., 2005). The postal system has around 500,000 employees (Ren B., 2005a). The postal savings system has a nationwide coverage and provides efficient, computerised remittances to any other outlet of the network. It is the largest remittance network in China (*China Postal Savings News*, 2006).

The postal system was established in 1953. Already in 1986 a first reform was introduced with the separation between PBOC and postal savings. At that time it had the function to attract excess liquidity in the system. It takes only deposits which are then deposited with PBOC where it can earn its spread (Yan M., 2005). In the early 1990s fresh proposals were made to reform and restructure it. The establishment of a new bank (*Southern Daily*, 2006), is expected for the second half of 2006, since both regulators and State Council have given their green light (*Asia Pulse*, 2006b). Under the name of POSBank (Post Office Savings Bank), it will become China's fifth largest bank in terms of assets. The focus of the new bank will be the provision of basic financial products, including loans, to urban and rural customers. It has already started trial lending activities in selected areas in April 2006 with loan amounts not exceeding CNY 100,000 and maturities of less than a year (*Dow Jones International News*, 2006).

For a long period of time, the deposits collected by the postal savings system were all deposited at PBOC at a subsidised rate of 4.6% p.a., and from August 2003 onwards 4.131% p.a. (for the first CNY 829 bln, while the newly collected deposits earned only the same as other financial institutions' deposits). Because of the large available funds, special attention in the reform process will be given to the management of funds in view of the new risks taken (Ren B., 2005b).

The postal savings system is now free to dispose of its resources and has increasingly invested them in deposits with other rural financial institutions as well as policy banks and in government bonds. Diversifying investment channels is difficult because of the lack of safe alternatives, the low level of experience of the savings system staff in that area, and the lack of proper risk management mechanisms (Ren B., 2005b).

The reform blueprint for the postal savings system into a full-fledged bank is not yet fully known because the separation between savings and postal activities poses a challenge. How will the postal office generate sufficient revenues in the future (because the finance arm of the postal office accounts for a 30% of its income) and how will the current network as well as the pool of employees be physically shared between office and bank? (Ren B., 2005a). There will be three entities spun off the old postal savings system: the Ministry for Post, the post office and the postal savings bank. In future the postal savings bank will become a fully fledged bank, independent and subject to banking regulatory requirements (Ren B., 2005b).

Rural cooperative funds (RCFs) – dismantled

The RCFs were established in the early 1980s to manage the funds of dismantled rural communes (they can be characterised as fund cooperatives owned by collectives and households, Cheng E. *et al.*, 2003). These are (quasi-) formal institutions: they were not regulated under the PBOC and operated without its approval, but had received permission in a 1986 central document, rules were set by the Ministry of Agriculture, complied with more or less the same prudential rules as for other FIs (Cheng E. *et al.*, 2003). Idle funds from former communes and individuals were managed by RCFs: they were similar to mutual funds in that they were not allowed to take deposits (but did it anyway, Girardin, 1997). These were operated by local authorities (by their respective local Agricultural Economic Management Station) at township level (Girardin, 1997). This also meant that they did not have to comply with reserve requirements as, for example, RCCs.

The RCFs showed a strong growth until the mid-1990s. In 1997 total deposits amounted to CNY 200 bln. The development was not that strong in all provinces, but RCFs accounted for 2.92% of all bank deposits in 1997. Their operational model had the following characteristics:

- lending only to members depositing money and those within their local reach
- employed agents to gather necessary information about borrowers
- credit limits where function of creditworthiness, enterprise size and manager character.

The model resulted in lower costs than at RCCs, higher returns and better portfolio quality, better financial intermediation than other rural FIs (Cheng E. *et al.*, 2003). While not all of them were fully successful, the model showed its commercial viability. In 1999, the State Council decided to dissolve them because of mismanagement (authorities were loosing control and NPLs were reaching unsustainable levels of 20%) and because they posed a competitive threat to the RCCs. The dismantling of RCFs reduced the local governments' budgets (which had to pay for the losses incurred) and sources of financing (Kwong and Lee, 2005). These were recuperated by RCCs and this meant losses amounting to 10% of the RCCs total assets (or CNY 108.3 bln) in 2000.

Their dissolution took place despite their push of competition in rural areas and the departure from previous lending practices in rural areas (in terms of interest rates, lending and taking deposits locally, etc.). RCFs were as semi-informal financial institutions in rural areas the source of a number of financial innovations (Holz, 2001). Their overhaul was more a sign of supervisory failure (no recognition of innovations, no learning from their failure and no specific regulatory framework for this type of institutions) rather than the failure of an actually competitive and innovative model (Cheng E. *et al.*, 2003).

Corporate governance requirements in rural FIS

Table: A.7 Corporate governance requirements in rural financial institutions

Mechanism	Responsibilities and function	Composition and further requirements
General shareholders' meeting	Highest organ of the FI. Defines and changes the statutes; determines the procedure rules; nominates/removes BoD, its chairman and SB (including their remuneration); approves work reports from SB and BoD; approves the development, operation and investment plan, the budget, the repartition of dividends or losses; decides to reduce or increase capital; decides the separation/merger/ dissolution/liquidation of the FI.	Meeting at least within 6 months of the closing of the year. Decisions are passed with a 2/3 majority for changes on statutes and separation, merger, dissolution, or liquidation of the FI (otherwise simple majority required).
BoD	Organises the shareholders' meeting and reports its work; implements the meeting's decisions; proposes the bank's operational plan and investment plan; proposes the repartition of losses/gains, the budget, or increases/decreases of capital; proposes the organisational structure, the basic management system; nominates the bank director (together with 2–3 vice-directors) and his remuneration; proposes any plans for merger/ dissolution/etc.	Composed of 7–19 members: bank employees should not make less than 1/4 and no more than 1/3 of the BoD, natural persons other than employees should not make less than 1/4 of BoD. Nominated for 3 years. Independent directors should also be on board, they should take special care of the rights of small shareholders and of depositors. BoD should meet at least 4 times a year. Each director must participate at least twice a year.
SB	Oversees BoD and senior management, can require BoD and senior management to rectify any actions (must be reported to shareholders); conducts auditing and inquiries of senior managers' and BoD's work; ensures audit of financial activities, of operational decisions, of risk management and internal controls; proposes a special shareholders meeting.	SB is composed of 5–9 members and includes representatives of the employees (no more than 1/3, chosen by meeting of employees) and of the shareholders (chosen by shareholders meeting). Members should not be from the BoD, senior management or finance and risk management. Appointed for 3 years.

Bank Director	Proposes senior managers, submits on behalf of senior management operational plan and organisation to BoD, delegates rights/responsibilities to senior managers to take upon operations, reports to BoD and SB any important events and takes action. Bank director is responsible before the BoD.	All activities should be audited yearly and reports submitted to BoD and SB.

Source: Based on References for Laws 23, 24, and 25.

Microfinance

Microfinance in China is mainly regarded as a poverty alleviation tool and thus the involvement of government agencies is strong and most projects often target the poorest farmers and counties in China (Situ, 2003). In urban areas a few microfinance schemes also target disadvantaged individuals such as laid-off workers. Programmes often take the form of modified Grameen Bank replications under the lead of either international NGOs or development institutions. Microfinance can be considered as still being in an experimentation phase (Shen M. and Cheng E., 2004).

At the end of the third quarter of 2005, some 71 mln Chinese farmers (i.e. 32% of all farmers, but double this percentage has lending requirements) had small or microloans outstanding amounting to CNY 567.6 bln (i.e. 37% of total loans in these areas, Jiao J., 2006). Almost half of these are short-term loans. Loans are small, on average between CNY 500–3000 and often require groups as collateral substitute as well as frequent repayments. Most of the government funds earmarked for microfinance schemes are channelled through RCCs.

Microfinance schemes in China suffer from very high NPLs ratios: between 12 and 24%, depending on the province (Brandt *et al.*, 2005b). They also are likely to charge high interest rates, higher than in other rural financial institutions, at around 12–18% (Shen M. and Cheng E., 2004).

The state took interest in microfinance as a poverty alleviation tool in the 1990s and has started only in the last years to actively promote it. The first microfinance programme was established in Hebei province in 1993 as an experiment with the Rural Development Institute of the Chinese Academy of Social Sciences (CASS).

International NGOs and development institutions also participate in the development of microfinance schemes. By 2004 there were more than 200 donor-funded programmes all over China, mainly in poor rural regions and counties (Shen M. and Cheng E., 2004). Donors cooperate with a local partner, which is often engaged in poverty alleviation work.

There are no specific regulations for microfinance institutions, although regulations are being drafted. Microfinance projects are based on single programmes and do not take institutionalised forms (Shen M. and Cheng E., 2004). Most programmes are of small scale, funds average between CNY 1–1.5 mln (Shen M. and Cheng E., 2004).

For Park *et al.* (2003), microfinance in China has been in some cases successful but suffers from a number of deficiencies: unclear status of NGOs in China, lack of specific regulations for microfinance and tight regulations for financial markets (Du X., 2005), as well as the lack of capacity in mainstream financial institutions for microfinance. Chinese microfinance lacks scale, flexibility (in that it is predominantly oriented towards group lending), outreach (poor households are only for a part reached), management experience, efficient information systems. Microfinance also suffers in China from poor governance in banks and lack of repayment incentives, capped interest rates, high level of short-term poverty alleviation orientation, and lack of clear government policy.

Basel II, the New Capital Accord

Table A.8 Basel Capital Accord[4]

	1988 Basel Accord: Basel I	2004 Basel Accord: Basel II
Objectives	To harmonise capital requirements for banks, to strengthen the sound and stable development of the banking system, and to reduce competitive inequalities among banks	To promote the safety and soundness of financial institutions, especially banks, to align more closely capital levels to actual risks incurred in the course of business by setting more risk-sensitive standards, to ensure competitive equality among institutions, and to enable and incentivise banks in using a more comprehensive approach to risk management. Raise market discipline by increasing transparency. It takes a much more distanced approach and lets banks realise how much risks they (wish to) take and how to manage these. Make bank more independent, responsible and self-reliant in terms of risk management.
Observance	Voluntary, does not have legal force, recognised in most countries in the world	Voluntary, does not have legal force. It applies to internationally active banks. Implementation is intended for January 2007 and some 88 non-BIS member countries which have also indicated their intention to implement the Accord.
Minimum capital requirements	Capital ratio = capital/risk-weighted assets >= 8%, some national regulators have taken the freedom to increase the required level to 11 or 12% (Brazil, Oman e.g.). Risk-weighted assets are the bank's exposures weighted according to their riskiness.	
Definition of capital	Tier 1 capital (core capital) = paid-in capital, preference shares and disclosed reserves (represent at least 50% of a bank's total capital). Tier 2 capital (supplementary capital) = perpetual securities, unrealised gains and losses, hybrid capital instruments, long-term subordinated debt (not exceed 50% of	

	tier 2 capital) and hidden reserves. Tier 3 capital = short-term subordinated debt eligible under certain conditions and to be used to cover market risk (limited to 250% of tier 1 capital).	
Scope	Credit risk, later also market risk	Pillar 1: minimum capital requirements (taking into account credit, market and operational risks), Pillar 2: supervisory review process, Pillar 3: market discipline
Operational risk	Not taken into account	New, with three different approaches, qualification criteria apply (see below).
Market risk	Recognises innovative models developed by banks to measure market risk (based on value-at-risk). The amendment on Basel I required banks to follow qualitative standards for the management of market risk as well as quantitative standards to measure the potential highest loss over a 10-day horizon.	
Risk weights	Few categories of risk weights depending on the type and origin of the borrower and of exposure. Off-balance sheets exposures are taken into account through risk weights and credit conversion factors.	Used under the standardised approach: Risk weights applied to each claim reflect the rating of that borrower or transaction. All unrated claims carry a 100% risk-weight. Credit conversion factors continue to apply to contingent claims.
Risk mitigation methods	Use of netting agreements only	Use of collateral (depending on maturity, currency, originator, etc.), netting arrangements (which were already available under the first capital Accord), guarantees and credit derivatives, and maturity mismatching. Haircuts, to account for risk mitigation, can be estimated by the bank itself or provided by the regulators as guidelines or required inputs.
Credit risk	Measured by risk weights, very simple approach. Regulatory arbitrage possible.	**Pillar 1**: more risk-sensitive. Three different approaches, incentives to move to more sophisticated credit risk management. All exposures must be rated.
Supervisory review	Not envisaged	**Pillar 2**: Regulatory review of meeting requirements and capital adequacy; early intervention promoted; principles for regulators for assessing the adequacy of banks' risk management techniques, standards and structures. Supervisors should encourage banks to develop

Table A.8 (Continued)

	1988 Basel Accord: Basel I	2004 Basel Accord: Basel II
		finer techniques to manage risks and should not prescribe a defined model. Banks must demonstrate the adequacy and effectiveness of their risk management.
Market discipline	Not envisaged	**Pillar 3**: to encourage more formalised information disclosure to banks' stakeholders. Part of the disclosure is mandatory. The information should entail details of the scope of application, capital structure and adequacy, credit risk and its mitigation, securitisation, other types of risks (market, operational, etc.).
Compliance requirements	No requirements in terms of good governance and of data (quality and quantity).	Sophisticated systems/controls and data collection. Each bank must show that the chosen system is able to recognise, differentiate, measure and manage adequately each type of risk incurred. Banks can choose from a wide range of methods the one that is best adapted to their needs, environment and capacities. Well-documented credit methodologies, policies and procedures.
NPLs	No specific treatment	Loans that are overdue for more than 90 days receive different risk weights, depending on the loss provisions raised (as a % of the outstanding amount).
Challenges	Inadequate differentiation of credit risk, lack of recognition of the probability of default of a borrower, of risks linked to various maturities, of hedging instruments, of collateral, of internal risk management processes, and of portfolio diversification.	**Data** (Qualitative as well as quantitative data is lacking in banks. Data is scarce when it comes to default track records and migration data. The collected data needs to be reliable, complete, accessible, detailed and available in sufficient amounts.) and **validation** (since credit defaults are relatively rare, it is very difficult to draw conclusions from historical data but banks should start with a comparison between the past rating and the current situation based on rating migration matrices).

For further research	Issue of double default (when borrower and risk mitigant both default), definition of eligible capital and innovations, use of regulatory capital vs. economic capital to calculate adequate buffers, and stress testing of risk parameters such as LGD.
Corporate governance	*Core Principles for Effective Banking Supervision*, 1997: Rating and estimation processes and procedures must be documented and approved by bank's board of directors. Senior management responsible for daily operations and implementation of risk management. Risk management function must be independent (responsibilities: overview of rating systems, reporting of risk profiles and activities, procedures around the management of risk and reviewing/updating of the relevant processes). Internal ratings are used for setting approval limits, internal controls, loan loss provisions, capital allocation and corporate governance functions. Ensure effective monitoring and work-out processes and procedures. Inputs must be validated regularly.

Table A.9 Risk approaches and parameters under the Basel Accord

	Credit risk approaches		
	Standardised approach (SA)	**Foundation IRB (F-IRB)**	**Advanced IRB (A-IRB)**
Description	Much akin to that of Basel I but based on externally available credit ratings.	Three steps: estimation of risk factors, mapping of these risk factors into risk weights and finally compliance with all relevant basic requirements. F-IRB and A-IRB differ in their depth and breadth of use of external vs. internal inputs or estimates for different types of products and borrowers.	
Risk parameters	External ratings from national or international rating agencies.	PD generated internally, others given by regulators.	All generated internally.
Risk mitigants	Some types of collateral recognised (especially real estate).	Similar terms as for SA.	No restrictions on the type of collateral to be used.
Requirements		Differentiation of credit risk between borrower and transaction (minimum 7 grades for performing loans and	Same as F-IRB but further includes: Differentiation, criteria for estimation and

Table A.9 (Continued)

	Credit risk approaches		
	Standardised approach (SA)	**Foundation IRB (F-IRB)**	**Advanced IRB (A-IRB)**
		minimum 1 grade for NPLs, no more than 30% of gross exposures should fall in any single grade). Each borrower must be assigned a rating before loan origination, procedure to update rating regularly depending on rating. Comprehensive documentation of process, standards and so on. Rating used for approval process, in pricing, for internal limits, for stress-testing, demonstrate use of systems for at least three years. Internal validation required	assignment of other risk parameters, minimum data observation of seven years, adequate consideration of collateral.
	Operational risk approaches		
	Basic indicator approach	**Standardised approach**	**Advanced measurement approach**
Calculation	Capital charge = 15% of average of gross income over three years	Capital charge = sum of charge for each business line based on gross income	Capital charge generated internally taking into account internal and external loss data, scenario analysis, and risk mitigation (up to 20% possible)
Requirements	No specific criteria, compliance with BIS "Sound practices for the management and supervision of operational risk"	Active involvement of board of directors and senior management, existence of specialised function based on sound OpRisk management processes, systematic gathering of loss data	Same as standardised, plus: measurement integrated in day-to-day risk management, numerous quantitative standards, 3–5 years of historical data required

	For operational and credit risk approaches	
	Basic approaches	**More complex approaches**
Advantages	Circumvents data and validation challenges, simplified.	More risk-sensitive. More closely adapted to the bank's own strategy, lower capital requirements to be expected. More accurate view of risk incurred. Higher capacity to withstand crises and to respond adequately and timely to challenges. Increase investors' confidence. Wealth of information generated for business. Better market access. Higher transparency.
Disadvantages	Higher capital requirements, less risk-sensitive. Less competitive. Issue of "competitive inequality". Lack of credit agencies coverage in many countries or for smaller enterprises.	Expensive. Requires high amount of data. Higher probability of fraud (use of systems that bring about lower capital requirements). Not calibrated for emerging markets. Issue of "competitive inequality". High requirements on management capabilities. Possible greater volatility of capital. Issues of stress testing and validation.

Table A.10 Risk components or parameters for each exposure

	Probability of default (PD)	**Loss given default (LGD)**	**Exposure at default (EAD)**	**Maturity (M)**
Definition	The probability of default reflects the likelihood of a borrower to default within a set period of time and is often linked to the risk rating of the borrower.	Loss given default quantifies the loss incurred by the lender at the time of default (expressed as percentage, or one minus recovery rate). LGD depends on borrower's capital structure, collateral, business	The exposure at default quantifies the total exposure of the lender at the time of default (this is especially important for marked-to-market instruments	Maturity is viewed as similar to duration.

Table A.10 (Continued)

	Probability of default (PD)	Loss given default (LGD)	Exposure at default (EAD)	Maturity (M)
		cycle and industry. Expressed as transaction risk rating.	and commitments or contingent liabilities).	
Calculation	PD = Number of borrowers with rating n that defaulted/ total number of borrowers with that rating	Loss given default = (workout expenses + outstan ding loan amount + interest foregone – realisation value of collateral)/ outstanding loan amount	EAD is calculated as the "committed but undrawn amount multiplied by a credit conversion factor (75%)" (BCBS, 2004a: 67).	Effective maturity (M) is determined for each exposure depending on the cash flow schedule. Maturity is defined as 2.5 years under the F-IRB.
Requirements	Use mapping to external credit ratings, internal default experience and statistical default models. Observation period = minimum 5 years from at least one source.	Under F-IRB: LGD = 45% for senior claims, 75% = subordinated claims. Observation period = last seven years at least from any source.	Calculate long-run averages. Should include any material driver or factor. Observation period = same as for LGD.	

Definitions and capital requirements calculations in the Basel II Accord

Risk-weighted assets are calculated in the same fashion as for Basel I: Risk-weighted assets (RWA) = $\sum_i i \times Ni$. (For each asset *i*, there is a notional principal amount *N* and a corresponding risk weight ω.)

Under the IRB approaches, the calculation takes into account the borrower, its rating, the collateral and the transaction type. The risk-based capital (RBC) ratio is then defined as:

$$\text{RBC ratio} = \frac{\text{capital under consideration of estimated losses}}{\text{RWA} \times 1.06}$$

In this equation, 1.06 represents a granularity adjustment to take into account risk mitigation. This may be adjusted by the Committee in the course of implementation. We have

$$\text{Risk-weighted asstes (RWA)} = K \times 12.5 \times \text{EAD}$$

where, for a performing exposure we have capital requirement (K)=

$$\left\{\text{LGD} \times N\left[(1-R)^{-0.5} \times G(\text{PD}) + \left(\frac{R}{1-R}\right)^{0.5} \times G(0.999)\right] - \text{PD} \times \text{LGD}\right\} \times (1 - 1.5 \times b)^{-1} \times [1 + M - 2.5 \times b]$$

N is the standard normal distribution and G is the inverse of the standard normal distribution first applied to PD to derive the default threshold [G(PD)] and secondly applied to confidence level to derive the conservative value of the systemic factor [G(0.999)] (BCBS, 2005).

$$\text{Correlation}(R) = 0.12 \times \frac{1-e^{-50 \times \text{PD}}}{1-e^{-50}} + 0.24 \times \left(1 - \frac{1-e^{-50 \times \text{PD}}}{1-e^{-50}}\right)$$

$$\text{Maturity adjustment } (b) = [0.11852 - 0.05478 \times \text{In}(\text{PD})]^2$$

$$\text{Effective maturity } (M) = \frac{\sum_t t \times CF_t}{\sum_t CF_t}$$

For SME exposures a firm size adjustment (F) is available: $F = 0.04 \times \left(1 - \frac{S-5}{45}\right)$ where S is the total annual sales expressed in EUR mln. In that case R becomes Correlation

$$(R) = 0.12 \times \frac{1-e^{-50 \times \text{PD}}}{1-e^{-50}} + 0.24 \times \left(1 - \frac{1-e^{-50 \times \text{PD}}}{1-e^{-50}}\right) - 0.04 \times \left(1 - \frac{S-5}{45}\right)$$

For retail exposures (IRB approaches), we have

$$\text{Capital Requirement } (K) = \left\{\text{LGD} \times N\left[(1-\text{R})^{-0.5} \times G(\text{PD}) + \left(\frac{R}{1-R}\right)^{0.5} \times G(0.999)\right] - \text{PD} \times \text{LGD}\right\}$$

$$\text{Correlation}(R) = 0.03 \times \frac{1-e^{-35 \times PD}}{1-e^{-35}} + 0.16 \times \left(1 - \frac{1-e^{-35 \times PD}}{1-e^{-35}}\right).$$

Table: A.11 Evaluation of Basel II

Positive points	**Criticisms**
Important innovation in risk management	Set value for correlation despite lack of data and lack of sensitivity as a result. Question of whether diversification (geographic, by industry, by maturities, by collateral etc.) within a loan portfolio is sufficiently incentivised. Diversification and correlation are not sufficiently reflected in capital calculations. Scaling factor (absolute term) has been introduced to dampen the capital reductions. Is it still purveying the right incentives?
More active and responsive quantitative risk management	Mapping a rating is critical for using the results downstream. Mapping is largely influenced by assumptions made for each model and each of its inputs (depending on the expert judgement, on the likelihood of default of a borrower, on different rating scales, weightings and methodologies; depending on target credit markets and countries).
Integrate international best practices	Operational risk: lack of data and experience. Questioning adequacy of a single ratio for operational risk while qualitative methods in managing operational risk would have more impact.
Increase of sensitivity to and knowledge about risk management	Less sophisticated banks will be inclined to use less risk-sensitive and complex approaches, so they might attract higher-risk borrowers which would be rejected by more sophisticated banks. This imbalance in the system would be produced by some banks having less appropriate capital for covering higher risk borrowers and some others carrying more adequate levels of capital (and less risky borrowers).
Banks will be less volume-driven and more risk-driven	SA over-reliant on credit rating agencies. Two issues arise: the professional capacity of rating agencies and the institutional capacity of regulators to effectively monitor them (especially in emerging markets).
More accurate and consistent capital allocation	Lending incentives: incentives arise for banks to lend to low-quality borrowers where premiums will be higher.
Promotes higher transparency and greater comparability among banks	Depends on how many countries implement the accord and how they will use their discretion right. If crucial points of the accord are implemented in different ways, then comparability and transparency might be negatively affected. Regulators will have to

	balance the objectives of Basel II with the necessity to adjust it to their national environments.
Move from a rules-based supervision to a process-based one	Lack of clear enforcement and clear sanctions: risk arbitrage by manipulating risk databases and internal rating systems, market discipline can only be effective when readers of the published information value it and have the power or capability to impose a negative cost on the bank when it publishes incomplete or incorrect information (moral hazard under the conditions of a deposit insurance system). Quantitative requirements can be set effectively for under-capitalised banks, but have only a marginal impact on the disclosure of well-capitalised banks.
Creation of competitive advantages	Competitive disadvantages for banks with less resources and capabilities (such as smaller ones or those in emerging markets, or those using less complex approaches).
Banks using risk weights reflecting the state of the economy move in tandem with economic cycles.	Researchers have wondered how much influence the Basel II accord will have on banks' behaviour over the economic cycle (pro-cyclicality). In economic downturns, banks are likely to find fewer borrowers with higher ratings and thus will lend less. The bank's own rating might also deteriorate and make capital raising for new business more difficult, so that the bank might need to restrain the use of its capital. Pro-cyclicality is reflected in all inputs which are critical to the implementation of Basel II. The choice of a rating system can itself highly influence pro-cyclicality.

Expected benefits	**Expected costs**
Higher effectiveness, competitiveness	Four possible areas which are likely to impact banks' profitability: charge-offs, margins and provisioning, operating expenses, risk mitigation.
More efficient, streamlined and integrated risk management process	Higher borrowing costs for low-quality borrowers
Increased ability to identify, measure and manage risks, pro-active risk management	Lower risk borrowers will tend to move to larger banks with the capability and resources to implement finer credit risk models
Reductions in required capital are different for banks with different types of portfolios, asset sizes, economic environment, legal environment (banking and tax issues, for example) and	Costs of the implementation of Basel II requirements include mainly two types of cost drivers: information technology-related costs and costs related to the

Table: A.11 (Continued)

finally, surely depend on the choice of approach. The more basic the model, the less onerous it will be but also the higher capital charge will be required.	employment of specialists. New costs: for small exposures previously not rated; increased communication costs; higher regulatory costs; and costs linked to the existence of pro-cyclicality.
QIS results show that on average, for all banks and all types of approaches, the likely reduction in capital required is in the 4–5% range (as based on EU data), but results show large discrepancies. On average, larger banks face lower reductions in capital than smaller ones. The standardised approach is not benefiting banks and even smaller banks are likely to find few incentives in the standardised approach. Larger institutions will benefit by using the advanced IRB approach, all others will not provide as much benefits, and smaller banks receive the highest reductions in capital requirements using the foundation IRB.	Costs will largely depend on: the current development stage of each bank, the legal environment, the bank size, the choice of risk management approach and the bank's loan portfolio structure.
For larger banks it may be more interesting to take the A-IRB approach, if their portfolio is geared more towards corporate SMEs and retail banking. For smaller banks with a large retail portfolio, the F-IRB would bring the largest benefits. Higher capital charges can be expected for low risk activities such as private banking and asset management because they face additional operational risk charges.	Cost estimates range from USD 1–100 mln range for a bank with an average balance sheet of USD 100 mln, or USD 100 mln for the initial implementation. Smaller banks should face lower costs (between EUR 30 and 60 mln).

General assumptions for Basel II impact estimation

Up to now in the literature, there has been no quantitative assessment of the impact of Basel II on Chinese banks. This is because of the lack of credit loss data compliant with Basel requirements that would make actual Basel II capital calculations exact and real. It is nevertheless possible to estimate the quantitative impact. This estimate would give an answer on one important incentive for implementing Basel II over the next few years.

One might argue that there are serious constraints to such estimates. This is completely true. In fact many simplifying assumptions need to be made in order to make the calculations feasible. Furthermore, Chinese banks will be analysed with regard to their present state, while full implementation is only likely in a few years. By then, the financial conditions of Chinese banks will have changed, their environment will have matured, and they will have more financial and human resources and understand better where the challenges lie.

Simplifying assumptions:

- takes into account credit risk only (thus final estimates would still require adjustment for other risks, such as market and operational risks),
- lending portfolio is made up of corporates, SMEs and retail loans (it thus does not take into account inter-bank lending and lending to sovereigns or quasi-sovereigns),
- not accounting for different risk weights assigned to different loan loss provisions,
- not differentiating between general and special loan loss provisions,
- does not account for risk grades distribution within a portfolio,
- only on-balance sheet exposures,
- does not account for the state of the economy (affecting the PD and LGD estimates).

The analysis will compare three approaches:

1. Basel I approach – assumptions: residential mortgages carry a risk weight of 50%, assumed as 9% of all loans.
   This calculation is necessary in order to understand the likely change from one Basel accord to another in terms of capital requirements.
2. Basel II standardised approach – assumptions:
   - 6.5% of the bank borrowers are estimated to be rated in China (Wu J., 2005), meaning that 93.5% of a loan portfolio of corporate borrowers will be risk weighted at 100%.
   - Risk weight for 6.5% borrowers: weight that represents the average of all ratings given by Basel II for corporate borrowers, that is 84%.
   - SMEs: 100% risk weight.
   - Retail exposures: 75% risk weight.
3. Basel II centralised IRB approach – assumptions.
   - For PD, because of lack of real data, figures from other countries will be taken: 1) the average default rate for 5 years for corporates in developing Asia is assumed to be 2.04% (Varma, 2004). 2) For SMEs, due to the lack of data the German weighted-average default rate is used as proxy (Dietsch and Petey, 2004): 2.69%. 3) Retail default rates were calculated by Jacobson, Linde and Roszbach (2004) for two Swedish banks, the average loss rate between the two is 0.78%.
   - For LGD, because of the difficulty to realise collateral and the high reliance of real estate as collateral if any, LGD will be set as 80%, implying a recovery rate of 20%, that is close to that of AMCs (on average for 2005 for all 4 AMCs, the asset recovery rate was 25.3% and the cash recovery rate was 20.8%) and reflecting the better position of AMCs in realising collateral.

– EAD: assumed as the actual loan amount.
– Maturity: average maturity of 2.5 years proposed by the BIS.
– Definition of SMEs: as defined by the China's National Bureau of Statistics SMEs, depending on their size, have sales averaging between CNY 100 mln (up to CNY 300 mln for the largest).

Cost of borrowings of Chinese banks – Assumptions and calculations

The cost of borrowings that Chinese banks receive from other international banks will also change following the implementation of the Basel II accord in countries where banks are headquartered which provide Chinese banks with credit lines.

Assumptions:

- LGD of 45% (as in F-IRB for senior claims)
- International bank aims at a 15% RoE
- Based on the international credit rating agencies' ratings for Chinese banks, these would result in a 50% or 100% risk weight.

From the above calculations (which are simplified and thus might not fully reflect the reality and do not account for customer relationship considerations), we can observe that the higher rated Chinese banks, that is the larger ones, are

Table A.12 Interest rates for loans to Chinese banks

	Basel I	Basel II – SA		Basel II – IRB		
		A+ to BBB–	BB+ to B–	A	BBB	BB
EAD	100	100	100	100	100	100
Risk weight (%)	20	50	100	18	65	145
Own funds (%)	1.6	4	8	1.44	5.2	11.6
Borrowed funds (%)	98.4	96	92	98.56	94.8	88.4
ROE (%)	15	15	15	15	15	15
Credit cost (%)	4	4	4	4	4	4
Net ROE (%)	11	11	11	11	11	11
Net cost of equity	0.176	0.44	0.88	0.1584	0.572	1.276
Interest rate (gross) (%)	**4.18**	**4.44**	**4.88**	**4.16**	**4.57**	**5.28**
Handling charges (%)	0.25	0.25	0.25	0.25	0.25	0.25
Risk premium (%)	1	1	2	1	2	3
Interest rate (net) (%)	**5.43**	**5.69**	**7.13**	**5.41**	**6.82**	**8.53**

Source: Own calculations based on Hennecke and Trück, 2005.

likely to win from the implementation of more complex approaches at internationally active banks and the smaller ones would benefit more by turning to less risk-sensitive banks for borrowings. For better banks the costs will be slightly lower (less than 1% difference). For the banks with the worst ratings among Chinese banks, the costs could increase substantially by 26 to 57%.

Cost of capital of Chinese banks – Assumptions and calculations

The cost of borrowing for Chinese banks will influence their overall cost of capital. The average balance sheet structure of banks in China shows that deposits make 83% of the balance sheet, while equity makes 4%.

Assumptions for the CAPM model:

- cost of deposits as PBOC interest rates: 2.25% for one year deposits
- risk-free rate as that of Chinese government Treasuries: short-term treasury notes yield between 2.12–3.14%
- required market return as represented by the average return on equity of Chinese banks: average RoE for the SOCBs, main JSCBs and some of the largest CCBs is 10.95%
- cost of equity estimated as ranging between 13.07%–14.09%
- tax rate of Chinese banks is 38%: business tax is 5% of revenue and income tax is 33% of profits.

Table A.13 Weighted average cost of capital for Chinese banks (under the current conditions)

	Average*	Cost	Tax rate	Weighted cost
Deposits (%)	83.47	2.25	38	1.17
Equity (%)	3.68	13.07–14.09		0.48–0.52
Other (%)	12.85	5.41–8.53		0.69–1.10
Total				**2.34–2.79**

* % of total assets.
Source: Own calculations.

Cost of borrowing for Chinese enterprises – Assumptions and calculations

As a consequence of higher weighted average cost of capital and of higher capital requirements for Chinese banks, the rates for lending to Chinese borrowers will be higher, all other things being equal, as banks transfer their higher costs to their customers. These are likely to be adjusted then for the true PD and LGD of each borrower.

Table A.14 Comparison of loan interest rates for Chinese borrowers

	Basel I	Basel II – SA	Basel II – IRB		
		Unrated	Corporate	SME	Retail
EAD	100	100	100	100	100
Risk weight (%)	100	100	16.62	15.85	5.81
Own funds	8	8	1.33	1.27	0.46
Borrowed funds	92	92	98.67	98.73	99.54
ROE (%)	10.95	10.95	10.95	10.95	10.95
Credit cost (%)	5.58	5.58	5.58	5.58	5.58
Net ROE (%)	5	5	5	5	5
Net cost of equity	0.4296	0.4296	0.0714	0.0681	0.0250
Interest rate (%)	**6.01**	**6.01**	**5.65**	**5.65**	**5.60**

Source: Own calculations based on Hennecke and Trück 2005.

Assumptions:

- banks' average return on equity: 10.95%
- base interest rate on loans: 5.58%
- PDs: 100% under the present accord, 100% as well for unrated claims under the SA – reflecting the fact that most enterprises are unrated, and 2.04, 2.69 and 0.78% on average for corporate, SME and retail claims under the IRB approach.

Compared with the simpler approach of Basel I and under the standardised approach, the borrowers are likely to win on average. Only risk weights of at least 100% would require higher interest rates.

Notes

1 Structure of the banking system

1. The State Council is the highest executive organ in the state administration. Under the State Council are ministries, commissions and bureaus. It is further represented through government authorities at provincial and local level. The National People's Congress (NPC) represents the legislature at national, regional and local levels. Current affairs are dealt with by their respective standing committees. The judicial power is represented by People's Courts. Preliminary administrative rules may be issued by the State Council, but the NPC must enact a proper law after a time (Wei W., 2005).
2. At the end of the references part, the reader will find a list of legal texts.
3. Two other banks have been granted a nationwide licence during that period, but were already existing entities: the result of either a name and business scope change (Hengfeng Bank, previously known as Yantai Housing Bank, approved in 2003, with total assets of CNY 37 bln as of December 2004 and concentrating in Shandong province) or a merger of a number of CCBs (Huishang Bank, created at the end of 2005 as a merger of local RCCs and CCBs).
4. These were established as joint ventures with foreign partners, such as Xiamen International Bank or Sino-German Bausparkasse.

2 Legal and regulatory environment

1. Central bank re-lending is an important tool of the state to adjust the timing and direction of financial flows in China (including disaster relief and any other policy-lending objective), especially in rural China (Park and Sehrt, 2001). The funds can also be directed at certain areas and to specific rural activities. Up to 2005, the central bank had issued CNY 1.02 trillion in relending, with more than CNY 146 bln issued each year on average, at the end of 2005, there were CNY 59.7 bln in such loans outstanding. Around 90% of these funds are designated for rural farmers and transferred through RCCs (*China Economic News Net*, 2006).
2. In April 2004, for example, CBRC released measures to curb growth and loan expansion in commercial banks. It required banks to disburse loans approved at the end of April only after the May holiday, and to reduce loans to infrastructure, natural resources and transportation industries. In May 2006, CBRC, together with other ministries, issued a further notice to constrain the growth of the so-called "bundle loans", that is fixed investment loans provided to local governments with their (illegal) guarantees (Guo Q. *et al.*, 2006b as well as Sun M., 2006).
3. Financial institutions under its supervision include commercial banks, credit cooperatives and policy banks that are also depositary institutions.

These furthermore include asset management companies, investment banks and trust institutions, finance companies and leasing institutions and any other financial institutions whose establishment has been approved by the State Council (see *Law on Banking Supervision and Administration*, Art. 2 §2–3).

4. At the end of the references part, the reader will find a list of legal texts.
5. A number of smaller institutions, based locally, have applied in the past for banking licences (EIU, 2006b). Up to now only Huishang Bank and Bohai Bank have been allowed to go ahead and regulators are moving cautiously in opening the domestic banking market to other private banks.
6. The CBRC collects supervisory fees amounting to a total of CNY 5 bln yearly from commercial banks (Shi C., 2004). The size of each bank's contribution reflects the depth and breath of supervisory work, depending on some 10 ratios (including size, operations, results, net assets, market share and level of riskiness). According to EIU (2006b), the fees are as follows: 0.2% on the first CNY 3 trillion of assets and 0.1% thereafter.
7. Rural financial institutions are excluded from these new rules. For credit cooperatives, the upper cap has been widened to 2.3 times, deposit rates are uncapped.
8. The following paragraphs are based on: *China Consumer Net*, 2005, *Xinhua Economic News*, 2005, *SinoCast China Business Daily News*, 2005, *Shanghai Securities Times*, 2004, *Dow Jones International News*, 2004, *Xinhua Net*, 2003 and Kelleher and Dyer, 2005, unless stated otherwise.
9. The data is based on short news published by the finance magazine *Caijing* in its January 23rd (2006) edition.
10. In the name of "state security", authorities could potentially enforce further strict requirements in terms of dissemination and reading of private information.
11. Loan certificates are issued by the PBOC to those enterprises which have a lending relationship with a financial institution. The information is then fed into a centralised database. For enterprises borrowing more than CNY 100 mln, PBOC requires an independent external rating.
12. Two publications cite 20 agencies currently operating, a number that came down from a high level of some 50 agencies, following mergers and closures (Chen and Everling, 2002; Wu J., 2005). Hong (2004) counts some 50 rating agencies while Wassmuth (2004) found some 90 agencies nationwide which were reduced to a current 50 agencies.

3 Exit mechanisms in banking

1. In practice some 90% of the proceedings are opened by debtors, because most creditors lack incentives to do so (Wormuth, 2004).
2. This case took 4 years to resolve and had an average recovery rate of 12.54 cents to the dollar (Wormuth, 2004).
3. The institutions targeted for closure are UCCs, whose names are not known (for fear of bank runs), located in Heilongjiang province (7 of them), Shanxi province (4), Xinjiang province (3) and one in each, Jiangxi, Yunnan and Jilin provinces.

4. The CBRC has classified CCBs according to their riskiness and profitability into six groups in order to increase specialisation in supervision. The repartition among the groups is as follows: first group: 31 banks, second: 18, third: 26, fourth: 30. The worst group is the sixth one. To this and the fifth group belong CCBs from Taiyuan, Qinhuang Island, Zhuhai, Fushun, Nanyang, Dandong, Kaifeng (Liu Y., 2006; CBRC, 2006c).

4 Role of the state

1. It is important to mention that while the words "state" or "authorities" confer the impression that it acts as one cohesive player, authorities actually include a number of competing and at times even conflicting agencies representing different interests.
2. At the end of 2005, 1378 companies were listed in Shanghai and Shenzhen. Together they had a market capitalisation of CNY 3.24 trillion. These exchanges are known for their lack of transparency and poor standards. For a succinct update on China's financial market's challenges, refer to *The Economist*, 2006a, and Pissler, 2002a.
3. In November 2004, the previously required party membership for middle management has been removed at BoC and CCB (Zhang X., 2004b).
4. Senior appointments at large banks and at regulatory authorities also require the approval of the Communist Party, through its Central Leading Group for Finance and Economics (EIU, 2006b). Party members must fill a minimum of four seats on the Board of Directors (BoD) in banks.
5. The eagerness of local authorities in investment projects can be explained by financial reasons: local governments can only run a deficit or take upon debt once it has been approved by local people's congresses. Thus they can only steer economic development and investments through companies fully under their control, which they often guarantee in front of lenders.
6. While it is prohibited by law for local governments to guarantee investment projects, they have in many cases given de facto guarantees (or letters of comfort) which in case of default could trigger a series of defaults. In the case of Guangdong ITIC, the local government had provided a letter of comfort but which in the event of the bankruptcy was said to be worthless (Zhang Y. and Li Z., 2006).
7. One exception to all this are the comments of Liu Mingkang. During a government press conference in December 2005 (*People's Net – Jiangnan Times*, 2005), he stated that "the state finances cannot be used to cover up the operational losses of commercial banks. Otherwise, this would be contrary to the principle of fair competition". Market mechanisms have to be used to resolve such crises. He thinks that banks after a full restructuring and market listing cannot anymore expect the state to save them and this should reduce moral hazard. This would also spare a "big bleeding" in the state finances. Liu also thinks that the government background in commercial banks can easily put the commercial aim off tracks and cannot promote a good corporate governance structure, thus creating bad loans.

5 Foreign banks in China

1. Limits on foreign ownership are meant only for companies that are not listed (*South China Morning Post*, 2005b) and stakes are calculated on a consolidated basis, meaning that foreign banks cannot use their own subsidiaries to enter Chinese banks' capital. Press articles at the end of 2005 had repeatedly reported that the CBRC was thinking about a further increase of the ceiling for failed banks, but any hopes came to a halt as regulators refused to let foreign investors take a majority stake in the ailing Guangdong Development Bank.
2. Shares in listed companies in China take mainly two forms: A-shares are CNY-denominated locally listed shares that only Chinese entities and qualified foreign institutional investors (QFII) can trade; B-shares are those USD- or HKD-denominated shares which can be traded by both foreign and Chinese investors. Chinese enterprises, especially state ones, also have large chunks of non-tradable shares which often also represent state stakes (the so-called "legal person shares"). Finally H-shares pertain to those Chinese enterprises which are listed in Hong Kong and red-chips to Hong Kong listed companies with high levels of revenues from China.
3. The criticisms by "economic nationalists" (Blume, 2002) should be seen less from the point of view of the single naive arguments, but much more within a tendency with older roots to call for China to free itself from foreign "imperialists" and to regain its lost sovereignty. This discussion can also be seen in a wider framework of general criticism towards the handling of the reform process combined with patriotic feelings (which may be understood as used by the authorities to divert the attention towards less contentious problems).
4. Some may argue that the Chinese leadership is progressively opening securities firms to foreign investors (Chen G., 2006). While this is a welcomed move and could give a boost to the Chinese securities industry, the comparison with Chinese banks is not directly possible. Securities companies do not hold the same significant amount of deposits from Chinese households as do banks.
5. At the end of April 2006, a first step in this direction was made, when the authorities allowed private investors to invest limited amounts of money abroad, albeit through established banks only (which must get approval before offering such services and licences will be granted based on the risk management capacity of the bank) and for products with regular returns only (*Xinhua News Agency*, 2006; *Asia Pulse*, 2006a).

6 Financial intermediation

1. The 172 central SOEs showed the following performance at the end of 2004 (compared to a year earlier) (Zhang D., 2005): assets of CNY 9.19 trillion (+12.3%), net assets of CNY 3.95 trillion (+11.8%), net worth of CNY 3.2 trillion (+11.5%), ROE 8.9% (+2.9% points), ROA 6.5% (+1.5% points), sales revenues of CNY 5.5 trillion (+25.8%), realised profits of CNY 0.478 trillion (+57.6%), tax revenues of CNY 0.429 trillion (+27%) and productivity of all employees: CNY 155,000 per employee per year (+ CNY 310 mln).
2. The SASAC's president said that by the end of 2002 some 2500 smaller SOEs had gone bankrupt. These had generated some CNY 240 bln in bad loans

(Green, 2004). This alone represents already 9% of all NPLs in 2002. In December 2005, the President of ICBC suggested that 81% of the bank's NPLs came from SOEs and collective enterprises (Jiang J., 2005).

3. Wu Jian (2005) has calculated that accounts of enterprises are reliable in 70–80% of all cases for manufacturing companies, in 60% of cases for commercial and real estate companies, in 80% of cases for large companies and in 50–70% of cases for small enterprises.
4. In China, land is owned by the State. The State grants enterprises and individuals the right of use for a limited period (70 years for residential purposes, 40 years for commercial and recreational purposes and 50 years for industrial, science/educational and other purposes). Land use rights (except for collectively owned rural land) can be collateralised (WTO, 2001c).
5. The TVEs were created as collective enterprises (at a time where there was no legal room for private enterprises). Since their privatisation at the end of the 1990s, some are now also owned by managers and employees, as well as by township or village administrations (Yusuf *et al.*, 2006).
6. Entertainment fees are relatively common in China and include all expenses paid to entertain important guests to induce favourable decisions.
7. The funds are deposited in a bank which is asked to further lend on the funds to the target enterprise. The terms of the loan (maturity, amount, purpose, borrower, etc.) are defined by the funding entity. In these cases banks only act as facilitators, as intermediaries and credit risk is carried by the depositor.
8. We do not take into account criminal and money-laundering activities here, even if drawing a line may be difficult.
9. There are a number of different revolving savings and loans associations in China: *lunhui* (轮会) where the turn of each member is predetermined, *yaohui* where members rotate according to draws, *biaohui* (标会) where members tender for making use of their funds, *taihui* which resemble pyramidal schemes and *bahui* where the money is divided according to group hierarchy (Ma Z., 2003b).
10. There are more than 1000 registered pawn shops in China which were forbidden in the PRC's early 40 years. They have seen a strong revival in the reform period. There is a specific regulation for pawn shop activities. Pawn shops in Beijing charge between 3.2% per month for collateralised loans and 4.7% per month for other loans (Yao K., 2006).
11. The SOEs and collective enterprises use the loans received from formal institutions to on-lend them to private enterprises which are not able to borrow directly (Tsai, 2001).

7 Non-performing loans

1. According to a survey (Yang J., 2005) at the end of September 2003, the amount of related parties transactions in the 14 surveyed banks reached CNY 44.3 bln, that is 10% of all outstanding loans, with most of these held by the SOCBs. Most of these loans went to manufacturing, communication and trade companies. Only 21% of the loans were without collateral. The average NPL ratio for these was 19%. These types of transactions are more risky because they are more difficult to monitor and because riskiness is often played down.

2. When CCB and BoC transferred again some USD 33.9 bln of NPLs, they witnessed strong loan growth, thus the nominal decrease in NPLs is exaggerated (Melka and Xu, 2004). To increase the speed of NPLs disposal, central authorities have also flushed CCB and BoC with fresh capital from foreign exchange reserves. This had a double effect: it did not create further liquidity or money and at the same time allowed for more NPLs write-offs as well as a higher CAR (Melka and Xu, 2004).
3. At some point regulators had asked banks to require new collateral for these loans, but in practice banks are unlikely to turn to their long-standing customers to ask for collateral for the first time (*China Business*, 2003b).
4. Ernst & Young (E&Y) published in May 2006 (E&Y, 2006) its estimate of the NPLs still in the banking system: USD 900 bln (including pre 1999 NPLs, and potential new ones), more than the official foreign exchange reserves. The report has been, after strong criticism of PBOC, swiftly withdrawn. Whatever the true figure, this discussion reveals that concerns over NPLs on both sides (Chinese authorities and foreign investors) are still high (*The Economist*, 2006g).
5. One journalist mentioned recently that, for example, an unsecured loan with arrears of 1 month is counted as "performing" at CCB, but as "special mention" at Bank of Communications (Lu Y., 2005).

8 Capital adequacy and risk management

1. As of December 2005, 40 commercial banks complied with the 8% capital requirements (CBRC, 2006b). They represent some 73% of the total commercial banking assets. But remain some 42 CCBs with negative equity and 67 of them with a CAR below 4% (*South China Morning Post*, 2006a).
2. Chinese regulators have called upon banks not to issue more than a combined amount of CNY 250 bln in subordinated debt.
3. Instead, CBRC has published a notice on operational risk management for banks which is written in general terms and requires banks to establish processes and codes, to define clear responsibilities and policies for control, to establish incentives and foster transparency (CBRC, 2005b). This goes hand in hand with sound internal controls practices (References for laws 22). The operational risk regulation is solely qualitative.
4. Those banks will have 2 months to submit a plan to get their capital adequacy in line and they might suffer restrictions in terms of asset growth, and so on, as CBRC sees fit. Those significantly undercapitalised will see their senior management removed and other sanctions could follow.
5. In a recent article, Xu Changyuan (2005) found that in a number of CCBs the management of capital adequacy had not reached the levels required by the new regulations (there was no capital account management, no plan for capital increase, etc.).
6. By mid-2005, 12 commercial banks have either already issued or announced that they plan to issue subordinated debt. In 2004, 7 of them issued some CNY 59 bln of which half was issued by the two state-owned banks, in 2005 already CNY 93 bln have been issued (January–October 2005). CBRC approval is required for including subordinated debts in capital. Issuance is

open only to commercial banks with among others sound governance structures, minimum 5% of core capital ratio and adequate LLP.
7. Only half of emerging markets countries is on average compliant with 10 out of 30 BCP.

9 Governance and corruption

1. Sheng *et al.* (2005) find that corporate governance structures cannot find a fertile ground for their long-term establishment as long as the property rights issue is not conclusively resolved. Property rights on equity, land and assets must enjoy an infrastructure in which they can be effectively transferred, exchanged, recognised, and clearly defined. Institutions such as registries, accounting standards (for defining and valuing rights), trading places (auctions and stock markets, for example), intermediaries (to facilitate transactions), settlement systems, rules and regulations, transparent and independent judiciary, efficient and reliable enforcement system, mandatory disclosure requirements, and public entities (such as consumer groups, etc.) are all part of the infrastructure. These permit the more efficient flow of wealth.
2. Starting from 2007, China is going to implement, at first for listed companies, the international accounting standards (IFRS).
3. The BoD's responsibilities include the definition of the operational strategy, choosing and supervising the senior management of the bank, proposing the allocation of resources, capital and earnings. In banks, the BoD also defines risk management and internal controls policies (including monitoring, auditing, related-parties transactions) and takes responsibility for information disclosure.
4. Some committees are mandatory: one for related transactions, one for internal audit and one for risk management. Banks with net worth of more than CNY 1 bln shall have further committees for remuneration, strategy and choosing managers.

10 State-owned commercial banks

1. In some cases, Bank of Communications is also considered the fifth SOCB. While its size is much larger than that of JSCBs, it is not directly under the State Council and its shares are spread among different state entities.
2. The remaining shares (as of June 2006) are held by a consortium of RBS, Merill Lynch and Li Ka-Shing Foundation 10%, Temasek 5%, UBS 2%, a domestic pension fund 5% and since the listing 11% are widely spread.
3. The remaining shares (as of June 2006) are held by state-owned entities: China Jianyin Investment Ltd 9.2%, China Power 1.3%, Shanghai Baosteel 1.3%, China Jiangtze Power 0.9% without any board seat, as well as Bank of America 8.5%, Temasek 5.9% and 11.4% widely held since the listing.
4. Stock market listings are often conducted in Hong Kong due to the greater access to investors, the higher liquidity of the markets, the better visibility and also the higher expected gains for the Chinese authorities. However, the idea of a double listing (Shanghai and Hong Kong) is also being discussed (Yu N., 2006) and was made reality by BoC and ICBC.

5. Ling H. (2005b) estimates that ABC's recapitalisation could cost as much as CNY 570 bln, that is more than what was paid for the other three SOCBs in 2004–2005 together. During previous reform efforts ABC already required some CNY 50 bln (Zhang D., 2006a).
6. It is unclear how high the NPL ratio for ABC was. Speculations abound, because very little information is being published. ABC's NPL ratio in 2001 was, according to the five-tier loan classification, 42% (thereof, commercial lending 36% and policy-related lending 74%, such loans make up 17% of the loan portfolio).

12 City commercial banks

1. A survey of some CCBs in 2005 showed that local governments directly hold an overall 24.2% share in the capital of the surveyed banks (Eastern China 22.3%, Central China 21.9% and Western China 28.9%), and indirectly, through wholly owned subsidiaries, 73.6%. Only an average of 23.75% is held by private enterprises or investors (*Financial News*, 2005a as well as SCDRC, 2005).
2. By way of a notice from the State Council in 1995, they were given their current designation of city commercial banks in 1998.
3. It should be noted that as of the end of 2005, only 23 complied with the 8% CAR, 67 had a CAR below 4% and even 42 CCBs still had negative equity (*South China Morning Post*, 2006a).
4. The discrepancies may be the result of poor information systems and some of the figures surely rely much on management's estimates.
5. In November 2005, Beijing Bank introduced two foreign bankers from ING Group to its management (in charge of personal banking and strategic development, and of risk management, *BBC News Asia Pacific*, 2005).
6. Apart from CCBs with negative equity, the majority of them shows on average that the loan volume to their 10 largest clients amounts to 200% of their equity on average (Zhong J., 2004; *China Industry and Economy Information Net*, 2005; Zhang J., 2005; Yan M., 2006).
7. While most in the survey had formally established a risk management function, only two institutions really used the developed risk management guidelines in their daily business. The remaining banks did not really use them. While, for example, the surveyed CCBs have NPL ratios averaging 14% (in Central China even 24.68%), the surveyed banks on average raised only 1.25% in LLP. The survey estimated that while they should raise some CNY 70 bln, in reality the banks raised only a fraction of that with CNY 6 bln (*Financial News*, 2005c; SCDRC, 2005).
8. Of accumulated net profits amounting to CNY 1.03 bln in 2002 and CNY 1.5 bln in 2003, only CNY 0.03 bln and CNY 0.3 bln remained after dividend payments. This represents a 97 and 80% payout ratio respectively. This underlines the strong short-term orientation of the banks' shareholders (*Financial News*, 2005c as well as SCDRC, 2005).
9. This view is contradicted by findings from Shih *et al.* (2005b) which show that they are important outliers in the data: for example, CCBs in Guangdong province, which has a vibrant private sector, are heavily weighted down by their NPL ratios.

13 Foreign banks

1. Under certain conditions and after meeting certain requirements, foreign banks can be approved to become QFII and invest funds in A shares (shares that were previously off limits for foreign investors and reserved to Chinese ones). Up to 2005, 27 foreign banks and financial institutions had received approval. The institutions can invest up to USD 3.75 bln in equity and bond markets. Chinese banks must act as trustees in this scheme.

14 Rural credit cooperatives

1. The ADBC supports state-owned agricultural entities with purchasing grain, cotton and oil.
2. The transfer of control of RCCs to the unions has advantages (the interference capacity of local governments at the level below the county is reduced because they cannot anymore efficiently influence the RCC in their locality and have to seek influence at county level; economies of scales are possible by centralising certain activities and sharing the benefits among member RCCs, increasing the capacity to withstand risks, reducing administrative expenses and increasing management capabilities) as well as negative aspects (the concentration of power and of influence at union level away from the locality and the conflict of interests arising between union and individual RCC, Liu M. *et al.*, 2005).
3. The RCCs were already established in the 1950 but lost their independence within the centralisation process of the banking system.

15 Retail banking

1. This is a more conservative estimate. Estimates found in the foreign literature vary widely: between 762 mln cards in issue at the end of 2004 of which 88% were debit cards (Yan M., 2005) and around 900 mln cards in issue at the end of 2005 (Robinson, 2006).

16 Impact of the new capital accord

1. Ba Shusong is Deputy Head of the Finance Research Institute of the Development Research Centre (DRC), which is under the State Council. He has published a number of articles related to Basel II in China (see among others Ba S., 2005a,b).
2. As Ba (2005b) also points out, delaying implementation allows CBRC to gain more flexibility. Chinese regulators are, as many other emerging markets regulators, very protective in their approach and this might also explain the rejection of a timely full implementation (Holland and Baglole, 2003).
3. Ward (2002) suggests that they should better concentrate on financial stability: regulations should target the collective behaviour of banks. Thus regulators should concentrate on creating the right incentives for banks to

move towards a more risk-sensitive management. Bankers should be fearful of failure. This would be a strong departure from the current practices.

4. Regulatory (capital) arbitrage is defined by Ong (1999: 22) as an activity used by banks to "effectively increase their regulatory capital ratios and their true capital cushions by reducing the size of their loan portfolios. [...] Two major approaches are based on the securitisation of assets and the use of credit derivatives".
5. As stated by the International Institute of Finance (IIF) (2005a) "a careful approach is needed for Basel II implementation in emerging markets, in particular regarding the necessary pre-conditions of supervisory resources, regulation and availability of technology, but the move toward the new framework is an important objective".
6. Ba S. (2005a,b), Chen Y. (2002), Liu M. (2005), Peng J. *et al.* (2005), Shen J. (2005), Tong M. (2005), Wu J. (2005), Wu S. (2004), Xu C. (2005), Zhang R. and Hou G. (2005) and Zhang Z. (2004), all treat the implementation of Basel II and credit risk modelling.
7. The assumptions presently used for estimating a realistic LGD have a strong impact on the capital requirements. This highlights the importance of the macro-environment (economic, legal, etc.) when implementing the Basel II capital accord. This further highlights the need to improve the external environment of banks at the same time as promoting best practices in credit risk management and financial restructuring.
8. The calculated ratios for all banks are quite high. This reflects the fact that the calculations are based on the loan portfolio only and do not include the large amounts of government securities they hold on their books. These large portions of government securities are likely to be reduced once banks find again the confidence for more lending.
9. Based on the work of Rixtel, van Alexopoulou and Harada (2003), "tactical implications relate to the day-to-day business operations of banks and how their operational framework may be affected (micro dimension). [...] Strategic implications focus on the structure of the banking system as such, the development of financial markets and services, and the overall functioning of the economy (macro dimension)".
10. Shortly after the issuance of the new regulations, the first asset securitisations were taken to the markets: CCB and China Development Bank separately issued a total of CNY 4.2 bln asset backed securities and CNY 3 bln in mortgage backed securities. This was hailed as a sign of innovation in the Chinese press (Li L., 2005a) and will help banks shorten their maturity gaps. This could also open the door to further foreign investments in the Chinese banking systems.

17 Entry to the World Trade Organisation

1. To this there is only one limitation: for the provision of local currency services, foreign banks must have been profitable in the last two consecutive years and have operated at least 3 years in China prior to their application for a local currency business licence.

Annexes

1. The authorities have created in August 2005 a fifth AMC called Huida AMC. This entity will deal with PBOC's bad loans stemming from re-lending activities of PBOC, amounting to a total of CNY 1.9 trln up to May 2005 (Chu *et al.*, 2006a and b).
2. The institutional organisation and background reflects the need to clarify who owns the AMCs (wholly state owned, but who is the state?), what is their legal and corporate status (not clarified in any law), who bears the losses incurred in the course of business (funds come from public money, but should depositors not have a say, especially when it comes to losses)?
3. The approval for participating in a debt–equity swap deal is given by the State Economic and Trade Commission (SETC), a government administration without any experience in restructuring or lending. The purpose of transferring the responsibilities to SETC was to avoid debt relief or debt amnesty to be granted by local governments to their enterprises. However, this is what exactly happened (Steinfeld, 2005).
4. The following are mainly based on: Altman and Sabato, 2005; BIS, 2004 and 2005; BCBS, 2003, 2004a/b/c and 2005; Cornford, 2005; Deloitte & Touche, 2005 a/b; Deutsche Bundesbank, 2005; Dichtl *et al.*, 2004; EU, 2003; FitchRatings, 2004; Gup, 2004b; IIF, 2005a, KPMG, 2003; Ong, 2004 and PwC, 2004b.

Bibliography

AFX Asia (2005), China CBRC detects 274 finance sector crimes last year involving 1.51 bln Yuan, 17 Jan.

AFX Asia (2006a), China to push reforms of banks but retain state control, 5 Mar.

AFX Asia (2006b), China to retain control over state-owned banks for 10 years – Central Huijin, 6 Apr.

AFX International Focus (2005), China "seriously considering" moving towards Basel II in 2007, 26 Sept.

Agence France Presse (2005), China says WTO deadline on banking to be met, no more bank bailouts, 5 Dec.

Allen, L. (2002), *Credit Risk Modelling of Middle Markets* (Zurich: Baruch College).

Allen, F., Qian, J. and Qian, M. (2004), *China's Financial System: Past, Present and Future* (Wharton School, University of Pennsylvania Working Paper).

Allen, F., Qian, J. and Qian, M. (2005), Law, finance and economic growth in China. *Journal of Financial Economics*, 77, pp. 57–116.

Altman, E. I. and Sabato, G. (2005), Effects of the new Basel capital accord on bank capital requirements for SMEs. *Credit Risk Evaluation Designed for Institutional Targeting in Finance: Proceedings of the Counterparty Risk Conference*, 22–23 Sept. (Venice: s.n.).

Andersen, L. (2003), Basel II: The path to promoting financial stability in the Asian and Pacific region? *Bulletin on Asia Pacific Perspectives*, 2003–04.

Anderson, J. (2005), The great Chinese bank sale. *Far Eastern Economic Review*, 23 Sept.

Areddy, J. T. (2006a), Policy change in China could hurt Foreign Banks – Beijing wants to blur structural differences with local lenders. *Wall Street Journal Asia*, 23 Feb.

Areddy, J. T. (2006b), China's plan to insure deposits may be costly for foreign banks. *Wall Street Journal*, 9 May.

Areddy, J. T. (2006c), U.S. auditor apologizes to Beijing. *Wall Street Journal Asia*, 16 May.

Asia Pulse (2004), China opens city commercial banks to foreign investors, 27 Sept.

Asia Pulse (2005a), Chinese banks adjusting risk management systems, 25 Jan.

Asia Pulse (2005b), Chinese banks seek to implement Basel II requirements, 21 Feb.

Asia Pulse (2006a), China allows commercial banks to invest overseas, 19 Apr.

Asia Pulse (2006b), China approves establishment of postal bank, 24 May.

Asia Pulse (2006c), Eight Chinese city comm'l banks prepare to launch non-local branches, 7 Jun.

Asia Pulse (2006d), China drafts revised rule for foreign lenders, 21 Jun.

Asiamoney (2005), China's Banks: Buying damaged goods, 27 Jun. Accessed online under http://www.gtnews.com/article/5995.cfm [25 Jan. 2006].

Ba, S. (2005a), Challenges confronting banking sector. *Business Weekly China*, 7 Feb.

[Ba, S.] 巴曙松 (2005b), 巴塞尔新资本协议对中国银行业的十大挑战 [The ten challenges brought by the new Basel capital accord to the Chinese banking industry]. *财经时报 [Finance News]*. 16 Jan. Accessed online under www.finance.sina.com.cn [25 Nov. 2005].

[Ba, S.] 巴曙松 (2005c), 金融改革：国际化亟需解决五大新问题 [Financial reform: internationalisation can help resolve five big new questions]. *中国经济周刊 [China Economic Weekly]*, 51.

[Ba, S.] 巴曙松 (2006a), 如何超越国有银行贱卖之争 [Getting behind the row over the sacrifice of state-owned banks]. *新浪财经* [*Sina Finance News*]. 20 Jan. Accessed online under http://finance.sina.com.cn/economist/jingjixueren/20060120/11082292985.shtml [20 Jan. 2006].

[Ba, S.] 巴曙松 (2006b), 落后的银行体系是金融安全最大威胁 [The backward banking system is the greatest threat to financial stability]. *商务周刊* [*Commercial Weekly*]. 15 Feb. Accessed online under http://finance.sina.com.cn [16 Feb. 2006].

[Ba, S.] 巴曙松 and [Chen, H.] 陈华良 (2005), 金融机构的政府救助对监管声誉的影响 [The influence of government rescues of financial institutions on the reputation of regulators]. *证券市场导报 [Securities Market Guide]*, 3.

[Ba, S.] 巴曙松, [Hua, Z.] 华中炜 and [Niu, B.] 牛播坤 (2005a), 城商行改革最佳路径——上海银行的外资模式、浙商行的股权多元化模式 [The best way to CCBs' reform: the foreign capital model of Bank of Shanghai and the ownership diversification model of Zhejiang Commercial Bank]. *《新财富》[New Wealth]*, 11.

[Ba, S.] 巴曙松 , [Liu, Q.] 刘清涛 and [Niu, B.] 牛播坤 (2005b), 中国资本充足监管框架的形成及其市场影响——兼论巴塞尔新资本协义与《商业银行资本充足率管理办法》的比较 [Shape of the regulatory framework for capital adequacy in China and its impact on markets – comparison of the Basel II capital accord and China's management guideline on commercial banks capital adequacy]. *《财经科学》[Finance and Economics Science]*, 1.

Baglole, J. (2003), China – opening up to private banks. *Far Eastern Economic Review*, 18 Sept.

Baglole, J. (2004), Chinese Credit Ratings – a huge leap of faith. *Far Eastern Economic Review*, 8 Jan.

Bai, C., Liu, Q., Lu, J., Song, F. M. and Zhang, J. (2003), *Corporate Governance and Market Valuation in China*. William Davidson Institute Working Paper 564.

Balfour, F. and Roberts, D. (2004), The leak in China's Banking System: Frustrated with low returns Chinese savers are taking money out of state banks and lending it themselves. *Business Week*, 67(3908), 15 Nov.

Balzarotti, V., Castro, C. and Powell, A. (2004), *Reforming Capital Requirements in Emerging Countries: Calibrating Basel II using Historical Argentine Credit Bureau Data and CreditRisk+*. Centro de Investigacion en Finanzas, 07.

Bank for International Settlements (BIS) (2004), *Implementation of the New Capital Adequacy Framework in Non-Basel Committee Member Countries – Summary of Responses to the Basel II Implementation Assistance Questionnaire*. Occasional paper (Basel: BIS).

Bank for International Settlements (BIS) (2005), *Studies on the Validation of Internal Rating Systems*. Working Paper 14 (Basel: BIS).

Bank for International Settlements (BIS) (2006), *Enhancing Corporate Governance for Banking Organisations* (Basel: BIS).

Barth, J., Caprio, G. and Levine, R. (2000), *Banking Systems Around the Globe: Do Regulation and Ownership Affect Performance and Stability*? Accessed online under www.auburn.edu/~barthjr/papers/Cheeca.pdf [5 Mar. 2006].

Barth, J. R., Koepp, R. and Zhou, Z. (2004), *Banking Reform in China: Catalyzing the Nation's Financial Future*. Milken Institute Working Paper.

Basel Committee on Banking Supervision (BCBS) (1997), *Core Principles for Effective Banking Supervision* (Basel: BIS).

Basel Committee on Banking Supervision (BCBS) (1999), *Credit Risk Modelling: Current Practices and Applications* (Basel: BIS).

Basel Committee on Banking Supervision (BCBS) (2000a), *Principles for the Management of Credit Risk* (Basel: BIS).

Basel Committee on Banking Supervision (BCBS) (2000b), *Range of Practices in Banks' Internal Ratings Systems* (Basel: BIS).

Basel Committee on Banking Supervision (BCBS) (2003), *Quantitative Impact Study 3: Overview of Global Results* (Basel: BIS).

Basel Committee on Banking Supervision (BCBS) (2004a), *International Convergence of Capital Measurements and Capital Standards* (Basel: BIS).

Basel Committee on Banking Supervision (BCBS) (2004b), *Modifications to the Capital Treatment for Expected and Unexpected Credit Losses in the New Basel Accord* (Basel: BIS).

Basel Committee on Banking Supervision (BCBS) (2004c), *Implementation of Basel II: Practical Considerations* (Basel: BIS).

Basel Committee on Banking Supervision (BCBS) (2005), *An Explanatory Note on the Basel II IRB Risk Weight Functions* (Basel: BIS).

BBC News Asia Pacific (2005), Chinese bank gets foreign vice-president. 4 Nov. Accessed online under http://global2.factiva.com.

Beck, T., Demirgüç-Kunt, A. and Maksimovic, V. (2004), *Financing Patterns Around the World: Are Small Firms different*? (Washington: World Bank). Accessed online under www.worldbank.org/research/projects/sme/Financing%20Patterns091604.pdf [10 Dec. 2004].

Becker, S. (2005), Smaller banks will be the winners with Basel II. *Securities Industry News*, 17 Jan.

Bekier, M. M. and Lam, K. (2005), What Chinese consumers want from banks? *McKinsey Quarterly*, Jun.

Bekier, M., Huang, R. and Wilson, G. (2005), How to fix China's banking system, *McKinsey Quarterly*, Jan.

Berger, A. N. (2004), *Potential Competitive Effects of Basel II on Banks in SME Credit Markets in the United States* (New York: Federal Reserve).

Berger, A. N., Hasan, I. and Klapper, L. F. (2003), *Further Evidence on the Link Between Finance and Growth: An International Analysis of Community Banking and Economic Performance*. World Bank Policy Research, 3105 Aug.

Best's Insurance News (2005), Ernst & Young: Trends point to global convergence of financial regulation, 19 May.

Bhattasali, D. (2005), Accelerating financial market restructuring in China. In Bhattasali, D., Li, S. and Martin, W. (eds), *China and the WTO: Accession, Policy Reform and Poverty Reduction Strategies* (Washington: World Bank), pp. 181–190.

Bhattasali, D., Li, S. and Martin, W. (eds) (2005), *China and the WTO: Accession, Policy Reform and Poverty Reduction Strategies* (Washington: World Bank).

Blume, A. (2002), *Chinas Beitritt zur Welthandelsorganisation aus Sicht der neuen politischen Ökonomie des Protektionismus [China's Entry to the WTO from the Point of View of the New Political Economy of Protectionism]* (Hamburg: Institut für Asienkunde).

Boston Consulting Group (BCG) (2002), *China Crossroads: Competitive Priorities for Chinese Banks* (s.l.: BCG).

Boston Consulting Group (BCG) (2005), *Banking on China: Where to Place the Chips?* (s.l.: BCG).

Boyreau-Debray, G. (2003), *Financial Intermediation and Growth: Chinese Style* (Washington DC: World Bank). Accessed online under econ.worldbank.org/files/25828_wps3027.pdf [14 Jun. 2004].

Boyreau-Debray, G. and Wei, S. (2005), *Pitfalls of a State-dominated Financial System: The Case of China* (s.l.: National Bureau of Economic Research).

Bradsher, K. (2004), China's informal lenders pose risks to its banks. *The New York Times*, 9 Nov.

Bradsher, K. (2005), A Chinese banker is convicted and a message is sent. *The New York Times*, 13 Aug.

Brandt, L. and Li, H. (2003), Bank discrimination in transition economies: Ideology, information, or incentives? *Journal of Comparative Economics*, 31, pp. 387–413.

Brandt, L., Li, H. and Roberts, J. (2005a), Banks and enterprise privatization in China. *Journal of Law, Economics, & Organization*, 21(2).

Brandt, L., Park, A. and Wang, S. (2005b), Are China's financial reforms leaving the poor behind? In Huang, Y., Saich, T. and Steinfeld, E. (eds), *Financial Sector Reform in China* (Cambridge: Harvard University), pp. 204–230.

Brehm, S. and Macht, C. (2004), Banking supervision in China: Basel I, Basel II and the Basel core principles. *Zeitschrift für Chinesisches Recht*, pp. 316–327.

Brehm, S. and Macht, C. (2005), Is a new broom sweeping clean? The emergence of the China Banking Regulatory Commission. *Aussenwirtschaft*, 60(2), pp. 169–207.

Bremner, B. (2006), Banking on China's reforms – western outfits are lining up to get into the hot Chinese lending market but fraud and a build-up of property loans are worrisome. *Business Week Online*, 6 Feb.

Browne, A. (2005), China agency spurs bank rift – state firm's role as investor heats up – financial-system tussle. *The Wall Street Journal*, 22 Aug.

Buckley, C. (2005), Lax management at China's banks remains a concern of regulators and investors. *The New York Times*, 8 Feb.

Buehler, K. S., D'Silva, V. and Pritsch, G. (2004), The business case for Basel II. *McKinsey Quarterly*, Jan.

Cai, E. (1999), Financial supervision in China: Framework, methods and current issues. In *Strengthening the Banking System in China: Issues and Experience*, Joint BIS/PBOC Conference proceedings, Beijing, 1–2 Mar. 1999 (Basel: BIS), pp. 169–173.

[Caijing Magazine] 财经 (2005a), 国有商业银行改革设定今年目标 [The state-owned banks' targets for this year], 25 Jul.

[Caijing Magazine] 财经 (2005b), 开发投资增幅回落 房贷潜在风险加大 [Development investments turn around, increased potential risks in real estate], 22 Aug.

[Caijing Magazine] 财经 (2005c), 转变增长方式与转变政府职能：吴敬琏、高尚全、江平、许小年四人谈 [Transform the growth path and the government Function: A discussion with Wu Jinglian, Gao Shangquan, Jiang Ping and Xu Xiaonian], 14 Nov.

[Cao, H.] 曹海丽 (2004), 上海银行：从幼稚起步 [Shanghai Bank: naive start off]. *《财经》[Caijing Magazine]*, 27 Dec.

[Cao, H.] 曹海丽 and [Ling, H.] 凌华薇 (2004), 浦发行：一张信用卡的故事 [Shanghai Pudong: a credit card story]. *《财经》[Caijing Magazine]*, 27 Dec.

[Cao, H.] 曹海丽 and [Lu, Y.] 卢彦铮 (2005), 交行上市变奏 [Change of rhythm at Bank of Communications' listing]. *《财经》[Caijing Magazine]*, 16 May.

[Cao, X.] 曹幸仁 and [Zhao, X.] 赵新杰 (2004), 国有商业银行公司治理改革问题研究 [Research into issues of corporate governance in SOCBs]. *金融论坛 [Finance Forum]* (01), pp. 3–8.

Carew, R. (2006), 中国银行：国内银行工作重点已由处置不良贷款转为拓展业务 [BoC: work focus of domestic banks changes from NPLs disposal to business expansion]. *道琼斯 [Dow Jones Chinese]*, 2 Mar.

Carey, M. (2002), A guide to choosing absolute bank capital requirements. *Journal of Banking and Finance*, 26, pp. 929–951.

Chang, G. C. (2003), China and the WTO: Progress, perils and prospects. *Columbia Journal of Asian Law*, 17, pp. 6–11.

Chen, A. and Everling, O. (2002), Finanzsystem und Rating in China [Financial system and rating in China]. *Die Bank*, 11, pp. 727–731.

Chen, G. (2006), China to allow foreign control of fund JVs-sources. *Reuters*, 18 May.

Chen, J. (2003), Capital adequacy of Chinese banks: Evaluation and enhancement. *Journal of International Banking Regulation*, Jun. (4.4), pp. 320–327.

[Chen, J.] 陈进忠 (2005), 城市商业银行发展定位与中小企业融资 [Development position of the CCBs and the financing of SMEs]. *中国金融 [China Finance]*, 11.

Chen, J. P. (2004), *Non-performing loan Securitization in the People's Republic of China* (s.l.: Stanford University).

Chen, S. (2004), 国际战略投资者对中资银行风险管理变革的作用 [The usefulness of international strategic investors in reforming the risk management of Chinese banks]. *中国金融 [China Finance]*, 23.

Chen, X. (2005), *Problemkredite und die chinesische Bankenreform in Anbetracht von asymmetrischer Information und institutionellen Anreizen [Problem loans and Chinese banking reform while considering information asymmetry and institutional incentives]* Diss. (Frankfurt/Main: Johann Wolfgang Goethe Universität).

Chen, X., Skully, M. and Brown, K. (2005), Banking efficiency in China: Application of DEA to pre- and post-deregulation eras 1993–2000. *China Economic Review*, 2.

[Chen, Y.] 陈燕玲 (2002), 新巴塞尔协议及其对我国银行业的影响 [The new Basel accord and its impact on China's banking system]. *中央财经大学学报 [Journal of the Central Economics and Finance University]*, 07.

Chen, Y. (2004), Safety line nearing final stage. *Business Weekly*, 16 Mar.

Chen, Z., Li, D. and Moshirian, F. (2005), China's Financial Services Industry: The intra-industry effects of privatization of the Bank of China Hong Kong. *Journal of Banking and Finance*, 29, pp. 2291–2324.

Cheng, E., Findlay, C. and Watson, A. (2003), Institutional innovation without regulation. In Findlay, C., Watson, A. and Cheng, E. (eds), *Rural Financial Markets in China* (Canberra: Asia Pacific Press), pp. 89–104.

[Cheng, S.] 成思危 (2004), *在学习贯彻《银行业监督管理法》座谈会上的讲话 [On the Conference for Studying the Implementation of the Law of the PRC on Banking Regulation and Supervision]* (s.l.: s.n).

Chien, K. (2006), China still faces bad-loan challenge – regulator. *Reuters News*, 27 Feb.

China Banking Regulatory Commission (CBRC) (2003), *刘明康主席致巴塞尔银行监管委员会主席卡如纳先生的信：中国银行业监督管理委员会对巴塞尔新资本协议的意见和建议 [Letter from Liu Mingkang, Chairman of the CBRC to Jaime Caruana, Chairman of the Basel Committee on Banking Supervision: Comments and Suggestions on the New Basel Capital Accord]* 31 Jul. (Beijing: CBRC).

China Banking Regulatory Commission (CBRC) (2004a), *《城市商业银行监管与发展纲要》 [Program for Regulations and Development of City Commercial Banks]* (Beijing: CBRC).

China Banking Regulatory Commission (CBRC) (2004b), *加强监管，促进城市商业银行的改革与发展 [Strengthening Regulations, Improving City Commercial Banks' Reform and Development]* (Beijing: CBRC).

China Banking Regulatory Commission (CBRC) (2005a), *中国银行业改革开放与监管的新进展 [The Reform and Opening of the Chinese Banking Industry and the Regulatory Outlook]* (Beijing: CBRC).

China Banking Regulatory Commission (CBRC) (2005b), *关于加大防范操作风险工作力度的通知 [Notice on Enhancing Work on Operational Risk Control]* (Beijing: CBRC).

China Banking Regulatory Commission (CBRC) (2006a), *刘明康在银监会 (2006) 年工作会议上强调以科学发展观统领监管工作全局 [Liu Mingkang Stresses at the CBRC (2006) Work Conference the Need for a Scientific Approach to Lead the Work of the CBRC]* (Beijing: CBRC).

China Banking Regulatory Commission (CBRC) (2006b), *农信社改革成效显著 [Effects of the RCCs' Reforms Start to Show]* (Beijing: CBRC).

China Banking Regulatory Commission (CBRC) (2006c), *2005 年城市商业银行风险处置工作取得阶段性成果 [Risk treatment work at CCBs has realised some partial results in 2005]* (Beijing: CBRC).

[China Business] 中国经营报 (2003a), 坏账指标期限紧逼基层 银行忙于粥锅掺水 [Running out of time for reducing NPLs, branches tend to dilute them], 28 Jul.

[China Business] 中国经营报 (2003b), 央行重庆报告：国有银行不良贷款下降玄机 [Report of the Central Bank in Chongqing: Secrets behind decreasing NPL levels at state-owned banks], 11 Aug.

[China City and Countryside Finance News] 中国城乡金融报 (2005), 新协议对中国银行业的影响 [The impact of the new accord on the Chinese banking industry], 22 Aug.

[China Consumer Net] 中国消费网 (2005), 央行个人征信开始发威 信用有污点全国封杀 [PBOC's credit registry starts showing results, "credit" finger prints nationwide to push out bad ones], 16 Dec.

[China Economic Information Net] 中国经济信息网 (2004a), 城商行，你们准备好了吗？[City commercial banks, are you ready?], 3 Dec.

[China Economic Information Net] 中国经济信息网 (2004b), 城市商业银行特色化经营发展研究 [Research into the business specificities of city commercial banks], 12 Oct.

[China Economic Information Net] 中国经济信息网 (2006), 民间资本达 8300 亿浙江金融理财产业异军突起 [Informal capital amounts to CNY 830 bln in Zhejiang, challenge for wealth management industry], 2 Mar.

[China Economic News Net] 中国经济信息网 (2005), 银监会拟明年出台 IRB 指引 [CBRC plans a guidance on IRB for next year], 22 Dec.

[China Economic News Net] 中国经济信息网 (2006), 改进农村金融服务：央行在行动 [Improve the rural financial services: The central bank is moving], 23 Feb.

China Economic Quarterly (CEQ) (2003), *China's Companies – A Special Issue*, 7(3) (London: Dragonomics Ltd).

China Economic Quarterly (CEQ) (2005), *Non-performing Loans – Voodoo Accounting*, 9(1) (London: Dragonomics Ltd).

[China Finance] 中国金融 (2005), 04 年度中国最大的 50 家商业银行排名 [Rankings of the 50 largest commercial banks in China at the end of 2004], 6 Dec.

China Industry Daily News (2005), 20 mainland banks included in 2005 "Asian Banker 300", 9 Nov.

[China Industry and Economy Information Net] 中国产业经济信息网 (2005), 城市商业银行 困境中寻机遇 [City Commercial Banks: Looking for opportunities in the middle of difficulties], 19 Sept.

[China INFOBANK Limited] 中国资讯行 - 新闻频道 (2005a), 工行力争 07 年底达到巴塞尔新资本协议初级法要求 [ICBC aims to reach foundation IRB approaches' requirements at the end of 2007], 29 Aug.

[China INFOBANK Limited] 中国资讯行-新闻频道 (2005b), 安徽省内 6 家城市商行合并步伐加快 [Six Anhui city commercial banks' merger gathers pace], 29 Aug.

[China Securities News] 中国证券报 (2006), 推进利率市场化央行将建再贴现率动态调整机制 [To improve the marketisation of interest rates, the central bank will have to introduce a dynamic adjustment mechanism for setting the re-discounting interest rate], 9 Feb.

[China Postal Savings News] 中国邮政报 (2006), 对邮政汇兑业务发展的几点建议 [Some suggestions for the development of remittance business in postal savings], 14 Jan.

[China Urban and Rural Finance Newspaper] 中国城乡金融报 (2005), 中国银行业实施内部评级法前景展望 [Perspectives and outlook of the implementation of the IRB approach in the Chinese banking industry], 26 Dec.

Cho, Y. J. (1999), The banking system of the PRC. In Asian Development Bank (ADB) (1999). *Rising to the Challenge in Asia: A Study of Financial Markets – Volume 4: People's Republic of China* (Manila: ADB).

Chu, C., Lin, K., Lin, L. and Marshall, D. (2006a), *China: Taking Stock of Banking System NPLs* (New York: FitchRatings).

Chu, C., Lin, K., Lin, L. and Marshall, D. (2006b), *The Chinese Banking System* (New York: FitchRatings).

Claessens, S., Demirgüc-Kunt, A. and Huizinga, H. (2001), How does foreign entry affect domestic banking markets? *Journal of Banking and Finance*, 25, pp. 891–911.

Clarke, D. C. (2003), *Corporate Governance in China: An Overview*. Working Paper. George Washington University Law School.

Clarke, G., Cull, R. and Martinez Peria, M. S. (2002), *Does Foreign Bank Penetration Reduce Access to Credit in Developing Countries? Evidence from Asking Borrowers* (Washington, DC: World Bank).

Clarke, G., Cull, R., Martinez Peria, M. S. and Snachez, S. M. (2003), Foreign Bank Entry: Experience, implications for developing economies and agenda for further research. *World Bank Research Observer*, 18(1), Spring, pp. 25–59.

Cornford, A. (2005), *Basel II: The revised Framework of June (2004)*. UNCTAD Discussion Papers, UNCTAD/OSG/DP/(2005)/2 (178) (New York: UNCTAD).

Coulton, B., Ngiam, A. L. and McCormack, J. (2004), *Credit Analysis of the PRC* (New York: FitchRatings).

Crystal, J. Dages, G. B. and Goldberg, L. (2001), Does foreign ownership contribute to Sounder Banks? The Latin American experience. In Litan, R.,

Masson, P. and Pomerleano. M. (eds), *Open Doors: Foreign Participation in Financial Systems in Developing Countries* (Washington, DC: Brookings Institution and the World Bank), pp. 217–266.

Cull, R. and Xu, L. C. (2000), Bureaucrats, State banks and the efficiency of credit allocation: The experience of Chinese state-owned enterprises. *Journal of Comparative Economics*, 28, pp. 1–31.

Dages, B. G., Kinney, D. and Goldberg, L. (2000), Foreign and domestic bank participation in emerging markets: Lessons from Mexico and Argentina. *Federal Reserve Bank of New York – Economic Policy Review*, 6(3), pp. 17–36.

Davydenko, S. and Franks, J. (2005), *Do Bankruptcy Codes Matter? A Study of Defaults in France, Germany and the UK* (London: London Business School).

Deloitte & Touche (2004), *Keeping Pace with the Times: Seeking Truth from the Facts* (London: Deloitte & Touche).

Deloitte & Touche (2005a), *From Framework to Execution: Effective Planning and Implementation of the Basel II Accord in Asia Pacific* (New York: Deloitte & Touche).

Deloitte & Touche (2005b), *Understanding the Framework: Adopting the Basel II Accord in Asia Pacific* (New York: Deloitte & Touche).

Denis, D. K. and McConnell, J. J. (2003), *International Corporate Governance*, European Corporate Governance Institute Working Paper No. 05/(2003).

Desombre, M. G. and Chen, W. (2004), New capital rules bring China's banking regulation up to global standards. *China Law and Practice*, 18(3), 28 Apr.

Desvaux, G., Wang, M. and Xu, D. (2004), Spurring performance in China's state-owned enterprises. *McKinsey Quarterly*, Special Edition.

Deutsche Bundesbank (2005), *Ergebnisse der vierten Auswirkungsstudie zu Basel II [Results from the Fourth QIS Study]* (Frankfurt/Main: Deutsche Bundesbank).

Dichtl, O., Hedde d'Entremont, L., Narita, K. and Kleinbaum, R. (2004), *Basel II: Overview and Key Effects* (Paris: BNP Paribas). Accessed online under www.openresearch.bnpparibas.com [4 Oct. 2005].

Dickie, M. (2005), China's banking system has made only patchy progress. *Financial Times*, 26 Mar.

Dietsch, M. and Petey, J. (2004), Should SME Exposures be treated as Retail or Corporate exposures? A comparative analysis of probabilities of default and assets correlations in French and German SMEs. *Journal of Banking and Finance*, 28(4), pp. 773–788.

Dolven, B. and Kuhn, A. (2004), Rural Credit Cooperatives – China's other big banking mess. *Far Eastern Economic Review*, 29 Apr.

Dong, F. and Featherstone, A. (2004), *Technical and Scale Efficiencies for Chinese Rural Credit Cooperatives: A Bootstrapping Approach in Data Development Analysis*. Working Paper WP 366, Iowa State University.

Dornbusch, R. and Giavazzi, F. (1999), Heading off China's financial crisis. *Strengthening the Banking System in China: Issues and Experience*. Joint BIS/PBOC Conference proceedings, Beijing, 1–2 Mar. (Basel: BIS), pp. 30–58.

Dougherty, S. and Herd, R. (2005), *Fast-Falling Barriers and Growing Concentration: The Emergence of a Private Economy in China*. OECD Economics Department Working Papers, No. 471 (Paris: OECD Publishing).

Dow Jones International News (2004), National individual credit database targeted '05. 16 Aug.

Dow Jones Chinese Financial Wire (2005), China bank regulator to extend reach of city commercial banks. 13 Dec.

Dow Jones International News (2006), China postal savings bureau begins small-scale loan trial. 19 Apr.

Du, X. (2005), *The Regulatory Environment for Microfinance in China*. Essays on regulation and supervisions, No. 11, University of Maryland.

[Du, Y.] 杜玉红 and [Xu, C.] 许传华 (2005), 城市商业银行公司治理结构问题探讨 [Discussing the issues in the corporate governance structure of CCBs]. *武汉金融 [Wuhan Finance]*, 4(64), pp. 9–11.

Duan, H. 段宏庆, Yu, N. 于宁, He, H. 何华峰, Guo, J. 郭琼 and Li, Z. 历志钢 (2006a), 2006 银行第一大案 [First bank corruption case in 2006]. *《财经》 [Caijing Magazine]*, 6 Mar.

Duan, H. 段宏庆 , Yu, N. 于宁 , He, H. 何华峰 , Guo, J. 郭琼 and Li, Z. 历志钢 (2006b), 反思"正规的地下金融"现象 [Reflecting on the phenomenon of normal underground finance]. *《财经》 [Caijing Magazine]*, 6 Mar.

Dyer, G. and McGregor, R. (2005), China goes to banks for 99% of financing, says report. *Financial Times*, 28 May.

Economist Intelligence Unit (EIU) (2006a), Newfangled investments? *Business China*, 13 Feb.

Economist Intelligence Unit (EIU) (2006b), *China Hand – Finance (2006)* (London: EIU).

Elizade, A. and Repullo, R. (2004), *Economic and Regulatory Capital – what is the difference*? CEMFI Working Paper 0422, Dec.

Ernst & Young (E&Y) (2004), *Asia-Pacific Basel II Survey* (Hong Kong: Ernst & Young).

Ernst & Young (E&Y) (2006), *Global Non-performing Loan Report 2006* (s.l.: Ernst & Young).

Estrella, A. (2004), Bank capital and risk: Is voluntary disclosure enough? *Journal of Financial Services Research*, 26(2), pp. 145–160.

European Commission (EU) (2003), *Review of the Capital Requirements for Credit Institutions and Investment Firms: Third Quantitative Impact Study, EU Results*. Document prepared by the Applied Statistics Group of the Ispra Joint Research Centre, Jul.

Euromonitor (2004), *Commercial Banking in China*. (s.l.: s.n.).

Euroweek (2004), Pressure mounts on mid-tier banks to adopt Basel II guides. 15 Oct.

Ewing, R. D. (2005), Chinese corporate governance and prospects for reform. *Journal of Contemporary China*, 14(43), May, pp. 317–338.

Fan, G. (2004), Créances douteuses et dette publique globale en Chine [NPLs and global public debt in China]. *Revue d'économie financière: Le devenir financier de la Chine*, 77.

Fan, S. (2003), Basel II: Its terms and its implications for Asian banks. *Asian Counsel*, Nov.

Fang, X. (2005), Reconstructing the micro-foundation of China's financial sector. In Huang, Y., Saich, T. and Steinfeld, E. (eds), *Financial Sector Reform in China*. (Cambridge: Harvard University), pp. 19–28.

Fang, Y. (2005), China to merge six city banks in industry overhaul. *Reuters News*, 23 Aug.

Ferri, G., Liu, L. and Majnoni, G. (2000), *How the Proposed Basel Guidelines on Rating-Agency Assessments Would Affect Developing Countries* (Washington: World Bank).

Foreign Investment Advisory Service (FIAS) and China Project Development Facility (CPDF) (2005), *China: Reforming Secured Transactions Laws in China* (Chengdu: FIAS/CPDF).

[Financial News] 金融时报 (2005a), 诚实商业银行抽象调查的一些重要结论 [Some important insights from the sample survey of city commercial banks], 7 Feb.

[Financial News] 金融时报 (2005b), 十年树木 百年树人 寄语城市商业银行十周年 [Wood with 10 years of age and talent of 100 years, speech at the 10th anniversary of the establishment of CCBs], 20 Jun.

[Financial News] 金融时报 (2005c), 资金联合投资显现活力 城商行: 夹缝中拓出生路 [Funds and Investments more lively – city commercial banks find a way through cracks], 29 Jul.

[Financial News] 金融时报 (2006), 银监会加强现场检查严处银行违规行为 [CBRC strengthened on-site inspections and uncovered unlawful activities in banks], 7 Feb.

Findlay, C., Watson, A., Cheng, E. and Zhu, G. (eds) (2003), *Rural Financial Markets in China* (Canberra: Asia Pacific Press).

[First Finance Daily] 第一财经日报 (2005), 南商行次级债中标利率 4.10% [The interest rate on Nanjing CCB subordinated debt is 4.10%], 24 Nov.

FitchRatings (2004), *Demystifying Basel II: A Closer Look at the IRB Measures and Disclosure Framework* (New York: FitchRatings).

Flouzat, D. (2004), Les défis de la transition du système financier chinois [The challenges of the transition of the Chinese financial system]. *Revue d'économie financière: Le devenir financier de la Chine*, 77.

Fu, X. and Shelagh, H. (2005), *China: The Effects of Bank Reform on Structure and Performance*. Cass Faculty of Finance Working Paper: WP-FF-19-(2005).

Gaenssmantel, F. (2003), China's debts: Mountain or molehill? *China Economic Quarterly*, 7(4) (London: Dragonomics Ltd).

Galati, G. (2002), Settlement risk in foreign exchange markets and CLS bank. *BIS Quarterly Review*, Dec.

Gapper, J. (2005), Company charged with clean-up of bad loans seeks fresh fields. *Financial Times*, 8 Nov.

García-Herrero, A., Gavilá, S. and Santabárbara, D. (2005), *China's Banking Reform: An Assessment of its Evolution and Possible Impact*. Documentos Ocasionales No. 0502 (Madrid: Banco de Espana).

Gerhardt, S. E. (2005), *Basel II im Wettstreit internationaler Regulierungsinteressen – Auswirkungen auf Transmission und Wettbewerb [Basel II in the Rivalry of International Regulatory Interests – Impact on Transmission and Competition]* Diss. (Wiesbaden: Deutscher Universitätsverlag).

Giles, T. and Milne, A. (2004), *Basel II and UK Banks – What are the Costs and Benefits of IRB Qualification*? Finance and Financial Products EU Practitioners Papers (London: Charles River Associates).

Gilley, B., Lawrence, S. V. and Murphy, D. (2002), China – Banks – China's Bankers: Rotten to the top. *Far Eastern Economic Review*, 31 Jan.

Gilligan, P. B. (2005), China's NPLs: Trends and future issues. *Technical Briefing*. Accessed online under http://www.deacons.com.hk/eng/knowledge/knowledge_225.htm [6 Mar. 2006].

Girardin, E. (1997), *Banking Sector Reform and Credit Control in China*. Organisation for Economic Cooperation and Development (Paris: Development Centre Studies).

Glantz, M. (2002), *Managing Credit Risk – An Introduction to Broad-Base Credit Engineering* (London: Academic Press).

Goodhart, C. and Zeng, X. (2005), *China's Banking Reform: Problems and Potential Solutions*. Financial Markets Group Special Paper sp163.

Green, S. (2004), Privatisation: The great state sell-down. *China Economic Quarterly*, Q2.

Gregory, N., Tenev, S. and Wagle, D. (2000), *China's Emerging Private Enterprises: Prospects for the New Century* (Washington: International Finance Corporation).

Griffiths, J. J. (2005), The use of CDO structuring for the disposal of non-performing loans in China. *Journal of Structured Finance*, 11(3), pp. 40–51.

Griffith-Jones, S., Segoviano, M. and Spratt, S. (2002), *Basel II and Developing Countries: Diversification and Portfolio Effects* (Brighton: Institute of Development Studies).

Griffith-Jones, S., Segoviano, M. and Spratt, S. (2003), *Submission to the Basel Committee on Banking Supervision: CP3 and the Developing World* (Brighton: Institute of Development Studies).

Grimm, M. (2005), *Das Finanzsystem Chinas zwischen Markt und Politik [China's Financial System Between Market and Politics]* (Baden-Baden: Nomos Verlagsgesellschaft).

Grobowksi, J. and Ho, B. (2002), Financial services sector. *Guide to China and the WTO* (Hong Kong: Baker & McKenzie), pp. 153–176.

Guerrera, F. (2005a), Bank offering might herald radical change – Chinese IPOs. *Financial Times*, 21 Oct.

Guerrera, F. (2005b), CCB's IPO world's biggest in 4 years. *Financial Times*, 21 Oct.

[Guo, L.] 郭立 (2005), 对当前民间融资的调查与思考 [Survey and thoughts on contemporary informal lending]. *金融理论与实践 [Financial Theory and Practice]*, 4(309), pp. 22–24.

[Guo, Q.], 郭琼 [Li, Z.] 历志钢 and [Yu, N.] 于宁 (2006a), 狙击信贷潮 [Snipe the loan tide]. *《财经》[Caijing Magazine]*, 1 May.

[Guo, Q.], 郭琼 [Li, Z.] 历志钢 and [Hu, J.] 胡蛟 (2006b), 博弈 "打捆贷款" [Game of "bundle loans"]. *《财经》 [Caijing Magazine]*, 15 May.

Gup, B. E. (ed.) (2004b), *The New Basel Capital Accord* (New York: Thomson Corp).

Hakenes, H. and Schnabel, I. (2005), *Bank Size and Risk-Taking under Basel II*. Publications 05–07 (Mannheim: Universität Mannheim).

Hale, K. (2004), Basel II – the pitfalls of delaying compliance, *GTNews, Basel II Special Report*, 17 May. Accessed online under http://www.gtnews.com/risk/creditrisk.cfm [14 Oct. 2005].

[Han, X.] 韩雪萌 (2006), 贷款五级分类：农信社改革涉足深水区 [Five Loan Categories: reform of RCCs enters deep waters]. *金融时报 [Financial News]*, 16 Feb.

Hansakul, S. (2004), *China's Financial Sector: Institutional Framework and Main Challenges* (Frankfurt/Main: Deutsche Bank Research).

Hansen, E. (2005), *Level of Preparedness of Asian Banks for Basel II* (Hong Kong: Ernst & Young).

Hansen, E. and Straley, P. (2004), *Asia-Pacific Basel II Survey* (Hong Kong: Ernst & Young).

Harner, S. M. (2004a), Bank reform: Earthquake! *China Economic Quarterly*, 8(3).

Harner, S. M. (2004b), China needs to stand by its new bank rules. *Financial Times*, 8 Jul.

[He, L.] 贺力平 and [Fan, X.] 范小航 (2004), 外资银行在华发展趋势概述 [Summary of the development trends of foreign banks in China]. *国际金融研究 [International Finance Research]*, 12, pp. 11–17.

He, Z. 何忠伟 (2004), 入世后农业信用合作社发展的制度分析 [System analysis of the RCCs' development after the WTO entry]. *调研世界 [Survey World]*, pp. 19–21.

Heilmann, S. (2005), Policy-making and political supervision in Shanghai's financial industry. *Journal of Contemporary China*, 14(45), Nov., pp. 643–668.

Helbekkmo, H., Shahram, E., Samuels, D. and Jameson, R. (2005), *The Ripple Effect: How Basel II Will Impact Institutions of All Sizes* (New York: ERisk).

Henneke, J. and Trück, S. (2005), *Capital Requirements for SMEs under the Revised Basel II Framework* (Universität Karlsruhe: s.n.).

Hoffbauer, A. (2005), Auslandsbanken warten in China noch auf die erhofften Gewinne [Foreign banks in China are still waiting for profits]. *Handelsblatt*, 15 Nov.

Holland, T. and Baglole, J. (2003), Banking In Asia: Bank regulation – Asia faces a stark choice. *Far Eastern Economic Review*, 25 Sept.

Holz, C. A. (2001), China's Monetary Reform: The counterrevolution from the countryside. *Journal of Contemporary China*, 10(27), pp. 189–217.

Hong, W. (2004), Die Rolle von Ratings, Ratingagenturen und Rating advisory in China [The role of ratings: Rating agencies and rating advisory work in China]. In Achleitner, A.-K. and Everling, O. (eds), *Handbuch Ratingpraxis [Handbook for Rating Practice]* (Wiesbaden: Gabler Verlag), pp. 689–696.

Hooke, P. (2006), Profile: China's banking sector. *Asia Pulse*, 10 Mar.

Hope, N. and Hu, F. (2005), *Foreign Investment in Chinese Banks*. Presentation at Stanford Center for International Development (SCID)'s Conference on China's Policy Reforms: Progress and Challenges, 29 Sept.–1 Oct.

Hope, N. and Hu, F. (2006), *Reforming China's Banking System: How Much can Foreign Strategic Investment Help*? Stanford Centre for International Development. WP 276.

Hu, F. (2002), *China Insight: Banking Reform in China* (Hong Kong: Goldman Sachs).

Hu, F. (2005), The truth about investing in China's banks. *Financial Times*, 18 Nov.

[Hu, J.] 胡蛟 (2005), GDP " 跳跃 " [GDP's leap]. *《财经》[Caijing Magazine]*, 26 Dec.

[Hu, S.] 胡舒立 (2006), 中国银行 IPO 凯旋之后 [After the triumph of the Bank of China IPO]. *《财经》[Caijing Magazine]*, 12 Jun.

[Hu, Z.] 胡祖六 (2005), 银行改革需要国际战略投资吗 [Does the Chinese banks reform require international strategic investors?]. *《经济观察报》 [Economic Observer]*, 12 Dec.

[Huan, G.] 宦国苍 (2005), 三问国有银行战略引资 [Three questions on the drawing of foreign strategic investors in SOCBs]. *《财经》[Caijing Magazine]*, 12 Dec.

Huang, Y., Saich, T. and Steinfeld, E. (eds) (2005), *Financial Sector Reform in China* (Cambridge: Harvard University).

Institute of International Finance (IIF) (2005a). Steering Committee on Regulatory Capital. *The Implementation of Basel II* (Washington: IIF).

Institute of International Finance (IIF) (2005b), *China: Economic Indicators* (Washington, DC: IIF).

Institute of International Finance (IIF) (2006), *Corporate Governance in China: An Investor Perspective*. IIF Task Force Report.

International Fund for Agricultural Development (IFAD) (2001), Rural financial services in China (Washington: IFAD).

International Monetary Fund (IMF) and World Bank (WB) (2002), *Implementation of the Basel Core Principles for Effective Banking Supervision, Experiences, Influences and Perspectives* (Washington: IMF/WB).

Intrater, M. (2004), Basel II for non-Basel II banks. *Bank and Accounting Finance*, Oct.–Nov., pp. 3–9.

Intrater, M. and Garside, T. (2003a), *The New Rules of the Game – Strategic Implications of the Basel II Capital Accord* (New York: Mercer Oliver Wyman [MOW]).

Intrater, M. and Garside, T. (2003b), *The New Rules of the Game – Strategic Implications of the Basel II Capital Accord for the European Banking Industries* (New York: MOW).

Jacobson, T., Linde, J. and Roszbach, K. (2004), *Credit Risk Versus Capital Requirements under Basel II: Are SME Loans and Retail Credit Really Different*? Sverige Riksbank Stockholm Working Paper Series, 162, Apr.

[Jiang, J.] 姜建清 (2005), *国有商业银行改革实践 [Reform Practices in SOCBs]*. Speech at the Caijing Magazine Annual Conference: "(2006): Forecasts and Strategies", Beijing, 12 Dec.

[Jiang, X.] 姜旭朝 and [Ding, C.] 丁昌锋 (2004), 民间金融理论分析：范畴、比较与制度变迁 [Analysis of the informal finance theory: Categories, comparison and system transition]. *金融研究 [Finance Research (PBOC)]*, 08, pp. 100–111.

[Jiangxi Daily] 江西日报 (2006), 农村信用社：六大举措支持新农村建设 [RCCs: Six measures to support the new rural infrastructure], 8 Feb.

[Jiao, J.] 焦瑾璞 (2006), 农村金融向何处去 [Where is rural finance heading to?]. *《财经》 [Caijing Magazine]*, 6 Feb.

[Jing, X.] 景学成 (2005), *走向现代金融制度 – 兼论中国金融业『入世』[Towards a Modern Financial System – China's Finance Industry Entering the WTO]* (上海 [Shanghai]: 上海财经大学出版社 [Shanghai Finance and Economics University Press]).

Kalish, I. (2006), *China and India: The Reality beyond the Hype* (New York: Deloitte & Touche).

Kamakura (2004), *China Everbright Bank Licenses Kamakura Risk Management and Basel II System*, Press Release (Honolulu: Kamakura).

Kelleher, E. and Dyer, G. (2005), Experian eyes China car market. *Financial Times*, 8 Sept.

King and Wood (2005), Reliable data and China's financial reforms (part I). *International Financial Law Review*, Nov.

Klein, D. (2005), Der Umbau des chinesischen Bankensystems: Maßnahmen in der Bankenaufsicht sowie Geld- und Wechselkurspolitik [Restructuring of the Chinese Banking System – measures for regulatory and monetary policies]. *Kreditwesen*, 8, pp. 421–424.

KPMG (2003), *Basel II. A Worldwide Challenge for the Banking Business*, Financial Services Basel Initiative. Accessed online under www.kpmg.com [04 Oct. 2005].

KPMG (2005), *China's City Commercial Banks: Opportunity Knocks*? (Hong Kong: KPMG Financial Services).

Krug, B. and Hendrischke, H. (2003), China incorporated: Property rights, networks and the emergence of a private business sector in China. *Managerial Finance*, 29(12).

Kupiec, P. H. (2004), *Capital Adequacy and Basel II*. FDIC Centre for Financial Research Working Paper, 02.

Kwong, C. C. L. and Lee, P. K. (2005), Bad loans versus sluggish rural industrial growth: A policy dilemma of China's banking reform. *Journal of the Asia Pacific Economy*, 10(1), Feb., pp. 1–25.

Kynge, J. (2002), Expectations look set to outstrip the reality. Survey: China and the WTO. *Financial Times*, 15 Mar.

Kynge, J. (2004), PwC set to certify Bank of China's NPLs. *Financial Times*, 21 Apr.

La Porta, R., Lopez-de-Silances, F. and Shleifer, A. (2000), *Government ownership of banks*. Discussion Paper 1890 (Harvard University: Harvard Institute of Economic Research).

Langlois, J. D. (2000), Shell Game: Taxing China's banks. *Asian Wall Street Journal*, 12 Oct.

Langlois, J. D. (2001), The WTO and China's financial system. *The China Quarterly*, 167, 09, pp. 610–629.

Lardy, N. R. (1999), The challenge of bank restructuring in China. *Strengthening the Banking System in China: Issues and Experience*, Joint BIS/PBOC Conference proceedings, Beijing, 1–2 Mar. (Basel: BIS), pp. 17–39.

Lardy, N. R. (2000), *When will China's Financial System Meet China's Needs*? Working Paper No. 54 (Stanford University: Center for Research on Economic Development and Policy Reform).

Lau, L. J. (1999), The macro-economy and reform of the banking sector in China, In *Strengthening the Banking System in China: Issues and Experience*, Joint BIS/PBOC Conference proceedings, Beijing, 1–2 Mar. (Basel: Bank for International Settlements), pp. 59–89.

Lee, J. L. (2006), Credit raters in China take generous view. *The Wall Street Journal*, 22 Mar.

Leung, M. K. and Chan R. (2006), Are foreign banks sure winners in post-WTO China? *Business Horizons*, 49, pp. 221–234.

Leung, M. K., Rigby, D. and Young, T. (2003), Entry of foreign banks in the People's Republic of China: A survival analysis. *Applied Economics*, 35(1), pp. 21–31.

[Li, C.] 李昌宇 and [Jie, S.] 解淑青 (2004), 论农村信用社的产权制度改革 [About the reform of the ownership system in RCCs]. *边疆经济与文化 [Frontier Economics and Culture]*, 1, pp. 83–85.

[Li, D.] 李德 (2006), 央行：中国资产管理公司运营状况分析 [PBOC: Analysis of the operational situation of Chinese AMCs]. *中国证券网 – 上海证券报 [China Securities Net – Shanghai Securities Newspaper]*, 14 Feb.

Li, H., Meng, L. and Zhang, J. (2006), Why do entrepreneurs enter politics? evidence from China. *Economic Enquiry*, doi:10,1093/ei/cbj031.

Li, K. and Ma, J. (2005), The economic intricacies of banking reform in China. *The Chinese Economy*, 37(4), Jul.–Aug., pp. 50–77.

[Li, L.] 李岚 (2005a), 资产证券化：开端有深意 前景更看好 [Asset Securitisation: A meaningful debut with even better prospects]. *金融时报 [Financial News]*, 16 Dec.

[Li, L.] 李利明 (2005b), 谁在反对银行业对外开放 [Who is against the opening of the banking industry?]. *《经济观察报》[Economic Observer]*, 8 Dec.

[Li, Q.] 李箐 and [Zhao, Y.] 赵逸荻 (2006), 外资入 A 股：模糊的信号 [Foreign Investors to Enter A-shares: an unclear signal]. *《财经》[Caijing Magazine]*, 23 Jan.

[Li, X.] 李晓君 (2005), 转轨经济背景下中国国有商业银行的产权改革 [Ownership reform of SOCBs within a transition economy]. *潍坊学院学报 [Journal of Weifang University]*, 5(3), pp. 68–71.

[Li, Y.] 李玉吉 (2005), 效率视角的公司治理与国有银行改革 [Corporate governance and state-owned bank reform from the point of view of efficiency]. *商业研究 [Commercial Research]*, 11(319), pp. 43–47.

[Li, Z.] 历志钢 (2006), 必须加强合规风险管理 [It is necessary to strengthen rules-based risk management]. *《财经》[Caijing Magazine]*, 1 May.

[Li, Z.] 李正华 (2004), 试论加入 WTO我国商业银行的发展战略 [About the development strategy of Chinese commercial banks in the WTO entry]. *吉林省经济管理干部学院学报 [Journal of Jilin Province Economic Management Cadre College]*, 18(6), pp. 8–10.

[Li, Z.] 李正华 (2005), 城市商业银行改革与发展的思考 [Reform of CCBs and thoughts about their development]. *吉林省经济管理干部学院学报 [Journal of Jilin Province Economic Management Cadre College]*, 1(19), Feb., pp. 46–48.

[Lin, Q.] 林靖 (2004), IFC 的中国经验 [IFC's China experience]. *《财经》[Caijing Magazine]*, 27 Dec.

[Ling, H.] 凌华薇 (2003), 贷款分类改革十年曲折 [Twisted road of 10 years of loan classification reform]. *《财经》[Caijing Magazine]*, 8 May.

[Ling, H.] 凌华薇 (2005a), 周小川谈建行改革 [Zhou Xiaochuan talks about CCB's reform]. *《财经》[Caijing Magazine]*, 28 Nov.

[Ling, H.] 凌华薇 (2005b), 农行重组尚无解 [Restructuring of ABC not yet decided]. *《财经》[Caijing Magazine]*, 17 Oct.

[Ling, H.] 凌华薇 (2006), 谁主导农行改革？[Who dominates ABC's reforms?]. *《财经》[Caijing Magazine]*, 29 May.

[Ling, H.] 凌华薇, Cao H. 曹海丽 and Lu, Y. 卢彦铮 (2005), 第一次握手 [The first handshake]. *《财经》[Caijing Magazine]*, 28 Jun.

[Ling, H.] 凌华薇 and [Guo, Q.] 郭琼 (2006), 银行: 较之激励机制的改革，银行人事制度改革更为本质，倘不能通过市场竞争选拔经理人, 单方面的薪酬体制改革只能南辕北辙 [Banking: compared with the reform of the incentives system, the reform of human resources system is more crucial: if managers are not chosen competitively in the market, the unilateral reform of the remuneration system will drive nowhere]. 中国 (2006) 反思之年 [Reflecting on China's year 2006]. *《财经》[Caijing Magazine]*, 6 Feb.

[Ling, H.] 凌华薇 and [Li, Q.] 李箐 (2005): 建行改革 在姑息与手术之间 [Reform of CCB: Between appeasement and surgery]. *《财经》[Caijing Magazine]*, 18 Apr.

[Ling, H.] 凌华薇 and [Lu, C.] 卢彦铮 (2004), 外资入股: 诱惑与困惑 [Foreign Entry: Between temptation and perplexity]. *《财经》[Caijing Magazine]*, 27 Dec.

[Ling, H.] 凌华薇 and [Zhang, X.] 张小彩 (2005), 工行改革难与易 [Hard and easy bits of the reform of ICBC]. *《财经》[Caijing Magazine]*, 25 Feb.

[Ling, Y.] 岭一晟 (2004), 谁降低了国有银行不良贷款率 [Who decreased the NPL ratio of state-owned banks]. *《财经》[Caijing Magazine]*, 24 Feb.

[Liu, D.] 刘丹丹 (2004), 在华外资银行的发展趋势与监管 [Development trends and supervision of foreign banks in China]. *云南财贸学院学报 [Journal of Yunnan Finance & Economics University]*, 19(4), pp. 36–38.

[Liu, L.] 陆磊 (2004), 利率调整与商业银行状况 [Adjustment of interest rates and the situation at commercial banks]. *《财经》[Caijing Magazine]*, 29 Nov.

[Liu, L.] 陆磊 (2006a), 再看建行 [Look once more at CCB]. *《财经》[Caijing Magazine]*, 6 Feb.

[Liu, L.] 陆磊 (2006b), 金融业国际化、监管国际化和风险传递 [Internationalisation of the finance industry and of supervision and risk transmission]. *《财经》[Caijing Magazine]*, 9 Jan.

[Liu, L.] 陆磊 , [Yu, N.] 于宁 and [Ling, H.] 凌华薇 (2005), 大博弈 – 中国银行业引资模式分析 [Big Game: Analysis of the model for attracting investments in China's banking industry]. *《财经》[Caijing Magazine]*, 19 Sept.

[Liu, L.] 陆磊 and [Zhu, X.] 祝晓平 (2003), 农信社改革十大难点 [Ten major problems in the reform of RCCs]. *《财经》 [Caijing Magazine]*, 10 Aug.

[Liu, M.] 刘明 (2004), 论农信社"革命": 难点与建议 [About the "Revolution" in RCCs: Difficulties and proposals]. *四川大学学报 [Sichuan University Journal]*, 132(3), pp. 10–15.

[Liu, M.] 刘明康 (2005), 新资本协议助力银行业公司治理迈上新台阶 [The new capital accord helps corporate governance in the banking industry to move to the next step]. *中国金融家 [China Financialyst]*, 01, pp. 19–21.

[Liu, M.] 刘民权 , [Xu, Z.] 徐忠 , [Yu, J.] 俞建拖 , [Zhou, S.] 周盛武 and [Zhao, Y.] 赵英涛 (2005), 农村信用社市场化改革探索 [Exploring the market reforms of RCCs]. *金融研究 [Finance Research (PBOC)]*, 4, pp. 99–112.

Liu, Q. (2006), *Corporate Governance in China: Current Practices, Economic Effects and Institutional Determinants*. Working paper CESifo Economic Studies, doi:10,1093/cesifo/ifl001.

Liu, S. (1999), China's experience in small and medium financial institution resolution. *Strengthening the Banking System in China: Issues and Experience*, Joint BIS/PBOC Conference proceedings, Beijing, 1–2 Mar. (Basel: BIS), pp. 298–303.

[Liu, X.] 刘兴桂 and [Liu, S.] 刘淑勤 (2004), 加入 WTO 与我国外资银行监管法律制度改革 [The WTO entry and the reform of the legal system for regulating foreign banks in China]. *广州大学学报 [Guanzhou University Journal]* 3(7), Jul., pp. 51–55.

[Liu, Y.] 刘永刚 (2005), 中国银行业面临六大挑战 [The Chinese banking industry's current six big challenges]. *《中国经济周刊》 [China Economic Weekly]*, 19 Dec.

[Liu, Y.] 刘洋 (2006), 最差城商行 : 退市还是扶持 [The Worst CCBs: Exit the market or get support]. *国际金融报 [International Finance News]*, 16 Jan.

Lo, C. (2004), Bank reform: How much time does China have? *China Business Review*, Mar.–Apr., Accessed online under http://www.chinabusinessreview.com/public/0403/chilo.html [26 Feb. 2006].

[Long, X.] 龙雪晴 (2004), 好事多磨深发展 [Shenzhen Development Bank: Road to happiness is full of hardships]. *《财经》 [Caijing Magazine]*, 27 Dec.

Longueville, G. and Ngo, N.-N. (2004), Le système bancaire chinois: un risque systémique [The Chinese Banking System: a systemic risk]. *Revue d'économie financière: Le devenir financier de la Chine*, 77.

Lou, J. (2000), China's Bank Non-performing Loan Problem: Seriousness and causes. *International Lawyer*, 34(4), pp. 1147–1192.

Lu, D., Thangavelu, S. M. and Hu, Q. (2005), Biased lending and non-performing loans in China's banking sector. *The Journal of Development Studies*, 41(6), Aug., pp. 1071–1091.

[Lu, M.] 陆锦文 (2004), 论国有商业银行公司治理结构与道德风险防范 [About the structure of corporate governance in SOCBs and preventing moral hazard]. *中山大学学报论丛 [Sun Yatsen University Forum]*, 124(16), pp. 219–224.

[Lu, M.] 陆岷峰 (2005), 城市商业银行个性风险特征和管理对策 [Characteristics and management response to specific risks of CCBs]. *青海金融 [Qinghai Finance]*, 6.

Lu, S. F. and Yao, Y. (2003), *The Effectiveness of the Law: Financial Development and Economic Growth in an Economy of Financial Depression: Evidence from China*. Center for Research on Economic Development and Policy Reform, 179.

[Lu, Y.] 卢彦铮 (2005), 建行 IPO: 阳光与阴影 [CCB's IPO sunshine and shadows]. *《财经》 [Caijing Magazine]*, 17 Oct.

[Lu, Y.] 卢彦铮 and [Long, X.] 龙雪晴 (2005), 广发行重组一波三折 [Restructuring of Guangdong Development Bank: one wave and three curves]. *《财经》[Caijing Magazine]*, 22 Aug.

[Luo, J.] 罗金生 (2002a), 何种银行产权安排更有利于经济转轨 [Which bank property rights arrangement is more auspicious to the economic transition?]. *《财贸经济》[Finance and Trade Economy]*, 4, pp. 20–24.

[Luo, J.] 罗金生 (2002b), 利益博弈与不良债权的形成 [Interest games and the apparition of non-performing debts]. *《经济理论与经济管理》[Economic Theory and Economic Management]*, 1, pp. 22–25.

Luo, P. (2003), *Challenges for China's banking sector and policy responses*, Speech at the Conference: "A Tale of Two Giants: India's and China's Experience with Reform and Growth", New Dehli, 14–16 Nov., Accessed online under www.imf.org/external/np/apd/seminars/2003/newdelhi/ping.pdf [15 Nov. 2005].

Ma, G. and Fung, B. (2002), *China's Asset Management Corporations*. BIS Working papers (Basel: BIS).

Ma, Z. (2003a), The evolution of the rural financial system and policies. In Findlay, C., Watson, A. and Cheng, E. (eds), *Rural Financial Markets in China* (Canberra: Asia Pacific Press), pp. 35–45.

Ma, Z. (2003b), Rural informal finance. In Findlay, C., Watson, A. and Cheng, E. (eds), *Rural Financial Markets in China* (Canberra: Asia Pacific Press), pp. 105–119.

Majnoni, G., Miller, M. and Powell, A. (2004), *Bank Capital and Loan Loss Reserves under Basel II: Implications for Emerging Countries*. World Bank Policy Research Working Paper 3437, Oct. (Washington: World Bank).

Manning, P. (2004), Basel II: Unfinished business. Global Association of Risk Professionals, *GARP News*, 20, Sept./Oct.

Marshall, D., Lin, K. and Lin, L. (2004a), *China Bank Prudential Regulations* (New York: FitchRatings).

Marshall, D., Lin, K. and Lin, L. (2004b), *Chinese Banks' Asset Quality and Capital Adequacy: Data and Trends* (New York: FitchResearch).

Marshall, D., Lin, K., Lin, L. and Tebbutt, P. (2005a), *Chinese Banks: 2004 Review and 2005 Outlook* (New York: FitchResearch).

Marshall, D., Tebbutt, P., Toritani, R. and Srivastava, A. (2005b), *Asian Banks and Basel II* (New York: FitchResearch).

Marshall, D., Lin, K., Lee, J. and Lee, S. (2006), *Managing Growth – The Challenge of Consumer Lending in Asia* (New York: FitchResearch).

Maude, D. J. (2006), *Global Private Banking and Wealth Management* (London: John Wiley & Sons).

McGregor, R. (2004), How to Transform a Banking System – Richard McGregor hears about the Government's hydra-like plans for reform and finds they have a long way to go. *Financial Times*, 7 Dec.

McGregor, R. and Pretzlik, C. (2003), China formally rejects Basel II rules. *Financial Times*, 16 Aug.

McIver, R. (2005), Asset Management Companies, State-owned Commercial Bank Debt Transfers and Contingent Claims: Issues in the valuation of China's non-performing loans. *Managerial Finance*, 31(12), pp. 11–29.

McKinsey Global Institute (MGI) (2006), *Putting China's Capital to Work: The Value of Financial System Reform* (Sydney: McKinsey & Co).

Melka, J. and Xu, W. (2004), Le poids des créances douteuses dans l'économie chinoise: existe-t-il un risque systémique? [The weight of NPLs on the Chinese

Economy: Is there a systemic risk?]. *Revue d'économie financière: Le devenir financier de la Chine*, 77.

Metcalfe, B. (2005), *Foreign Banks in China* (Hong Kong: PwC).

Miller, T. (2005), Private enterprise: Faster, higher, stronger. *China Economic Quarterly* Q12005, pp. 47–49.

Mitchell, T. and Lau, J. (2006), A Piece of the Action: Why investors are fired up by Chinese IPOs. *Financial Times*, 1 Jun.

Mo, Y. K. (1999), A review of recent banking reforms in China, *Strengthening the Banking System in China: Issues and Experience*, Joint BIS/PBOC Conference proceedings, Beijing, 1–2 Mar. (Basel: BIS), pp. 90–109.

Montes-Negret, F. (1995), China's Credit Plan: An overview. *Oxford Review of Economic Policy*, 11(4), Winter, pp. 18–25.

Moody's KMV. (2005), *Moody's KMV Internal Rating Platform and the Basel II IRB Approaches: Addressing Issues Raised by the New Basel Capital Accord's Internal Ratings-based Approach* (New York: Moody's).

Mori, J. (2003), *China's WTO Accession and Its Impact on China's Financial System*. Institute for International Monetary Affairs, Paper prepared for presentation at the Kyoto University China Project – Workshop on China's Economic Development and Structural Change in East Asia, Kyoto University, 8–9 Feb.

Mrak, M. (2003), *Implementation of the New Basel Capital Accord in Emerging Market Economies: Problems and Alternatives* (Warwick: University of Warwick).

Nasution, A. (1999), Recent issues in the management of macroeconomic policies: the PRC. In Asian Development Bank (ADB) (eds), *Rising to the Challenge in Asia, A Study of Financial Markets – Volume 4: People's Republic of China* (Manila: ADB).

Ng, C. Y. M. (2002), One Country, Two Systems: Insolvency administration in the PRC. *Managerial Auditing Journal*, 17(7), pp. 363–373.

[Niu, M.] 钮明 , [Zhang, X.] 张欣 and [Lin, H.] 邻淮 (2004), 民间借贷: 现状与抉择 [Informal lending: Current situation and choices]. *金融理论与实践 [Financial Theory and Practice]*, 6(299), pp. 15–18.

Nouy, D. (1999), Strengthening the Banking System: Issues and exposures, In *Strengthening the Banking System in China: Issues and Experience*, Joint BIS/PBOC Conference proceedings, Beijing, 1–2 Mar. (Basel: BIS), pp. 211–220.

Ong, M. K. (1999), *Internal Credit Risk Models – Capital Allocation and Performance Measurement* (London: Risk Books).

Ong, M. K. (ed.) (2002), *Credit Ratings: Methodologies, Rationale and Default Risk* (London: Risk Books).

Ong, M. K. (ed.) (2004), *The Basel Handbook: A Guide for Financial Practitioners* (London: Risk Books).

Organisation for Economic Cooperation and Development (OECD) (2004a), *Principles of Corporate Governance* (Paris: OECD Publishing).

Organisation for Economic Cooperation and Development (OECD) (2004b), *China in the Global Economy: Rural Credit and Credit Infrastructure in China*. Proceedings from a workshop of the OECD organised in Paris in October 2003 (Paris: OECD Publishing).

Organisation for Economic Cooperation and Development (OECD) (2005), *China OECD Economic Survey* (2005)/13, Sept. (Paris: OECD Publishing).

Park, A., Ren, C. and Wang, S. (2003), *Microfinance, Poverty Alleviation and Financial Reform in China*. Workshop on Rural Finance and Credit Infrastructure in China, 13–14 Oct., Paris, France.

Park, A. and Sehrt, K. (2001), Tests of financial intermediation and banking reform in China. *Journal of Comparative Economics*, 29, pp. 608–644.

Peerenboom, R. (2002), Social Networks, Rule of Law and Economic Growth in China: the elusive pursuit of the right combination of private and public ordering. *Global Economic Review*, 31(2), Research paper 03–3.

Pei, M. (2006a), China is stagnating in its "trapped transition". *Financial Times*, 24 Feb.

Pei, M. (2006b), How rotten politics feeds a bad loan crunch in China. *Financial Times*, 8 May.

[Peng, J.] 彭建刚 , [Xiang, S.] 向实 and [Wang, J.] 王建伟 (2005), 内部评级法的基本思想及其对我国银行业发展的影响 [The basic thinking behind the IRB approach and the impact on the development of China's banking industry]. *财经的理念与实践 [Theory and Practice of Finance and Economics]* 26(133), Jan.

People's Bank of China (PBOC) (2003), *Almanac of Banking and Finance* (Beijing: PBOC).

People's Bank of China (PBOC) (2004), *中国中小企业金融制度调查 [Survey on SME Financing Structure in China]*, Internal report (unpublished).

People's Bank of China (PBOC) (2005a), *Monetary Policy Report 1st Quarter* (Beijing: PBOC).

People's Bank of China (PBOC) (2005b), *Monetary Policy Report 2nd Quarter* (Beijing: PBOC).

People's Bank of China (PBOC) (2005c), *Monetary Policy Report 4th Quarter* (Beijing: PBOC).

People's Bank of China (PBOC) (2005d), *中国金融稳定报告 (2005) [China Financial Stability Report 2005]* (Beijing: PBOC).

[People's Net – Jiangnan Times] 人民网 – 江南时报 (2005), 国家不再为银行经营亏损埋单[The state will not cover up operational losses of banks] 7 Dec.

Pissler, K. B. (2002a), Corporate Governance in der VR China: Neue Vorschriften für börsenzugelassene Gesellschaften [Corporate Governance in China: New rules for listed companies]. *China Analysis* No. 17.

Pissler, K. B. (2002b), Auswirkungen des WTO-Beitritts auf das chinesische Bank- und Börsenrecht [Impact of China's entry to the WTO on Chinese banking and securities regulations]. *China Analysis* No. 11.

Pitsilis, E. V., Woetzel, J. R. and Wong, J. (2004), Checking China's vital signs. *McKinsey Quarterly*, Special Edition.

Podpiera, R. (2006), *Progress in China's Banking Sector Reform: Has Bank Behavior Changed*? IMF Working Paper (WP/06/71, Mar.) (Washington, DC: IMF).

PomerleaNo, M. (1999), The Framework for Financial Supervision in China: Offsite supervision and credit information, In *Strengthening the Banking System in China: Issues and Experience*, Joint BIS/PBOC Conference proceedings, Beijing, 1–2 Mar. (Basel: BIS), pp. 189–210.

Powell, A. (2002), *A Capital Accord for Emerging Economies*? (Washington: World Bank).

Powell, A. (2004), *Basel II and Developing Countries: Sailing Through the Sea of Standards*. Policy Research Working Paper 3387 (Washington: World Bank).

PriceWaterhouseCoopers (PwC) (2004a), *Basel II Navigator Tool* (s.l.: PwC).

PriceWaterhouseCoopers (PwC) (2004b), *Study on the Financial and Macroeconomic Consequences of the Draft Proposed New Capital Requirements for Banks and Investment Firms in the EU* (Brussels: European Commission).

PriceWaterhouseCoopers (PwC) (2004c), *China NPL Investor Survey 2004* (s.l.: PwC).

PriceWaterhouseCoopers (PwC) (2004d), *China's Proposed New Bankruptcy Law – the Practical Implications* (HongKong: PwC).

PriceWaterhouseCoopers (PwC) (2005), *NPL Asia* (s.l.: PwC).

PriceWaterhouseCoopers (PwC) (2006), *NPL Asia* (s.l.: PwC).

[Qian, X.] 钱小安 (2004), 市场化改革中的资金配置机制、结构及其影响 [The funds allocation mechanism, structure and its influence in the market-driven reforms]. *金融研究* [*Finance Research* (PBOC)] 03, pp. 16–27.

Ramos, R., Ma, N., Meng, J. and Inamdar, T. (2005), *China Banks – The USD 10 bln Question: Where to for Bank Reform*? (New York: Goldman Sachs).

[Ren, B.] 任波 (2005a), 邮政改革揭幕 [Start off for the reform of the Postal savings bank]. *《财经》[Caijing Magazine]*, 25 Jul.

[Ren, B.] 任波 (2005b), 催生邮储银行 [Giving birth to the postal savings bank]. *《财经》[Caijing Magazine]*, 8 Aug.

[*Reuters Chinese*] (2006), *路透社* 发改委主任称继续推进国有银行股改，并坚持绝对控股 [NDRC chairman calls for continuing the SOCBs shareholding reforms, but maintaining a controlling share], 2 Mar.

Reuters News (2006), China to implement new Basel II for some banks, 10 Apr.

Rime, B. (2005), Will Basel II lead to a specialization of unsophisticated banks on high-risk borrowers? *International Finance*, 8(1), pp. 29–55.

Rixtel, A., van Alexopoulou, I. and Harada, K. (2003), *The New Basel Capital Accord and its Impact on Japanese Banking: A Quantitative Analysis*. Centre for Economic Institutions Working Papers Series (Tokyo/Frankfurt/Main: Institute of Economic Research).

Robinson, J. (2006), Business Strategies – China: Overcoming the challenges. *Cards International*, 10 Feb.

Rodman, J. and Chan, P. K. (2004), (2003) *Annual Review: Non-Performing Loans in China* (s.l.: Ernst & Young).

Rojas-Suarez, L. (2001), *Can International Capital Standards Strengthen Banks in Emerging Markets*? (Washington: International Institute for Economics).

Sapienza, P. (2004), The effects of government ownership on bank lending. *Journal of Financial Economics*, 72, pp. 357–384.

Saurina, J. and Trucharte, C. (2004), The impact of Basel II on lending to small- and medium-sized firms: A regulatory policy assessment based on Spanish credit register data. *Journal of Financial Services Research*, 26(2), pp. 121–144.

Schlotthauer, N. (2003), *Unternehmens- und Bankenreform in China [Enterprise and Banking Reform in China]* (Frankfurt/Main: Peter Lang).

Schmidt Bies, S. (2005), *Community Banks – A Regulatory Update*, Remarks at the American Bankers Association CFO Exchange Conference.

Schmitz, E. (2004), *Bankenreform und geldpolitische Steuerung in der Volksrepublik China: Entwicklung, Stand und Perspektiven [Banking Reform and Monetary Policies in the PRC: Development, Situation and Perspectives]* (Düsseldorf: s.n.).

Schobert, F. and Schulte, A. (2005), Chinese Financial Markets – How have they evolved and where may they go to? *China Aktuell* 5.

Schüller, M. (2006), Ausländische Banken drängen nach China – Marktchancen werden höher als Risiken eingeschätzt [Foreign banks push towards

China – market chances are estimated as being higher than risks]. *China Aktuell*, 15 Feb.

Segoviano, M. A. and Lowe, P. (2002), *Internal Ratings, the Business Cycle and Capital Requirements: Some Evidence from an Emerging Market Economy*. BIS Working Papers 117 (Basel: BIS).

[Shanghai Securities Times] 上海证券报 (2004), 央行加快中央基础信用信息系统建设 [PBOC accelerates the establishment of a central basic credit information system], 21 Oct.

[Shen, J.] 沈钧 (2005), 新巴塞尔协议与我国银行业监管改革 [The new Basel accord and the reform of the Chinese banking supervision]. *华东经济管理 [Eastern China Economic Management]*, 19(4), Apr.

[Shen, L.] 沈理明 and [Hua, J.] 华金辉 (2005), 加入 WTO 后外资银行地位及竞争策略 [The position and competitive strategy of foreign banks after the WTO entry]. *黑龙江对外经贸 [Heilongjiang Foreign Economic Relations and Trade]*, 5(131), pp. 37–39.

Shen, M. and Cheng, E. (2004), *Restructuring China's Rural Financial System: Existing Approaches, Challenges and the Future of Microfinance*. Background Paper for the German Agency for Technical Cooperation (GTZ).

Sheng, A., Xiao, G. and Wang, Y. (2005), Property rights and "original sin" in China. *Perspectives*, 6(1).

[Sheng, H.] 盛洪 and [Jiang, P.] 江平等 (2004), 专家谈地下融资 [Experts talk about informal finance]. *银行家 – 农村金融 [The Banker – Rural Finance]*, pp. 124–128.

[Shi, C.] 石朝格 (2004), 银监会似向监管对象征收 50 亿年费？[Can CBRC take CNY 5 bln in fees yearly from supervised banks?]. *世纪经济报道 [World Economic News]*, 12 Mar.

Shih, V. (2004), Factions Matter: Personal networks and the distribution of bank loans in China. *Journal of Contemporary China*, 13(38), Feb., pp. 3–19.

Shih, V. (2005), China's uphill battle for stronger banks. *Far Eastern Economic Review*, 168(10), Nov.

Shih, V., Huang, L. and Lee, J. (2005a), Stuck in the quicksand. *China Economic Quarterly*, Q4, pp. 48–51.

Shih, V., Zhang, Q. and Liu, M. (2005b), *Comparing the Performance of Chinese Banks: A Principal Component Approach* (Chicago: Northwestern University).

[Shu, M.] 舒眉 (2005), 要不要重思银行改革路径? [Shall we rethink the banking reform path?]. *《南方周末》[Southern Weekend]*, 1 Dec.

[Sina Finance News] 新浪网财经新闻 (2004), 四大商业银行短期难达到"新巴塞尔协议" [In the short-term the Big four are unlikely to reach Basel II], 4 Jun.

[Sina Finance News] 新浪网财经新闻 (2005), 新巴塞尔协议明年实施 刘明康称中国需要过渡期 [Implementing Basel II Next Year: Liu Mingkang thinks China needs a transition period], 19 May.

[Sina Financial News] 新浪财经 (2005), 交通银行十级评级试验 [BoCom's 10 rating grades on trial], 14 Oct.

SinoCast China Business Daily News (2005), PBC to establish state credit bureau, 16 Jun.

SinoCast China Business Daily News (2006), Enterprise Credit Database to be Connected Nationwide, 1 Mar.

SinoCast China Financial Watch (2005a), China city banks in capital build-up spree, 29 Jun.

SinoCast China Financial Watch (2005b), ICBC to scrap five-category lending, 26 Jul.

SinoCast China Financial Watch (2005c), Rabobank to buy Liaoning RCCU stake, 29 Dec.

SinoCast China Financial Watch (2006a), Banks prefer bonds to loans, 26 Jan.

SinoCast China Financial Watch (2006b), Global banks tap needs of China wealth management, 27 Apr.

SinoCast China Financial Watch (2006c), Foreign bankers keen on China SMEs, 6 Jun.

Situ, P. (2003), *Microfinance in China and Development Opportunities* (Frankfurt/Main: GTZ).

South China Morning Post (2005a), ICBC heeds Call to Boost SME Lending – Mainland's biggest commercial bank has increased funds to small firms by 31.8 bln yuan since the beginning of the year, 29 Dec.

South China Morning Post (2005b), Mainland marks first with hybrid lender, 29 Dec.

South China Morning Post (2006a), One Third of China City Banks "Broke" – scathing report says only 23 of the 117 lenders meet international capital adequacy ratio standards, 18 Mar.

South China Morning Post (2006b), Residential mortgage loans show bad signs, 21 Apr.

South China Morning Post (2006c), Vehicle finance idea faces cultural hurdle with mainland buyers, 5 Jun.

[Southern Daily] 南方日报 (2006), 邮储银行破冰叩问邮政体制改革 [The new POSBank raises questions about the reform of the postal system], 25 Jan.

[Southern Weekend] 南方周末 (2005), 城商行未来怎么走 [Which way ahead for city commercial banks], 4 Jul.

State Council Development Research Centre (SCDRC) (2005), 城市商业银行调查 [Survey of city commercial banks]. *发展 [Development]*, 07.

Steinfeld, E. (2005), China's Program of Debt-Equity Swaps: Government failure or market failure? In Huang, Y., Saich, T. and Steinfeld, E. (eds), *Financial Sector Reform in China* (Cambridge: Harvard University).

Stephanou, C. and Mendoza, J. C. (2005), *Credit Risk Measurement under Basel II: an Overview and Implementation Issues for Developing Countries*. World Bank Policy Research Paper 3556 (Washington: World Bank).

Studwell, J. (2002), *The China Dream – The Elusive Quest for the Greatest Untapped Market on Earth* (London: Profile Books).

[Study Group for Urban Finance in Wuhan] 武汉市城市金融学会课题组 (2004), 国有商业银行公司治理结构的特殊性及其改革 [Reform and specifics of the corporate governance structure of SOCBs]. *金融论坛 [Finance Forum]*, 03, pp. 16–21.

[Sun, M.] 孙铭 (2005), 独立董事与党委是什么关系？ [What is the relation between the directors and the Party Committee?]. *发展月刊 [Development Monthly]*, 1(171), pp. 14–15.

[Sun, M.] 孙铭 (2006), 五部委紧急叫停打捆贷款进一步加强宏观调控 [To increase macro-economic adjustments, five ministries and agencies urge to end the provision of bundle loans]. *21 世纪经济报道 [21st Century Business Herald]*. 12 May.

Suyter, A. (2004), Neue Leitlinien für ratingorientiertes Risikomanagement [Guidelines for a rating-based risk management]. In Achleitner, A.-K. and Everling, O. (eds), *Handbuch Ratingpraxis [Handbook for rating practice]* (Wiesbaden: Gabler Verlag), pp. 243–258.

[Tang, H.] 唐宏飞 (2004), 加入 WTO 中国银行法制面临的挑战及对策 [Challenges faced by Chinese banks' legal system through the WTO entry and their responses]. *甘肃农业 [Gansu Rural Industry]*, 12(221), pp. 89–90.

Tenev, S., Zhang, C. and Brefort, L. (2002), *Corporate Governance and Enterprise Reform in China: Building the Institutions of Modern Markets* (Washington: IFC).

The Asian Banker (2004a), CBRC on regulation governing capital adequacy of commercial banks, 15 Mar.

The Asian Banker (2004b), China: CBRC introduces risk assessment system for joint-stock commercial banks, 15 Mar.

The Asian Banker (2005a), Fitch: Long-run benefits for Asian banks from Basel II, 31 Jan.

The Asian Banker (2005b), City banks band together, 15 Feb.

The Banker (2004), Reality check on Basel II. Special supplement, Published in association with Accenture, Mercer Oliver Wyman and SAP, 1 Jul.

[The Banker] 银行家(2006), 商业银行竞争力排名出炉 招行综合竞争力居榜首 [Competitive rankings of Chinese commercial banks, Merchants is most competitive], 14 Mar. Accessed online under http://www.ce.cn/economy/bank/main/news/200503/12/t20050312_3304277.shtml [23 Mar. 2006].

The Economist (2003), Reforming China's Banks: don't bank on a bail-out, 4 Dec.

The Economist (2004a), Bothersome Basel, 15 Apr.

The Economist (2004b), Now for the hard part, 13 May.

The Economist (2005a), Who rates the raters? 23 Mar.

The Economist (2005b), Billion-dollar Gamble: Foreign investment in China's banks, 3 Sept.

The Economist (2005c), A Great Big Banking Gamble – China's banking industry, 27 Oct.

The Economist (2006a), Fixing broken brokers, 9 Feb.

The Economist (2006b), Survey: China – Coming out, 24 Mar.

The Economist (2006c), Of angels and banking, 30 Mar.

The Economist (2006d), Rot in the vaults, 6 Apr.

The Economist (2006e), Struggling to keep the lid on, 27 Apr.

The Economist (2006f), Survey: International banking, 18 May.

The Economist (2006g), A muffled report, 18 May.

The Economist (2006h), Atomised, 1 Jun.

The Wall Street Journal (2005), Four to bid on Guangdong stake, 11 Nov.

Thompson, J. (2005), Governance of banks in China. *Financial Market Trends*. OECD, Nov. (2), 89, pp. 67–105.

[Tian, H.] 田华臣 and [Zhang, Z.] 张宗成 (2004), 我国银行业改革与引进外资的开放竞争策略 [Reform of Chinese banks and the competition strategy of opening to foreign banks]. *金融论坛 [Finance Forum]*, 06, pp. 57–61.

[Tian, Q.] 田启林 (2006), 房地产: 经济学家预言的"泡沫破裂"也许已成过去, 但仍需经 历痛苦的吸收, 2006 年远非乐观的一年上海隐患, [Real Estate: Economists warn of the "bursting of a bubble", however this could have already happened, the painful experience is still to come, 2006 is far from optimistic in view of Shanghai's troubles]. 中国 2006 反思之年 [Reflecting on China's year 2006]. *《财经》[Caijing Magazine]*, 6 Feb.

[Tong, M.] 童梦 (2005), 经济资本管理的引入分析: 以城市商业银行为例 [Introductory Analysis of the Management of Economic Capital: based on the example of CCBs]. *银行管理 [Bank Management]*, 7(289).

Transparency International (2005), *Global Corruption Report 2006* (Berlin: s.n.).
Tsai, K. S. (2001), *Beyond Banks: The Local Logic of Informal Finance and Private Sector Development in China*. Paper prepared for the conference on Financial Sector Reform in China, China Public Policy Program at the Kennedy School of Government, Harvard Business School and Massachusetts Institute of Technology, Cambridge, MA. 11–13 Sept.
Tsui, E. (2005), Securing China's financial future China Construction Bank finds itself at the vanguard of reform as the first securitisation rules are drawn up. *Financial Times*, 3 Nov.
Varma, P. (2004), *Default and Recovery Rates of Asia-Pacific Corporate Bond Issuers 1990–2003* (New York: Moody's).
von Emloh, D. A. and Wang, Y. (2004), Retail banking in China. *McKinsey Quarterly*, Special Edition.
[Wang, C.] 王聪 (2005), 加快建立存款保险制度势在必行 [Speeding up the establishment of a deposit insurance scheme is a must]. *《中国金融》[China Finance]*, 27 Oct.
Wang, H. (2006), *Basel II Challenges and Implications for Asia*, Speech at ADB Conference Challenges and Implications of Basel II for Asia, ADB Annual Meeting, Philippines, 3 May.
[Wang, L.] 王兰 (2005a), 汇金公司之辨 [The characteristics of Central Huijin Co,]. *《财经》[Caijing Magazine]*, 8 Aug.
[Wang, L.] 王磊 (2005b), 信达动用自有资金接手上海银行 30 亿不良资产 [Cinda uses own funds to take over CNY 3 bln in NPLs from Shanghai Bank]. *每日经济新闻 [Daily Economic News]*, 22 Dec.
[Wang, X.] 王晓青 and [Huang, Y.] 黄友萍 (2004), 中国的商业银行改革: 产权结构、公司治理与市场竞争 [Reform of Chinese Commercial Banks: ownership structure, corporate governance and market competition]. *济南金融 [Ji'nan Finance]*, 7, pp. 10–13.
[Wang, Y.] 王玉侠 (2004), WTO 对商业银行的影响及商行的对策 [Impact of the WTO on commercial banks and their response]. *宿州教育学院学报 [Suzhou Education College Paper]*, 7(4), Dec., pp. 16–19.
Ward, J. (2002), *The New Basel Accord and Developing Countries: Problems and Alternatives*. ESRC Centre for Business Research Working Paper 4 (Cambridge: Cambridge University).
Wassmuth, D. (2004), *Rating in China – Entwicklung von Kreditrisikosystemen, Risikokultur und die Standards von Basel II [Rating in China – Development of Credit Risk Systems, Risk Culture and Basel II Standards]* (Wiesbaden: Deutscher Universitätsverlag).
Watson, A. (2003), Financing farmers. In Findlay, C., Watson, A. and Cheng, E. (eds), *Rural Financial Markets in China* (Canberra: Asia Pacific Press), pp. 63–88.
Wei, W. (2005), *The Banking Law System in Transitional China – a Comparative Review in the Light of EU Banking Rules* (Zürich: Schulthess Juristische Medien).
Wen, Y. (2005), 银行业反腐三题 [Three topics on corruption in the banking industry]. *《财经》[Caijing Magazine]*, 26 Dec.
Wilson, E. (2004), Small banks urged to get bigger. *The Standard*, 31 Aug.
Woo, W. T. (2004), Les obstacles structurels au contrôle macroéconomique en Chine [Structural obstacles to macroeconomic controls in China]. *Revue d'économie financière: Le devenir financier de la Chine*, 77.

World Bank (WB) (2000), *Bankruptcy of State Enterprises in China – a Case and Agenda for Reforming the Insolvency System* (Washington: World Bank).
World Bank (WB) (2003), *贷款分类和准备计提的现行做法的调查报告 [Results of the Review of the Current Treatment of Loan Classification and Provisioning]* 巴塞尔核心原则联络小组成员国 [Liaison group for Basel core principles] (Beijing: World Bank).
World Bank (WB) (2004), *Doing Business Report 2004: Understanding Regulations* (Washington: World Bank).
World Bank (WB) (2005), *Doing Business Report 2005: Removing Obstacles to Growth* (Washington: World Bank).
World Trade Organisation (WTO) (2001a), *Report of the Working Party on the Accession of China*. Ministerial conference 4 session, Doha, 9–13 Nov., WT/MIN(01)/3, 10 Nov.
World Trade Organisation (WTO) (2001b), *Report of the Working Party on the Accession of China – Addendum 1*. Ministerial conference 4th session, Doha, 9–13 Nov., WT/MIN(01)/3/Add1, 10 Nov.
World Trade Organisation (WTO) (2001c), *Report of the Working Party on the Accession of China – Addendum 2*. Ministerial conference 4th session, Doha, 9–13 Nov., WT/MIN(01)/3/Add2, 10 Nov.
World Trade Organisation (WTO) (2001d), *Accession of the People's Republic of China*. Ministerial conference 4th session, Decision, Doha, 9–13 Nov., WT/L/432, 23 Nov.
Wormuth, M. (2004), *Das Konkursrecht der VR China – Kontinuität und Wandel [The Bankruptcy Law of the PRC – Continuity and Change]* (Hamburg: Institut für Asienkunde).
Worthington, S. (2003), The Chinese Payment Card Market: An explanatory study. *International Journal of Bank Marketing*, 21(6/7), pp. 324–334.
Worthington, S. (2005), Entering the Market for Financial Services in Transitional Economies – a case study of credit cards in China. *International Journal of Bank Marketing*, 23(5), pp. 381–396.
[Wu, J.] 武剑 (2005), 中国实施巴塞尔新资本协议的战略构想 [The strategic concepts for China's implementation of the new Basel capital accord]. *海南金融 [Hainan Finance]*, 5.
[Wu, S.] 吴松汉 (2004), 中国银行业实施巴塞尔新协议的重点 [The key points of the Chinese banking industry implementing the new Basel accord]. *银行家 [The Banker]*, 11.
Wu, X. (2005), *Conditions and Environment for Improving Corporate Governance Structure of China's Financial Enterprises*. Speech by Ms Wu Xiaoling, Deputy Governor of the PBOC, at the 2005 China International Finance Development Forum, 23 Apr.
Wyatt, K. (2004), CP3's standardised approach for credit risk and current capital requirements. *Journal of Financial Services Research*, 26(2), pp. 103–120.
[Xi, H.] 奚慧 (2004), 入世后国有商业银行的竞争战略 [Competition strategy of SOCBs after the WTO entry]. *市场周刊 – 管理探索 [Market Weekly – Management Probe]*, Oct., pp. 140–141.
[Xiao, Z.] 萧灼基 (ed.) (2006), *中国金融市场分析与预测 – 2006 年金融金皮书 [Analysis and Forecast of the Chinese Financial Markets – 2006 Finance Gold Book]* (北京 [Beijing]: 经济科学出版社 [Economic Sciences Publishing House]).

[Xiao, Z.] 萧灼基 (ed.) (2005), *中国金融市场分析与预测 – 2005 年金融金皮书 [Analysis and Forecast of the Chinese Financial Markets – 2005 Finance Gold Book]* (北京 [Beijing]: 经济科学出版社 [Economic Sciences Publishing House]).

Xie, D. 谢登科 (2005), 近 30 家高风险城市商业银行初步摆脱困难局面 [Almost 30 high-risk CCBs start freeing themselves from their difficulties]. *新华网 [Xinhua Net]*, 6 Jul.

Xie, P. 谢平 (2006), 与不良资产有关的十大串谋 [Ten collusions related to non-performing assets]. *《财经》[Caijing Magazine]*, 20 Mar.

[Xie, P.] 谢平 and [Lei, L.] 陆磊 (2005), 金融腐败求解 [Financial corruption report]. *《财经》[Caijing Magazine]*, 24 Jan.

Xie, P., Xu, Z., Cheng, E. and Shen, M. (2005), *Establishing a Framework for Sustainable Rural Finance: Demand and Supply Analysis in Guizhou Province of the PRC* (Manila: Asian Development Bank).

[Xie, P.] 谢平, [Xu, Z.] 徐忠 and [Shen, M.] 沈明高 (2005a), 农信社改革得失调查 [Investigation into success and failure of the reform of RCCs]. *《财经》[Caijing Magazine]*, 12 Dec.

[Xie, P.] 谢平, [Xu, Z.] 徐忠 and [Shen, M.] 沈明高 (2005b), 农信社改革下一步 [Next step in the reform of RCCs]. *《财经》[Caijing Magazine]*, 12 Dec.

[Xie, P.] 谢平, [Xu, Z.] 徐忠 and [Shen, M.] 沈明高 (2005c), *农村信用社改革: 我们做了什么？我们还需要做什么？[Reform of RCCs: What Have We Done? What do we Still Need to do?]* (Beijing: Development Research Center).

[Xinhua Economic News] 新华社经济信息 (2005), 中国个人信用数据库继 2004 年 12 月七城市试运行后, 目前已基本实现 [Since the first trial of the individual borrower database in seven cities at the end of 2004, it is now becoming reality], 31 Aug.

Xinhua Financial Network (XFN) News (2005a), China Basel II risks high, but slow implementation prudent – S&P, 1 Mar.

Xinhua Financial Network (XFN) News (2005b), China CBRC says 30 banks met Basel capital-adequacy standards at end-(2004), 7 Mar.

Xinhua Financial Network (XFN) News (2005c), China commercial banks subordinated debt quota 250 bln yuan, 21 Oct.

Xinhua Financial Network (XFN) News (2006), China's banking regulator warns of rising NPLs from Shanghai mortgages, 17 Feb.

Xinhua News Agency (2006), China allows its citizens to invest in foreign financial market, 21 Apr.

新华社经济信息 [*Xinhua News Agency Economic Service*] (2005), 为支持小企业发展, 工行目前已建成一整套适应小企业风险特点的信用风险评级体系, 以确保在有效防范信贷 [In order to support the development of SMEs and to mitigate adequately risks, ICBC has established a credit risk rating system especially for small enterprises], 26 Aug.

Xinhua's China Economic Information Service (2006), Economic Review: China vows to press ahead state-owned bank reforms, stressing state holding, 7 Mar.

Xinhua's China Economic Information Service (2005a), China's banking industry, 17 Jan.

Xinhua's China Economic Information Service (2005b), Local governments bailout city commercial banks, 6 Jun.

新华网 [Xinhua Net] (2003), 人民银行: 银行信贷登记咨询系统实现全国联网 [PBOC: Banks loan registration system goes online nationwide], 9 Jun.

[Xu, C.] 徐昌元 (2005), 加强对城市商业银行资本充足率管理 [Strengthening the capital adequacy management at CCBs]. *银行管理 [Bank management]*, 5(287).

Xu, L. C., Zhu, T. and Lin, Y. (2002), *Politician Control, Agency Problems and Ownership Reform: Evidence from China*. SSRN Working paper.

[Xu, N.] 许南 and [Wang, Z.] 王忠生 (2005), 试论外资银行进入中国的经济效应分析 [Analysis of the economic efficiency of the entry of foreign banks into China]. *海南金融 [Hainan Finance]*, 2, pp. 24–26, 30.

Xu, S. S. (2006), Risky Business: Why foreign companies should worry about possible reversals in China's economic policy this year. *Economist Intelligence Unit – Business China*, 27 Feb.

[Xu, Y.] 徐樱 (2006), 调整银行信贷结构势在必行 [The imperative of adjusting banks' loan structures]. *《现代商业银行》[Modern Commercial Bank]*, 1.

Yan, M. (2005), *China – Reforms on Track, but More Needed. Banking System Outlook* (New York: Moody's).

Yan, M. (2006), *China City Commercial Banks: Uncovering the Myths* (New York: Moody's).

[Yang, D.] 杨大明 (2004), 高西庆、唐旭、汤敏、季卫东谈金融改革 [Gao Xiqing, Tang Xu, Tang Min and Ji Weidong discuss financial reform:]. *《财经》[Caijing Magazine]*, 30 Nov.

Yang, G. and Gu, A. (2006), Rescue plan for Agricultural bank. *The Standard*, 19 Jan.

[Yang, J.] 杨家才 (2005), 新理念下的银行监管 [Banking supervision under the new concepts] (北京 [Beijing]: 中国金融出版社 [China Finance Publishing House]).

[Yang, X.] 杨小苹 and [Shen, S.] 沈松庆 (2004), 改革农信社产权制度 , 完善法人治理结构 [Reform the ownership system of RCCs, perfect the corporate governance structure]. *浙江金融 [Zhejiang Finance]*, 6, pp. 10–13.

[Yang, Z.] 杨昭 (2006), 银监会列出城市商业银行重组四项原则 [CBRC outlines four principles for restructuring CCBs]. *新华网 [Xinhua Net]*, 11 Jan.

Yao, K. (2006), China's trapped entrepreneurs fuel pawn broking boom. *Reuters*, 27 Feb.

[Ye, W.] 叶伟强 and [Hu, J.] 胡蛟 (2006), 吴晓灵谈金融改革 [Wu Xiaoling discusses financial reforms]. *《财经》[Caijing Magazine]*, 20 Feb.

Ye, X. 叶向阳 (2004), 公司治理: 基于债权融资视角的分析 [Corporate Governance: analysis from the point of view of debt financing]. *经济体制改革 [Economic System Reform]* 5, Sept., pp. 91–94.

[Ying, W.] 应维云 , [Tan, Z.] 覃正 and [Li, X.] 李秀 (2005), 国有商业银行公司治理特殊性的理论和实证研究 [Theoretical and practical research into the specifics of corporate governance at SOCBs]. *改革与战略 [Reform and Strategy]*, 01, pp. 104–107.

[Yu, F.] 余丰慧 (2005), 金融股权外卖盲目跟风不好 [Blind selling of financial shares is a negative fashion]. *证券时报 [Securities Times]*, 7 Nov.

[Yu, L.] 羽良 (2006), 地下信贷转正是否能成为创造性破坏 [Can the formalisation of underground finance wreak creativity?]. *《董事会》[Board of Directors]*, 7 Mar.

[Yu, N.] 于宁 (2005a), 民生银行引资两难 [Two difficulties in attracting capital at Minsheng]. *《财经》[Caijing Magazine]*, 14 Nov.

[Yu, N.] 于宁 (2005b), 中行引资开揭底牌 [Inside the attracting of funds at BoC]. *《财经》[Caijing Magazine]*, 22 Aug.

[Yu, N.] 于宁 (2005c), 中行引资接近终点 [Attracting funds at BoC approaches the end]. *《财经》[Caijing Magazine]*, 8 Aug.

[Yu, N.] 于宁 (2005d), 细解央行再贷款 [Explaining central on-lending]. *《财经》[Caijing Magazine]*, 25 Jul.

[Yu, N.] 于宁 (2006), 中行工行上市渐行渐难 [One step forward, one step backward in BoC's and ICBC's market listings]. *《财经》[Caijing Magazine]*, 20 Feb.

[Yu, N.] 于宁 and [He, Y.] 何禹欣 (2003), 农信社有限改革 [Limited reforms in RCCs]. *《财经》[Caijing Magazine]*, 10 Aug.

[Yu, N.] 于宁 and [Ji, M.] 季敏华 (2005a), 广发行招标渐入佳境 [The bidding for Guangdong Development Bank is getting nicer]. *《财经》[Caijing Magazine]*, 12 Dec.

[Yu, N.] 于宁 and [Ji, M.] 季敏华(2005b), 广发行竞标"加时赛" [Guangdong Development Bank's bidding is running out of time]. *《财经》[Caijing Magazine]*, 26 Dec.

[Yu, N.] 于宁 and [Li, Z.] 历志钢 (2006), 银监会特急警示票据风险 [CBRC urgently calls attention on bills' riskiness]. *《财经》[Caijing Magazine]*, 1 May.

[Yu, N.] 于宁, Li, Z. 历志钢 and Zhang, J. 张洁 (2006), 房贷之危 [the risks in real estate lending]. *《财经》[Caijing Magazine]*, 29 May.

[Yu, N.] 于宁 and [Ling, H.] 凌华薇 (2005), 中行引资未了局 [Agency casts doubt on Bank of China's restructuring]. *《财经》[Caijing Magazine]*, 31 Oct.

[Yu, Y.] 于研 (2003), *信用风险的测定与管理 [Measurement and Management of Credit Risks]* (上海 [Shanghai]: 上海财经大学出版社 [Shanghai Finance and Economics University Press]).

[Yu, Y.] 余云辉 and [Luo, D.] 骆德明 (2005a), 谁将掌控中国的金融？[Who wants to control the Chinese finance industry?]. *《上海证券报》[Shanghai Securities Newspaper]*, 25 Oct.

[Yu, Y.] 余云辉 and [Luo, D.] 骆德明 (2005b), 全球化背景下的中国金融版图告急 [The Chinese finance domain is in a state of emergency in the context of globalisation]. *《董事会》[Board of Directors]*, 26 Oct.

[Yuan, J.] 袁剑 (2005), 金融改革的困局与赌注 [Predicament and stakes of the financial sector reform]. *新浪财经 [Sina Finance News]*, 22 Nov.

[Yue, G.] 岳刚 (2005), 设副部级理事会 年内有望推出 – 存款保险运作路径解析 [A vice-ministerial council set up, their propositions expected for deposit insurance expected within this year, analysis of the operations]. *经济观察报 [Economic Observer]*, 17 Jan.

[Yue, X.] 岳晓明 (2004), 外资参与条件下的银行体制变迁 [Transition in the banking system in the context of foreign banks' participation]. *对外经济贸易大学学报 [Journal of the Foreign Trade and Economics University]*, 2, pp. 42–45.

Yusuf, S., Nabeshima, K. and Perkins, D. H. (2006), Under New Ownership: Privatizing China's state-owned enterprises (Washington: World Bank/Stanford University Press).

Zhang, D. (2005), *The Function and the Legal Bases of SASAC*. Director General of Bureau of Policies, Laws and Regulations SASAC. OECD: Second Policy Dialogue on Corporate Governance, Beijing, 19 May.

Zhang, D. (2006a), ABC Bank to restructure by end of '06. *China Daily*, 18 Jan.

Zhang, D. (2006b), Local banks must prepare for shock. *China Daily*, 9 Mar.

[Zhang, H.] 张宏 and [Cheng, M.] 程明霞 (2003), 财政为四大行买单千亿"输血" 金融能持续多久 [100 billions for paying the bills of the SOCBs, how long can we sustain the transfusion?]. *经济观察报 [Economic Observer]*, 6 Dec.

[Zhang, J.] 张吉光 (2005), 中国城市商业银行十大发展特征 [Ten main development characteristics of CCBs]. *数字财富 [Digital fortune]*, 10 Jan., pp. 65–71.

[Zhang, J.] 张继伟, [Yu, N.] 于宁 and [Guo, Q.] 郭琼 (2006), 杨凯生: 工行自有路 [Yang Kaisheng: ICBC's own way]. *《财经》[Caijing Magazine]*, 15 May.

Zhang, L. (2005), The impact of China's post-1993 financial reforms on SOEs – the case of Shanghai. In Huang, Y., Saich, T. and Steinfeld, E. (eds), *Financial Sector Reform in China* (Cambridge: Harvard University), pp. 29–49.

[Zhang, M.] 张淼 (2005), *商业银行信贷风险管理 [Credit Risk Management of Commercial Banks]* (上海 [Shanghai]: 上海财经大学出版社 [Shanghai Finance and Economics University Press]).

[Zhang, R.] 张燃 and [Hou, G.] 侯光明 (2005), 内部评级法与我国商业银行信用风险管理 [IRB approach and credit risk management in China's commercial banks]. *北京理工大学学报 [Journal of Beijing University of Technology]*, Apr., 7(2).

[Zhang, X.] 张小彩 (2004a), 利率市场化 "行路难" [The difficult way to marketisation of interest rates]. *《财经》 [Caijing Magazine]*, 29 Nov.

[Zhang, X.] 张小彩 (2004b), 专访中央汇金公司总经理谢平 [Interview with Xie Ping, General Manager of Central Huijin Co,]. *《财经》 [Caijing Magazine]*, 2 Nov.

[Zhang, Y.] 张宇哲 (2006), 国开行火线重组城商行 [China Development Bank in the front line to restructure CCBs]. *《财经》 [Caijing Magazine]*, 1 May.

[Zhang, Y.] 张宇哲 and [Li, Z.] 历志钢 (2006), " 渝富 ": 一场没有完成的演化 [Yufu Company: an unfinished evolution]. *《财经》 [Caijing Magazine]*, 3 Apr.

[Zhang, Z.] 章彰 (2004), *解读巴塞尔新资本协议 [Understanding the New Basel Accord]* (北京 [Beijing]: 中国经济出版社 [China Economic Publishing]).

Zhao, M. 赵明霄, Huang, P. 黄萍 and Xu, Q. 许菁 (2004), 新巴塞尔资本协议解读 – 兼论 WTO 条件下我国银行业的风险管理 [Understanding the New Basel Capital Accord – Chinese banks' risk management under the WTO conditions]. *兰州商学院学报 [Journal of Lanzhou Commercial College]*, 20(1).

Zhao, R. (2003), China not ready for Basel II. *China Daily*, 18 Sept.

Zhao, R. (2005), Banks value Basel II requirements. *China Daily*, 21 Feb.

[Zhao, S.] 赵霜茁 (ed.) (2004), *现代金融监管 [Modern financial supervision]* (北京 [Beijing]: 对外经济贸易大学出版社 [Foreign Economic Trade University Press]).

[Zhao, Y.] 赵逸茯 and [Fu, T.] 付涛 (2006), 中诚信穆迪 "同床异梦" [Chengxin and Moody's "in the same bed with different dreams"]. *《财经》 [Caijing Magazine]*, 15 May.

[Zhao, Z.] 赵志宏 (2003), 距巴塞尔之途还太远 [Still too far from the Basel way]. *《财经》 [Caijing Magazine]*, 20 Sept.

[Zheng, L.] 郑录军 and [Cao, Y.] 曹延求 (2005), 我国商业银行效率及其影响因素的实证分析 [Analysis of the efficiency of Chinese commercial banks and its influencing factors]. *金融研究 [Finance Research (PBOC)]*, 1, pp. 91–101.

Zheng, Y. (2003), Financial systems, credit policies and development in rural areas. In Findlay, C., Watson, A. and Cheng, E. (eds), *Rural Financial Markets in China* (Canberra: Asia Pacific Press), pp. 1–12.

[Zheng, Y.] 郑宇 (ed.) (2005), 中国商业银行竞争力排名榜单出炉 [Ranking of Chinese commercial banks is out]. *Business.sohu.com*, 14 Mar.

[Zhong, J.] 钟加勇 (2004), "整编" 城市商业银行 [Reorganising CCBs]. *商务周刊 [Business watch]*. 20 Oct.

[Zhong, W.] 钟伟, [Ba, S.] 巴曙松, [Gao, H.] 高辉清 and [Zhao, X.] 赵晓 (2004), 中国金融风险评估报告 [Evaluation report of China's financial risks]. *中国改革 [China Reform]*, 3.

[Zhong, Y.] 钟永红 and [Li, Z.] 李政 (2004), 在华外资银行盈利能力影响因素的实证分析 [Analysis of the influencing factors of the profitability of foreign banks in China]. *国际金融研究 [International Finance Research]*, 09, pp. 45–49.

[Zhou, S.] 周韶扬 (2004), 试析入世后外资银行入股中资银行的可行性 [On the feasibility of foreign banks becoming shareholders in Chinese banks after the WTO entry]. *安康师专学报 [Journal of Ankang Teachers College]*, 16, pp. 22–24, 27.

Zhou, W. 周伟 (2005), 城市商业银行的引资之惑 [The temptation of attracting new capital for CCBs]. *中国信贷风险信息库 [News database for china credit risk]*, 24 Nov.

Zhou, X. (2004a), *Capital Accord II and Regional Disparities in Financial Risks*, Speech of Governor Zhou Xiaochuan at the Seminar on risk management and internal control of the commercial banks, 8 Jan.

Zhou, X. (2004b), *Improve Corporate Governance and Develop Capital Market*, Speech by Mr Zhou Xiaochuan, Governor of the PBOC at the "China Forum: Capital Market and Corporate Governance", 1 Dec.

Zhou, X. (2004c), *Improve legal system and financial ecology*, Speech by Mr Zhou Xiaochuan, Governor of the PBOC at the "Forum of 50 Chinese Economists", 2 Dec.

Zhou, X. (2005), 周小川：国有商业银行如何充实资本 [Zhou Xiaochuan: How SOCBs should replenish their capital]. *《财经》[Caijing Magazine]*, 28 Nov.

[Zhu, H.] 朱华明 (2004), 制度、流动性与农村信用社支农绩效的实证研究 [Analysis of system, liquidity and performance of RCCs in supporting rural areas]. *金融研究 [Finance Research (PBOC)]*, 12, pp. 119–127.

Zhu, J. (1999), Closure of financial institutions in China. In *Strengthening the Banking System in China: Issues and Experience*, Joint BIS/PBOC Conference proceedings, Beijing, 1–2 Mar. (Basel: BIS), pp. 304–320.

References for laws and regulations

1. 中华人民共和国商业银行法 (修正) [Commercial banking law], first issue 1995, revision 2003.
2. 中华人民共和国银行业监督管理法 [Law of banking supervision and administration], 2003.
3. 中华人民共和国中国人民银行法 (修正) [Law of the People's Bank of China], first issue 1995, revision 2003.
4. 金融企业会计制度 [Accounting system for financial companies], 2001.
5. 商业银行风险监管核心指标 (试行) [Core indicators for the risk supervision of commercial banks (trial)], 2006.
6. 商业银行市场风险管理指引 [Directive for the risk management of market risks in commercial banks], 2004.
7. 股份制商业银行董事会尽职指引 (试行) [Directive on the duty of directors in JSCBs], 2005.
8. 商业银行集团客户授信业务风险管理指引 [Directive regarding the risk management and approval authorities for group exposures], 2003.
9. 商业银行授信工作尽职指引 [Directive regarding authorities and approval limits at commercial banks], 2004.
10. 贷款风险分类指导原则 (试行) [Directive principles for the categorisation of loan risks (trial)], 2001.
11. [Guidelines on rural household micro-credit by RCCs], 2001.
12. 中国银行、中国建设银行公司治理改革与监管指引 [Guidelines on corporate governance reforms and supervision of BoC and CCB], 2004.

13. 中华人民共和国外资金融机构管理条例实施细则 [Implementation details of the management rule regarding foreign-invested institutions], 2004.
14. 合作金融机构行政许可事项实施办法，外资金融机构行政许可事项实施办法，中资商业银行行政许可事项实施办法，行政许可实施程序规定 [Implementation rule for licensing of cooperative financial institutions, of foreign invested financial institutions, for Chinese-invested commercial banks, and for the licensing procedures], 2006.
15. 贷款通则 [Loan principles], 1995.
16. 金融企业呆账准备提取管理办法 [Management rule regarding bad loan provisions at financial companies], 2005.
17. 商业银行与内部人和股东关联交易管理办法 [Management rule regarding commercial banks and transactions with insiders and shareholders], 2004.
18. 外资金融机构驻华代表机构管理办法 [Management rule regarding representative offices of foreign-invested financial institutions in China], 2002.
19. 境外金融机构投资入股中资金融机构管理办法 [Management rule regarding the entry of foreign financial institutions into Chinese financial institutions], 2003.
20. 个人债权及客户证券交易结算资金收购意见 [Opinion on purchasing personal creditor's rights and client securities transaction liquidation funds], 2004.
21. 商业银行服务价格管理暂行办法 [Provisional management rule regarding the service prices of commercial banks], 2003.
22. 商业银行内部控制评价试行办法 [Provisional rule for assessing internal controls at commercial banks], 2004.
23. 农村信用社省（自治区、直辖市）联合社管理暂行规定 [Provisional regulation for the management of RCCs' unions], 2003.
24. 农村商业银行管理暂行规定 [Provisional regulation for the management of rural commercial banks], 2003.
25. 农村合作银行管理暂行规定 [Provisional regulation for the management of rural cooperative banks], 2003.
26. 商业银行不良资产监测和考核暂行办法 [Provisional rule regarding the supervision and assessment of NPLs at commercial banks], 2004.
27. 商业银行信息披露暂行办法 [Provisional rule for the information disclosure at commercial banks], 2002.
28. 商业银行资本充足率管理办法 [Regulation governing the capital adequacy of commercial banks], 2004.
29. 股份制商业银行风险评级体系（暂行）[Risk grading system for JSCBs (provisional)], 2004.
30. 外资银行并表监管管理办法 [Rule governing the consolidated supervision of foreign banks], 2004.
31. 金融机构撤消条例 [Rule on dissolution of banks], 2001.
32. 商业银行次级债券发行管理办法 [Rules on the issuance of subordinated bonds by commercial banks], 2004.
33. 金融机构信贷资产证券化试点监督管理办法 [Trial supervisory management rule regarding the asset securitisation at financial institutions], 2005.
34. 国有商业银行公司治理及相关监管指引 [Directive regarding the corporate governance in state-owned commercial banks and related supervision], 2006.
35. 关于加强宏观调控整顿和规范各类打捆贷款的通知 [Notice concerning the strengthening of macro-economic adjustments to clean and normalise bundle loans], 2006.
36. 中华人民共和国外资金融机构管理条例 [Management rule regarding foreign-invested institutions], 2002.

Websites

Bank for International Settlements	www.bis.org
China Banking Regulatory Commission (CBRC)	www.cbrc.gov.cn
China Insurance Regulatory Commission (CIRC)	www.circ.gov.cn
China Securities Regulatory Commission (CSRC)	www.csrc.gov.cn
International Institute of Economics	www.iie.com
International Institute of Finance	www.iif.com
Internation Monetary Fund	www.imf.org
Organisation for Economic and Cooperation Development	www.oecd.org
People's Bank of China (PBOC)	www.pbc.gov.cn

Banks' annual reports

Industrial and Commercial Bank of China	2005 (preliminary), 2004
Bank of China	2005, 2004
Agricultural Bank of China	2005 (Fitch data), 2004
China Construction Bank	2005, 2004
Bank of Communications	2005, 2004
China Merchants Bank	2005, 2004
CITIC Industrial Bank	2005 (Fitch data), 2004
Shanghai Pudong Development Bank	2005, 2004
China Minsheng Banking Corp.	2005, 2004
Industrial Bank	2005, 2004
Huaxia Bank	2005, 2004
Shenzhen Development Bank	2005, 2004
Bank of Beijing	2005, 2004
Shanghai Bank	2005, 2004
Chongqing City Commercial Bank	2004 (without notes)
Xi'an City Commercial Bank	2004 (without notes)
Nanjing City Commercial Bank	2005, 2004 (without notes)
Shenzhen City Commercial Bank	2004 (without notes)
China Everbright Bank	2005 (unaudited, press release)

China Everbright Bank and Guangdong Development Bank are both undergoing restructuring exercises and for 2004 no annual report has yet been published. All are audited, unqualified, PRC-GAAP (except for CCB 2005, BoComm 2005 according to IFRS).

Sources of news and information

Factiva	www.factiva.com
Sina News	www.sina.com.cn
Economic Observer	www.eeo.com.cn
Cajing Magazine	www.caijing.hexun.com
Southern Weekend	www.nanfangdaily.com.cn
21st Century Business Herald	www.nanfangdaily.com.cn/jj/
Cajing Magazine	www.caijing.hexun.com

Index

Subentries are ordered by importance or by page numbers.
Figures in **bold** indicate main entries (for those entries where page numbers are numerous).